T0329630

# THE CAPACITY TO INNOVATE

**Studies in Comparative Political Economy and Public Policy**

Editors: MICHAEL HOWLETT, DAVID LAYCOCK (Simon Fraser University), and STEPHEN MCBRIDE (McMaster University)

*Studies in Comparative Political Economy and Public Policy* is designed to showcase innovative approaches to political economy and public policy from a comparative perspective. While originating in Canada, the series will provide attractive offerings to a wide international audience, featuring studies with local, subnational, cross-national, and international empirical bases and theoretical frameworks.

*Editorial Advisory Board*

For a list of books published in the series, see page 189.

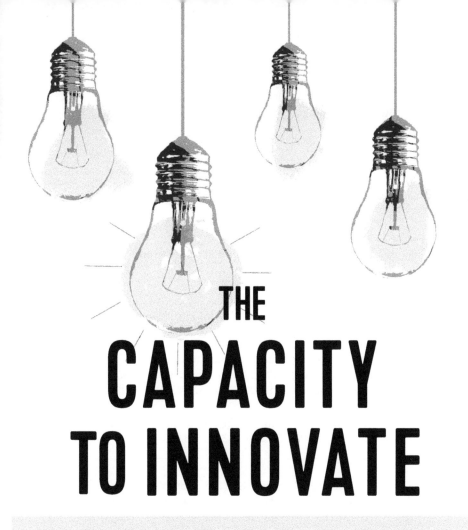

# THE
# CAPACITY
# TO INNOVATE

CLUSTER POLICY AND MANAGEMENT
IN THE BIOTECH SECTOR

SARAH GIEST

UNIVERSITY OF TORONTO PRESS
Toronto  Buffalo  London

ISBN 978-1-4426-5006-0 (cloth)
ISBN 978-1-4426-2215-9 (EPUB)
ISBN 978-1-4426-2214-2 (PDF)

---

**Library and Archives Canada Cataloguing in Publication**

Title: The capacity to innovate : cluster policy and management in the biotech
    sector / Sarah Giest.
Names: Giest, Sarah, 1986– author.
Series: Studies in comparative political economy and public policy ; 60.
Description: Series statement: Studies in comparative political economy
    and public policy | Includes bibliographical references and index.
Identifiers: Canadiana (print) 20200412515 | Canadiana (ebook) 20200412647 |
    ISBN 9781442650060 (cloth) | ISBN 9781442622142 (PDF) | ISBN
    9781442622159 (EPUB)
Subjects: LCSH: Industrial clusters. | LCSH: Biotechnology industries.
Classification: LCC HC79.D5 G54 2021 | DDC 338.6/042–dc23

---

University of Toronto Press acknowledges the financial assistance to its
publishing program of the Canada Council for the Arts and the Ontario Arts
Council, an agency of the Government of Ontario.

Canada Council    Conseil des Arts
for the Arts      du Canada

ONTARIO ARTS COUNCIL
CONSEIL DES ARTS DE L'ONTARIO
an Ontario government agency
un organisme du gouvernement de l'Ontario

Funded by the     Financé par le
Government        gouvernement     Canada
of Canada         du Canada

# Contents

# Tables and Figures

**Tables**

**Figures**

# THE CAPACITY TO INNOVATE

# 1 Introduction

Clusters have received a great deal of attention ever since the success of Silicon Valley; and similar regions elsewhere have also produced high levels of innovation. The idea of local agglomerations of economic activities in related industries is not new, but it has created significant buzz connected to high-tech sectors. Clusters have been shown to generate outsized economic output, and are therefore used to increase the growth of regional and national economies and to promote employment. Increases in innovation levels, efficiency, and productivity have also been attributed to regional clustering (Baily and Montalbano 2017). National governments around the world have therefore attempted to emulate Silicon Valley to channel success in innovative fields, such as telecommunications, biotechnology, and artificial intelligence (AI). And clusters remain part of the policy language to facilitate innovation in those areas (Dutton 2018). Canada, Denmark, and Germany, for example, have all developed cluster strategies linked to AI.

Using the clustering of high-tech industries to boost economic growth is controversial, however, when it comes to the level of government involvement and the way cluster policy is shaped, raising larger questions around the role and impact of government and the types of interventions required to boost innovation. Furthermore, discussion is ongoing about the evidence of the success or failure of government involvement. Some researchers caution direct involvement, due to short-sighted initiatives, partial information about the innovation process, and the limited effects of financial incentives (Bresnahan and Gambardella 2004; Lerner 2009; Wallsten 2004). Others criticize the "blanket enthusiasm" surrounding cluster measures, paired with a lack of proper evaluation of policy instruments linked to them (Duranton 2011; Martin and Sunley 2003). Despite these discussions, considerable amounts of time and (public) money have been invested in supporting local agglomerations.

These efforts range from institutional changes to consumer acceptance campaigns (Birch 2017; Pisano 2006). The main challenge arising from these diverse strategies is that, although reducing the barriers to the transfer of scientific and technical knowledge is at the core of enhancing innovation, the ways to address these bottlenecks are multiple and their evaluations rather vague (Borrás 2011). The high-tech industry challenges governments to adapt policies to dynamic knowledge transfer processes. Such fields are moving at a fast pace, and as technologies mature, they change industry structures and supply-and demand conditions. Cluster policy is thus a complex undertaking since it has to be multidimensional, contain a diverse set of policy instruments, and is often informed by a combination of rationales rooted in industrial, regional, and innovation policies (Nauwelaers 2001; Uyarra and Ramlogan 2016). This has resulted in several failed attempts in which it seems decision makers were unable to balance immediate needs with long-term goals and ensure regional economic integration (Giest 2017).

Given the equivocal evidence concerning government involvement, in combination with the challenge of identifying effective cluster policies, this book aims to answer the question: how can government identify gaps in cluster development and implement effective policies tailored to the innovation context? Although discussions are ongoing about the degree of involvement by government, about the types of direct or indirect initiatives that should be implemented, or even about the value of clustering more generally, this research proposes that there are common, underlying patterns that apply to all clusters linked to *capacity*. Capacity describes the ability of stakeholders to absorb and use knowledge relevant for innovation processes. The capacity framework assumes that collaboration and knowledge exchange are at the core of innovative clusters. Capacity tools are thus public initiatives that enable individuals, groups, and organizations to act based on informational, educational, or training resources (Schneider and Ingram 1990). This approach acknowledges the complexity of the interplay within the cluster, while providing a range of policy instruments that work with the high-tech innovation dynamic. In short, the book develops *a capacity framework for the coordinated effort by government and cluster organizations to support capacity elements lacking in the local cluster in order to improve knowledge-sharing activities.*

Today's research on clusters is largely dominated by developing measures to link network characteristics and social interactions to performance outcomes, such as patents. This trend to quantify local agglomerations and their ability to innovate is one important research stream unravelling the dynamics within clusters that can inform policy making. The trend overlooks, however, some of the more detailed mechanisms that enable the interplay between structural factors and activities within clusters. By focusing on capacity, the book touches upon something that is mentioned in much of the literature but never systematically analysed. In recent years, various publications have pointed towards elements that can be summoned under the capacity label. For example, Lundvall et al. (2003, 231) talk about the "learning capability of individuals, organizations, and regions." Lindqvist, Ketels, and Sölvell (2013) develop a framework of three pillars – cluster identity and attractiveness, innovation and research and development (R&D), and business development – on which cluster organizations build. Several researchers find that "a weak capacity to absorb knowledge from outside the region and a thin structure of supporting organizations" leads to innovation system failures (Trippl, Asheim, and Miorner 2015, 4; see also Doloreux and Dionne 2008; Karlsen, Isaksen, and Spilling 2011). Murphy, Huggins, and Thompson (2016, 1049) also point to the "softer elements of innovation"; for example, "knowledge absorption, transformation and creation capture the benefits of local agglomeration that ultimately benefit overall cluster development." The idea of a "fragmented" regional innovation system raises a similar issue by highlighting the importance of networking and knowledge exchange for collective learning (Blazek and Zizalova 2010). The capacity concept developed in this book is divided into collaborative and absorptive capacity, where collaborative capacity targets the networking elements of innovation, such as structure, resources, and communication, while absorptive capacity describes the ability to integrate and exploit knowledge from inside and outside the cluster.

In this context of cluster policy that targets capacity elements, *cluster organizations play a key role in organizing knowledge-sharing activities and supporting government in implementing cluster policies.* Cluster organizations are those entities in the network that can create favourable conditions for cooperation and knowledge exchange among industry and research stakeholders by being experts with a certain skill set (Rutter et al. 2012). Such an entity fills a central position in the network, and is closely connected to the cluster stakeholders, while keeping in touch with government. The idea of such facilitators is similar to the establishment in the 1970s of clientele or administrative units by government to target network mobilization and activation (Howlett 2011) and to the concept of network administration organizations developed by Provan and Kenis (2007). Cluster organizations or initiatives are widely seen as important in order to offer services and to support the coordination and development of joint projects within the cluster (European Commission

2002; Gerolamo et al. 2008; Ketels, Lindqvist, and Sölvell 2008; Sölvell. Lindqvist, and Ketels 2003). This means that cluster organizations potentially can compensate for limited capabilities at the individual or company level by facilitating overall institutional thicknesses along the lines of collaborative and absorptive capacity building. They can, for example, promote a shared vision, provide a common communication infrastructure, or create local spaces for collaboration. In recent years, governments increasingly have focused on existing cluster organizations to boost cluster development (EU 2016). For example, Denmark's cluster strategy defines establishing and improving the quality of cluster organizations as key to boosting collaborative structures. This is done by allocating funds to regional and local government entities, establishing a quality label for cluster organizations, and evaluating their efforts (Denmark 2013). In addition, the national program, "Cluster Excellence Denmark," acts as a nation-wide cluster organization by providing a number of services, such as competence development, branding, and networking (EU 2016). At the continental level, the European Secretariat for Cluster Analysis (ESCA) specifically promotes cluster management excellence through benchmarking and quality labelling of clusters and cluster management organizations (ESCA 2017). ESCA has also established a management-quality-labelling scheme, with Bronze, Silver, and Gold identifying different levels of "cluster management quality" (EU 2016).

Thus, cluster organizations can take on different organizational forms, depending on local circumstances. Findings from the Global Cluster Initiative Survey (Sölvell, Lindqvist, and Ketels 2003) suggest that almost all cluster initiatives have a dedicated cluster organization that is initiated by government, industry, or both (Nallari and Griffith 2013). This book identifies three variations of cluster organizations ranging from government-initiated to industry-initiated linked to the regional set-up. Cluster organizations are largely region- or even country-specific, based on the economic development and political system (Ketels, Lindqvist, and Sölvell 2008), and so this study reveals three models that correspond to these regional characteristics: a public-private model in Europe (Medicon Valley, spanning Denmark and Sweden), an industry-driven one in North America (Chicago and Vancouver), and a government-initiated one in Asia (Singapore), with cases from each focusing specifically on the biotechnology industry.

## Biotechnology

The biotechnology sector is defined as the "application of science and technology to living organisms ... to alter living or non-living materials for production of knowledge, goods and services" (OECD 2005, 9). The field is well known for relying heavily on local agglomerations due to its dependence on scientific knowledge from a diverse set of stakeholders. Innovative advancements in biotechnology are further heavily dependent on the financial resources of bigger companies or on government funding, because the production of, for example, a new medication requires large up-front costs and long development times. Similarly, the work being done requires individual skill sets obtained by university graduates and an environment in which to carry out the work, such as a wet lab (special ventilation and piped utilities) or a research hospital. These mutual interdependencies explain the tendency for these actors to agglomerate close to one another (Cooke 2002b; Feldman and Francis 2004; Zeller 2001). Indeed, it is argued that clustering and biotechnological advancement go hand-in-hand: as biotechnology grew as an industry, clustering became more prominent (6 et al. 2006).

Biotechnology has several unique characteristics. The sector is based on the commercialization of knowledge, which is largely done in the form of intellectual property (IP). There are also "dedicated biotech firms" that specialize in economic rent seeking via the ownership and out-licensing of IP assets, rather than developing new products or services (Birch 2017; Mirowski 2012). Biotechnology is thus described differently depending on the focus of the industry in the specific country. "Bio-economy," "bio-based economy," "life sciences," and "biomedical applications" all describe an aspect of biotechnology. Life sciences, for example, put emphasis on more fundamental research in biology, whereas biotechnology focuses on the application of such research. Different labels thus appear throughout the book, depending on the language used in the policy documents of the particular region and the aspect of biotechnology on which the industry mostly focuses.

Overall, these characteristics make biotechnology an industry favoured by many to show cluster effects. The cases presented in this book – Chicago, Medicon Valley, Singapore, and Vancouver – are not unique: the cluster spanning Denmark and Sweden (Medicon Valley) and the Singaporean efforts, in particular, have been widely discussed (e.g. Asheim and Moodysson 2008; Finegold, Wong, and Cheah 2004; Halkier 2011; Jensen and Richardson 2004; Maskell 2004; Moodysson, Coenen, and Asheim 2010; Nauwelaers, Maguire, and Marsan 2013; Wong 2011). This is advantageous for the purposes of this book, as, beyond the in-person interviews carried out for this research, the cases give additional information about different aspects of the relevant government and cluster organization activities, revealing a more complete picture of the capacity elements within those local agglomerations.

## Methodology

The study is based on a two-stage research process: a survey and four case studies. The survey helps to answer the more general question of how clusters are structured and how this affects knowledge-sharing activities by stakeholders. The cases help to gain an in-depth understanding of how (cluster) policy and management shape the collaborative and absorptive capacity elements within the cluster.

### The Survey

The theoretical context for the survey, which was undertaken in 2012 and 2013, was based on commonalities that research has identified in the structure of clusters, which consist of three groups: government, industry, and research institutions. This triple-helix structure forms the basis for interactions within the cluster. Looking at a diverse set of clusters from a triple-helix perspective enables a stable and observable structure that defines separate analytical areas (Leydesdorff and Meyer 2006). This helps to map the existing relationships within the cluster that feed back into the institutional arrangements surrounding it (Leydesdorff and Etzkowitz 1998). In analysing these relationships, the literature has identified three main themes.

One theme is the existence and role of cluster management, which in recent years has come to the forefront as a key factor influencing cluster excellence (Schretlen et al. 2011; zu Köcker and Rosted 2010). Thereby, the idea of cluster management shows up in the literature under different names, such as trust facilitators (Mesquita 2007), network brokers (Visser and Atzema 2008), or intermediaries (Baxter and Tyler 2007). More management-oriented scholars also describe them as managers, promoters, or leaders (Goduscheit 2014; McEvily and Zaheer 2004; Provan, Isett, and Milward 2004). (For a more in-depth analysis of this literature, see Chapter 3.) Current analyses struggle, however, to identify the shape and role these organizations or individuals play and the activities they carry out. As a competing or parallel model to cluster organizations, some scholars emphasize the role of "star scientists" (Florida 2005; Maier, Kurka, and Trippl 2007; Zucker and Darby 2006) or "anchor firms" (Dhanaraj and Parkhe 2006). Both suggest that these companies or individuals are able to unite cluster stakeholders, attract investment, and are carriers of knowledge beyond industry and geographical boundaries (Baglieri, Cinici, and Mangematin 2012; Maier, Kurka, and Trippl 2007).

A second main theme in the literature is the importance of an entrepreneurial culture in the region for a cluster to flourish. This strand of literature is unclear, however, about the causal direction – whether clusters enhance entrepreneurial culture or whether entrepreneurial culture increases the likelihood of clusters to flourish (Malecki 1994; Reynolds et al. 2001; Rocha 2004). The leading idea for this research is that entrepreneurial culture affects the investment decisions of venture capitalists as well as the relocation of stakeholders into the region, and thereby contributes to overall cluster performance (Majocchi and Presutti 2009).

The third strand of the literature concerns government policies. This is a wide set of literature tackling a variety of policy instruments that affect clusters either directly, such as through patent regulation, or indirectly, such as in housing prices (e.g. Agranoff and McGuire 2001; Borras 2011). This strand also looks at the role of government more generally and letting cluster members point towards specific policies.

The structured online questionnaire addressed these dimensions by including a large number of clusters all over the world. The clusters were identified based on their online presence, with the websites, set up either by government or by the cluster itself, determining if an agglomeration of firms, universities, and government was in fact a cluster. Those websites identifying a cluster were the sources for contact information of affiliated institutions, firms, and government departments. After determining the list of clusters, a sample was taken within each cluster from among firms and research facilities, the objective being to cover the perspectives of both small and larger firms – in other words, the survey made sure that companies and research facilities were not chosen based on popularity (through being featured on a website, for example) or mere size. Universities and government institutions usually appeared in smaller numbers, and were all contacted with the survey link invitation.

Survey questions covered characteristics of the cluster, such as its structural set-up and relationships among different entities at the individual and institutional levels. Responses were received from 9.2 per cent of the 1,400 stakeholders that were targeted, located in twenty-nine different countries. The data were then used to complement some of the existing research and to draw attention to specific aspects of cluster policy and organization, discussed in Chapter 3, as well as to add structural context to the cases examined in Chapter 4. The responses were spread evenly across companies, cluster organizations, and research institutes or universities (~30 per group), while there were fewer government and non-profit organizations (~15 per group). The response population was mainly from Europe (~64 responses) and North America (~32 responses).

To show the results for this diverse set, the clusters were categorized along different levels of competitiveness ranging from low performance to nationally competitive to high performance, with the latter two categories grouped together under "high performance clusters." From data acquired through external sources such as the World Bank, the Organisation for Economic Co-operation and Development (OECD), Eurostat, and the statistical bureaus of relevant countries, each cluster was assigned to one of these categories based on a combination of performance indicators, including the unemployment rate, the number of patents in the according industry within that region or state, the share of the labour force employed in medium-, high-tech, and knowledge-intensive sectors, the number of new enterprises established, and, for some of those ranked by the OECD, the performance of local business clusters in the knowledge economy. Clusters fell into the high-performance category if they had high levels of patent count, firm creation, and medium-, high-tech, and knowledge-intensive employment. An OECD ranking gave further indication of international recognition of that sector. Nationally competitive clusters were those known within the country, but not recognized beyond its borders. Compared with higher-performing clusters, these nationally competitive clusters were only average in patent counts, employment, and firm creation in relationship to the relevant industry. Low-performing clusters compared badly across all or most indicators, and were either just starting out or not gaining momentum in building up industry in that area.

*The Case Studies*

Based on preliminary insights from the survey and current theoretical discussions, the goal of the case studies – all of which operate within the same industry, biotechnology – was to offer a more in-depth look at how cluster policy and management shape collaborative and absorptive capacity elements within a cluster – more specifically, how the level of government involvement and the visibility of cluster management affect those capacity dynamics. To analyse these aspects, only clusters that have some variation of cluster management were chosen, which allows a focus on how this is linked to government involvement and levels of capacity within the cluster.

Survey respondents indicated that cluster organizations facilitated linkages among clusters, firms, and research institutions, as well as providing a communication platform, advice on funding opportunities, the creation of new projects for cooperation, and advertising the cluster on the (global) market. Further, over 90 per cent of respondents pointed out that, because of the cluster organization, there were better or stronger connections among cluster stakeholders. The case studies thus can give additional insights into the day-to-day activities of cluster organizations and the collaboration of companies, research institutes, and government entities. Previous research further points out that, for clusters to be successful, new channels of communication and intermediation are needed horizontally among, for example, government departments or cluster stakeholders and vertically across levels of policy making and planning (Borras and Tsagdis 2008; Halkier 2011). The literature remains vague, however, about how this is to be structured and which activities these "forums" or "spaces" carry out (Borras and Tsagdis 2008). From the strand of management and organizational studies, different scholars give different weight to cluster organizations in their explanation of innovation performance. Some see them as day-to-day managers embedded in the larger historical structures of the region and part of a multilevel policy construct. Others emphasize their ability to implement innovation-related policies and to serve as connectors for new entries to the established core of the cluster (Crespo, Suire, and Vicente 2014).

Since the activities carried out by cluster organizations and their impact remain vague in the current literature, the case selection was based on a higher level of abstraction: the visibility of a cluster manager or unit. This then helped to identify activities in the analysis of the cases. Rather than pre-emptively speculating about the role and effect of cluster management, one was thus able to choose cases based on how visible cluster management was in the first place, whether high, medium, or low. A highly visible cluster organization was one that was identified as such, by itself, by other stakeholders in the cluster, and in policy documents or websites marketing the cluster. A cluster organization with medium visibility was either not as well known or not the only one fulfilling a similar role for some of the stakeholders. Finally, a low visibility organization was one that had the goal of being a link among cluster members, but had not been identified as a node in the network, due to limited or weak linkages to key stakeholders.

For the second case selection dimension, government involvement, survey respondents identified a variety of policies as relevant, with immigration, infrastructure, and taxation mentioned as the top three policies areas hindering cluster development. These results mirror the challenges described in the literature, where clusters are portrayed as complex constructs with dynamic and connected components (Bauer et al. 2012). In order to accommodate heterogeneous components, government requires a combination of broad-spectrum policies and specific policy initiatives (Borras 2011). Since a mix of policies ranging from broad to more specific initiatives affects clusters, the dimension defined for this research looks at government involvement in the case study clusters, whether high, medium, or low. These more open-ended categories have the goal of accommodating different versions of government involvement, which differs by jurisdiction. Some governments use clusters to provide sharper tools for interventionist policies; others use regional agglomerations to identify and try to overcome market failures in an otherwise market-oriented setting. Government also operates at different levels: although most involvement is at the local or regional level, involvement also comes from the national or even supranational level (Enright and the Competitiveness Institute 2000).

For the purpose of this research, a high level of government involvement is where specific programs target the cluster and/or government has a visible presence in the cluster's development – for example, a local start-up program that funds university spin-offs to increase entrepreneurship and business ventures within the cluster. Medium involvement is where government programs exist, but they are not specifically designed with the cluster in mind. The program might be applicable to other industries or clusters as well, even as a local government is clear about offering it to stakeholders in a specific cluster. Finally, low government involvement is where government is not actively involved in the cluster through institutional linkages or programs or policies targeting the local network, although again there might be larger programs that favour the cluster, into which stakeholders are able to tap without support from local officials.

*Case Selection*

The cases were selected based on their variation on the two key dimensions identified above: the visibility of cluster management and the level of government involvement (see table 1.1). The contextual conditions were kept somewhat similar by selecting cases that are part of the same sector and can be categorized as "emerging" clusters. Emerging clusters differ from established ones in that they are consciously created by government, and cluster management is used to facilitate these developments. Established clusters evolve largely organically, based on the collective behaviour of individuals and firms, rather than as a coordinated effort by government and industry (Casper 2007). As table 1.1 shows, the cases chosen represent both ends of the spectrum (low/low and high/high for government involvement and visibility of cluster management, respectively), while medium/medium is covered

Table 1.1. Levels of cluster management visibility and government involvement, selected cases

|  |  | Visibility of cluster management | | |
|---|---|---|---|---|
|  |  | Low | Medium | High |
| Government involvement | High | | Singapore | Medicon Valley |
|  | Medium | | Chicago | |
|  | Low | Vancouver | | |

by Chicago, and Singapore gives some variation with high government involvement and medium cluster management visibility. Not all categories along the continuum of the two dimensions are covered, but this is a first step towards a more contextual understanding of their variation. This follows the logic summarized by Seawright and Gerring (2008) to choose both extreme values (high and low), as well as and the mean or median.

Each case also represents a typical one for its respective geographic location. Medicon Valley is an example of network management embedded in a European multilevel governance system, similar to that in many European Union member states, as the EU currently trains and benchmarks cluster organizations, making network management more visible there. In the Chicago case, there is limited government involvement – typical for the United States, where public input is largely unwanted. In Singapore, government involvement is high in terms of both funding and organizing the life sciences network. This is true for most of Asia, as governments are trying to fast-track the development of high-tech industries.

In analysing the four selected cases, the goal was to triangulate data sources by looking at primary and secondary data, as well as by conducting interviews. Interview partners were chosen based on the idea, noted above, that clusters consist of a triple-helix structure that consists of research institutes and universities, companies, and government departments. Thus, for each cluster, interview partners from each group were identified and contacted. The analysis draws on empirical data from twenty-seven semi-structured interviews conducted in 2012 and 2013 with representatives from these groups in the regional agglomerations picked for this research: five interviews in Vancouver, five in Medicon Valley (all on the Danish side), eleven in Singapore, and six in Chicago. The interview questions consisted of three parts. The first set addressed the position and relationships of interviewees and their institution in the cluster. The second set asked about government involvement, and covered aspects hypothesized to be linked with cluster management, such as communications channels, funding opportunities, and links to other clusters. The third part concerned the future of the cluster, possible improvements, and its competitive advantage relative to others in the industry. For primary sources, a variety of (public) strategy and policy documents was consulted; secondary sources consisted of research that had previously examined these clusters.

## Outline of the Book

Chapters 2 and 3 are a combination of theoretical concepts and policy-related characteristics that evolve around the idea of knowledge transfer and the role of cluster management. Chapter 2 gives an overview of research developments in the geography and systems of innovation literature as well as network sociology and clusters. The goal is to draw out findings that point towards common features in clusters and the dynamics among network members that foster innovation. Taken together, this review of past research enables the development of the collaborative and absorptive capacity framework. Chapter 3 also draws on previous research and results from the survey conducted for this book to identify the relevance and role of cluster organizations and how they connect to government, innovation, and cluster policy. The enabling factors for knowledge transfer developed in the capacity model conclude chapter 3 and build the foundation for chapter 4, which focuses on the different cluster cases and draws out their collaborative and absorptive capacity elements in combination with local cluster management models, the genesis of the cluster, its current status, and public initiatives supporting it. The comparative case analysis sheds light on the linkages among knowledge-sharing activities, the role of cluster organizations, and the cluster policy initiatives relevant to supporting capacity elements. Chapter 5 offers a bird's-eye view of stakeholders' issues that came to light during the interviews, and how they connect to both the role of cluster organizations and the design of cluster policies. Chapter 6 concludes the book by presenting final thoughts on the collaborative and absorptive capacity framework, and how government can identify gaps in cluster development in order to implement effective policies tailored towards innovation.

# 2 Capacity Concepts in Cluster and Innovation Research

In reviewing the geography and systems of innovation, as well as network sociology and cluster literature, the goal of this chapter is twofold. The first is to draw out findings that point towards common features in cluster relationships. The literature addresses elements of capacity indirectly or in passing, but here I focus on those existing elements and situate them in the current debate among the fields mentioned above. The second goal, based on this, is to develop the collaborative and absorptive capacity framework, which highlights capacity-related activities at the network level, embedded in the larger policy and cluster management setting.

As the literature has captured, a cluster can be broken down into several core elements, which include more stable components – such as actors, the network, the regional component or place, as well as the multilevel governance structure – and more dynamic elements that look at evolutionary or life-cycle developments within clusters. There are also relational components. Several attempts have been made to categorize different types of clusters and policies around them. For example, Gordon and McCann (2000) distinguish among three basic forms of clustering: pure agglomeration, the industrial complex, and the network model. Each corresponds to a literature stream that looks at different aspects of these clusters, such as proximity, sectoral activity, and relationships, respectively. Policy has also found different ways of approaching clusters under the umbrella of industrial, technology, or regional policy, emphasizing different aspects of clusters and innovation. And even non-cluster policy instruments, such as housing or education policy, can affect cluster development (Giest 2016; Uyarra and Ramlogan 2016).

Further, there is a temporal dimension to the research connected to clusters. Whereas some research points towards the path-dependent development of regional agglomerations, which sees prior industries and potential institutional legacies as determining factors for innovation success in a specific location (Sternberg 2010; Acemoglu and Robinson 2012; Spolaore and Wacziarg 2012), more policy-oriented research focuses on the impact of current policies. The regional path development stream, in particular, has highlighted aspects of economic renewal and new path development in regions, distinguishing among path extension, path renewal, and new path creation (Boschma 2014; Hassink 2010; Trippl, Asheim, and Miorner 2015). These developments, in turn, are linked to the characteristics of the regional innovation system. In other words, the capacity of a region to renew itself is highly relevant (Boschma 2014; Trippl, Asheim, and Miorner 2015). In addition, researchers such as Enright (2003) and Ffowcs-William (2005) have developed a life-cycle model of cluster development in which each stage potentially requires a different set of resources and policies.

A major criticism of past cluster research was the lack of an overarching framework for clusters because of the reliance on individual case studies. This has changed in recent years as the European Cluster Observatory and the US Cluster Mapping Project have taken shape, providing data on various clusters and drawing conclusions based on a larger set of cases and sources. The question that Bathelt (2005) asks, however, remains: which mechanisms create consistent behaviour within a cluster?

This is a question many policy makers ask themselves when designing cluster and other policies that might affect the creation and sustainability of innovative local agglomerations. This has to do with two main aspects. First, the research on clusters lies at the intersection of several fields that do not always agree on the drivers of local innovation. Second, cluster policy is at the intersection of industrial, regional, and innovation policy. This makes clusters as a policy target a complex, multilevel, multilayered phenomenon.

These themes in the literature are not mutually exclusive, as they incorporate elements from each other to develop arguments about innovation and clusters. This is not to say that, on some elements, deep-seated conceptual and empirical controversies remain that go beyond the scope of this book (Uyarra and Ramlogan 2016). The literature is thereby summarized here under the following headings in order to draw out capacity-related aspects from current research:

- *The geography of innovation*: This is the intersection of spatial analyses of networks and their impact on places and regions, combining micro-level dynamics of knowledge transfer with more macro-level, structural elements; this line of research highlights that innovative capacity is not only about the place, but also about the integration in a network.

- *Systems of innovation*: This literature stream focuses on the system context in which clusters are embedded, including the national and regional innovation system. This stream also spans the idea of a triple-helix set-up in which research, industry, and government entities need the capacity to collaborate in order to innovate.
- *Network sociology*: With an eye on the relational, dynamic elements within networks, this research focuses on the capacity of individuals and firms to identify, interpret, and exploit knowledge, and includes the dimension of trust in sharing knowledge with other stakeholders. The analyses thereby address these aspects at the individual, organizational, network, and cluster levels. Evolutionary economic geography and cluster life cycles further show how these relationships evolve over time.
- *The institutional layer*: This focus has the goal of singling out the institutional make-up of a cluster to differentiate institutions that support the capacity to exchange knowledge and learning from the idea of a national or regional innovation system.

Taken together, these research strands sketch the landscape of the literature on clusters in a broader sense, including a multilevel perspective in combination with relational, spatial, and temporal dynamics. With special attention to capacity, this section intends to show that, as research highlights, innovation – a complex process in itself – requires several types of capacities, which are combined under the concept of collaborative and absorptive capacity. This framework focuses on capacity-related activities at the network level embedded in a larger framework of multilevel institutions. Much of the literature distinguishes between a cluster's internal and external knowledge exchanges. This is captured by separating collaborative capacity, which speaks to internal collaborative and knowledge structures, from absorptive abilities, which describe the inclusion of external knowledge.

The structure of the following theory section moves from the geography of innovation and the dynamics of networking more generally towards a focused discussion around the concept of clusters and their evolution. The establishment of the capacity framework constitutes a separate subsection in order to distinguish capacity from other concepts, as well as to define collaborative and absorptive capacity specifically.

## The Geography of Innovation

The geography of innovation has its roots in neoclassical growth theory, which describes the role of labour and capital in production (Stough, Stimson, and Nijkamp 2011). After a so-called relational turn in the study of economic geography, the field moved towards a more endogenous growth interpretation, including a turn away from macroeconomic to micro-level factors, such as the behaviour of individual firms in the market (Vaz et al. 2014; Williamson 1995). Specifically, network evolution has become a subject of study driven by findings about the cumulative character of network relationships. Economic geography research aims to understand the mutual connection "between the spatial evolution of networks and the imprint of network dynamics on the development of places and regions considering endogenous change and the concept of network trajectories" (Glückler and Doreian 2016, 1127).

Among the themes emerging from this literature are a region's economic preconditions, on which high-tech sectors and cluster development strategies build. The availability of human capital is often mentioned as one factor relevant to innovative performance. The economic geography literature accordingly has moved away from the assumption of geographically bound knowledge spillover to the existence of voluntary knowledge relationships (Boschma 2005; Breschi and Lissoni 2001; Crespo, Vicente, and Amblard 2016). In a second step, the combination of knowledge and the localized nature of knowledge flows then produce a cluster (Normaler and Verspagen 2016). Government policy plays a role in this by providing the conditions for relational connections to evolve in a specific location (Grillitsch and Asheim 2015).

Micro-level factors within the cluster also span more intangible elements – for example, networking and social capital. This is where research on network sociology and that on innovation geography clearly intersect. The latter stream incorporates ideas of interfirm relationships and knowledge transfer, whereas the literature on networks has gained an economic dimension to co-location, pointing towards cognitive and organizational proximity that can enhance innovation (Boschma 2005). The geography-of-innovation perspective further brings forward relevant factors for driving innovation in local agglomerations, including local public or private demand, specialized institutions, and the structure of business (Delgado, Porter, and Stern 2014; Porter 1990; Saxenian 1994). Thus, the most recent economic geography research on innovation and clusters centres on questions of the effect of structural dynamics on the network and collective outcomes for actors (Glückler and Doreian 2016). Ultimately, this research stream shows that enhancing a firm's innovative capability is not just a matter of being in the right place, but also being in the right network (Crespo, Vicente, and Amblard 2016).

## Systems of Innovation

The geography-of-innovation approach is predominantly a spatial analysis for capturing the economic and institutional structures affecting innovation; here, clusters are smaller entities than national and regional innovation systems. This approach has incorporated some of the geography-of-innovation findings by focusing on the location of innovation. Both the geography and systems of innovation literature are based on the assumption that the concentration of innovative activities is based on voluntary knowledge relationships and the positive effects of network embeddedness (Crespo, Vicente, and Amblard 2016).

The systems perspective goes back to List (1841), who developed the "national system of production" approach, which takes into account a wide set of national institutions, such as those involved in education and training (Lundvall et al. 2003). Basically, each country has some form of national innovation system, which has a variety of regional innovation systems that can cross national boundaries. Within those regional innovation systems, universities and companies can then cluster in a particular locale. The systems-of-innovation approach defines "all important economic, social, political, organizational, institutional and other factors that influence the development, diffusion and use of innovations" (Edquist 1997, 14; 2005).

Asheim and Gertler (2005) further distinguish between different types of regional innovation systems: territorially embedded regional innovation systems; regionally networked innovation systems, which have a planned character because they are strategically set up locally and gain access to a wider pool of knowledge globally; and regionalized national innovation systems, in which exogenous actors and relationships play a larger role (science parks, for example). Using administrative and political borders as the basis for thinking about innovation has already taken root in Europe. The European Innovation Scoreboard (European Commission 2017a) uses national innovation systems as an entity to measure innovation performance. An extension of this is the Regional Innovation Scoreboard (European Commission 2017b), which looks at regional innovation systems within and across countries. A narrower understanding of the systems-of-innovation approach focuses on the roles of universities, public and private research institutes, and companies in R&D. This is captured in the triple-helix concept (Etzkowitz and Leydesdorff 2000; Asheim and Gertler 2005).

The triple-helix framework identifies interactions within the network, based on collaboration among research, industry, and government entities (Etzkowitz 2003). This relationship can be observed at different levels, national or local, depending on the unit of analysis (Lundvall 1992). The triple helix thus offers a structural perspective on clusters by mapping the institutional interface and potential changes in the dynamics among these entities (Etzkowitz 2003; Leydesdorff and Etzkowitz 1998). Critics of this approach point out that it "captures only part of the process" and that an "analytical territories approach" would allow one to focus on the "fluidity of action across local, regional and national boundaries" (Aylward and Turpin 2003, 4–5). The alternative being offered operates in an economic space, rather than a political one, by moving away from individual institutions towards a more geographic understanding of innovation.

## Network Sociology

### Learning and Trust

At the intersection of the systems literature and the network literature, attention has increasingly been paid to learning among stakeholders, rather than pure knowledge transfer. This means separating the structural component from the institutional one, and focusing on the latter by looking at the capacities of actors to learn. Fischer, Scherngell, and Jansenberger (2006), for example, point out that smaller firms within a cluster need to interact with other firms and organizations in order to gain the benefits of co-location and to compensate for their size with learning.

This idea further includes "learning regions" and even "learning economies" (Morgan 1997; Ratanawaraha and Polenske 2007). Learning regions refers to the combination of "innovation systems, technology complexes including the knowledge spillover phenomena, post-Fordism new industry clusters, technology policy, local and regional institutions, and community action" (Stough, Stimson, and Nijkamp 2011, 11). According to Florida (1995), learning regions provide the environment and infrastructure that facilitate the flow of knowledge and, ultimately, the opportunity to learn. An important aspect of this is that proximity is not sufficient for learning to take place – in fact, it can be a disadvantage if there is limited access to a diverse set of information. This loops back to the capacity of individual organizations within the network to identify, interpret, and exploit new knowledge (Boschma 2005; Cohen and Levinthal 1990). Also relevant for learning is the source of the knowledge – whether it is available locally, within the cluster, or globally. Belussi and Sedita (2010) distinguish between local learning, including the transfer of knowledge among network members in a certain location, and a global pipeline of knowledge, whereby stakeholders are able to learn from outside sources or even to substitute a lack of local learning with global knowledge transfer.

Another factor that affects the ability to learn is trust. Trust, indeed, has a key function, as collaboration is voluntary, while competition is fierce (Beugelsdijk and Van Schaik 2005; Putnam 1993). Stakeholders who experience intense competition have to choose whether or not to disclose certain information (Zucker et al. 1995) – in other words, for knowledge transfer and learning to take place, actors in the network need to trust one another to disclose what they know. This is a cumulative process, where co-location creates a collaborative dynamic, and repeated interaction improves trust (Klijn et al. 2016; Reagans and McEvily 2003). In short, trust creates collaborative dynamics in a competitive setting. This is best described in the economics literature as a "stag hunt": a game-theoretic approach to collaboration in a competitive environment that indicates that the viability of cooperation depends on mutual beliefs and rests on trust (Skyrms 2004). The approach ties attitudes about trust to specific behavioural patterns that could generate macro-level outcomes, arguing that trust causes prosperity, since a change in attitude leads individuals to make different decisions in settings where their decisions have economic consequences (Bosworth 2013).

This literature is particularly relevant for identifying how trust evolves through third parties, such as another person or an organization. As McEvily, Perrone, and Zaheer (2003, 94) point out, "two people who have little or no knowledge of each other can develop trust for each other relatively quickly when they share trust in a common third party." These dynamics also play out such that individuals transfer trust to other members of the group with whom they have no history (McEvily, Perrone, and Zaheer 2003). This indicates that knowledge of the trustworthiness of a stakeholder can be transferred from one network member to another through a third party or intermediary (Coleman 1990; Hardin 2002; McEvily, Perrone, and Zaheer 2003). This gives cluster organizations the opportunity to create connections among network members by being trusted entities (Giest 2019), in a position to broker among stakeholders, and thereby enhance collaboration and knowledge sharing (Giest 2015; Gulati 1995; Klijn et al. 2016).

*Social Capital*

Linked to trust is the social capital research stream. This literature describes how companies and other organizations gain access to knowledge through relationships that are based on trust. A widely accepted definition of social capital is "the sum of the actual and potential resources embedded within, available through, and derived from, the network of relationships possessed by an individual or social unit" (Nahapiet and Ghoshal 1998, 243). The creation of social capital is based on four main mechanisms. Relationships enhance, first, the flow of information, second, the influence on other network members, and, third, give access to specialized resources. Finally, social connections create a social group that is recognized beyond the immediate network (Filieri et al. 2014; Uzzi 1996).

Generally speaking, two schools of thought are contributing to the idea of social capital. One follows Putnam's (2000) idea of social capital, whereby people invest in relationships with the expectation that the favour will be returned later. The idea is based on concepts of civil society and civic participation that predate the social capital concept (Burt 1992; Foley and Edwards 1999). The second school treats social capital investment as a private asset of a group that wants to enhance its economic returns (Granovetter 1985; Huggins, Johnston, and Thompson 2012; Murphy, Huggins, and Thompson 2016), and has been widely applied to networks in order to understand knowledge transfer in these settings.

To establish social capital, network members can pursue relationships within a group of individuals or a community ("bonding"), and reach out to those beyond the group ("bridging"). This potentially opens up the opportunity to gain access to skills and resources currently not present in the network (Burt 1992; Putnam 2000; Woodhouse 2006). Bonding and bridging are both based on the assumption that prior relationships need to be established before individuals exchange information, and that this knowledge will first circulate within the group before it reaches stakeholders beyond the group (Burt 2002). Although bonding includes strong ties (which create cohesion within small groups), the research in this book focuses predominantly on bridging, where social capital enables contact and collaboration among members of diverse groups (Estrin, Korosteleva, and Mickiewicz 2014). This is again linked to trust by distinguishing between "thick" trust for members of the same group and "thin" trust for relationships beyond the immediate network (Anheier and Kendall 2002).

*The Network as an Entity*

The focus of most of these studies is the network as a whole, or the relationships among individual organizations and other network members. Provan, Fish, and Sydow (2007) distinguish here between network-level and egocentric theories. Both concern the network, but the latter focus on structural issues and, for example, the role of individual members in the network setting. This includes questions such as whether they take on the role of connecting or brokering among several organizations and what the implications are for these organizations (Burt 1992; Gulati 1995; Uzzi 1996). Research looking at the network as a whole focuses more on its properties and characteristics: "This perspective presumes that a network involves many organizations collaboratively working towards a more or less common goal and that the success of one network organization may or may not be critical to the success of the entire networking its customer or client group" (Provan, Fish, and Sydow 2007, 485). The network perspective can highlight how organizational action is embedded in existing relationships through conducting social network analysis.

**Clusters**

The idea of clusters taps directly into many of these findings by combining the relevance of the local agglomeration of innovation with collaboration and knowledge exchange on the basis of proximity and social capital (Audretsch and Feldman 1996; Cooke, Uranga, and Etxebarria 1997; Uyarra 2010). Clusters are further based on the idea of specialized localization put forward by Marshall (1890), who identified "industrial districts" as "local availability of inputs, presence of a skilled labour force and knowledge spillover" (quoted in Giuliani 2005, 270). In his research, Marshall described the metallurgical and textile-producing areas of Britain. Almost sixty years later, Becattini (1979, 132) found similarities between the British industry and certain areas in Italy, and refers to these Marshallian industrial districts as a localized social and productive "thickening," held together by a "complex and tangled web of external economies and diseconomies of joint and associated costs, of historical and cultural vestiges, which envelops both inter-firm and interpersonal relationships." Along these lines, a widely used definition today is that by Porter (1998) – namely, that clusters appear when densely linked companies and research institutions in a common industry locate in the same geographic area. Following the original cluster concept, several disciplines developed the idea further, and used different versions influenced by their specific perspectives (Bathelt 2005). This created some definitional and conceptual elasticity for the cluster concept (Martin and Sunley 2003), and led to "conceptual and empirical controversies about what clusters are and how they can be identified, how they emerge and evolve, why they matter and how they can be used by policy" (Uyarra and Ramlogan 2016, 197).

Specifically, the boundary between networks and clusters has been a challenging one. The term "network" refers to a group of stakeholders who cooperate on a joint project – complementing one another and specializing in order to overcome problems, achieve collective efficiency, and conquer markets beyond their individual reach. "Clusters" refers to a sectoral and geographical concentration of enterprises that produce and sell a range of related or complementary products, and are thus faced with common challenges and opportunities. The network literature thus is not so much concerned with the concentration of firms in particular areas, but rather with the process that leads them to establish cooperative links, even if they operate in different regions. In contrast, the basic assumption from a cluster perspective is that geographic proximity plays a role in the relationships among stakeholders. Due to this spatial dimension, the regional-innovation-system perspective plays a role in conceptualizing clusters. For example, the definition put forward by the European Commission actively uses "the concept of regional innovation system to denote regional clusters plus 'supporting' institutions" (European Commission 2002, 14). The Commission further states that the relationships among firms within the cluster through which they exchange ideas, information, and knowledge define their competitive advantage (European Commission 2002). Similarly, the Silicon Valley model of clusters (Saxenian 1994) identifies collective learning, informal communication, and collaboration as trademarks of clustering.

*Cluster Life Cycles*

A large portion of the literature approaches clusters from an evolutionary or life-cycle perspective. Borrowing from the 1950s literature on product profiles over time, this research is based on observations that clusters come and go, might undergo reinvention and transformation, and might decline or even disappear (Martin and Sunley 2011).

There are several ways to define and identify the different stages that constitute a life cycle or cluster evolution. Klepper (1997) identifies three stages of the industry life cycle, after which theories about cluster development have been shaped. There is wide-ranging agreement on the stages of birth, growth, maturity, and decline or reinvention (Bergman 2007; Brenner 2004; Klepper 2007; Menzel and Fornahl 2010; Sainsbury 1999; Sölvell 2008), but several scholars have taken a slightly different perspective on specific aspects of such developments. For example, instead of focusing on the dynamics of the rise and decline of clusters, some look at the potential of a cluster's being "locked into" a specific way of doing things or being "path dependent" when it comes to institutional structures (Malmberg and Maskell 2002). A growing strand of the literature is also moving away from an industry-driven understanding of the cluster life cycle and towards a logic that suggests that "cluster development can be found in more autonomous processes specific to clusters themselves" (Martin and Sunley 2011, 1302; see also Maskell and Malmberg 2007; Potter and Watts 2008, Tavassoli and Tsagdis 2014). This means that localization externalities have their own life cycle and that local cluster developments do not necessarily follow the cycle of their respective industry (Menzel and Fornahl 2010). This is linked to contextualizing the life-cycle stages in a more complex system of production and innovation (Menzel and Fornahl 2010) – which Martin and Sunley (2011) label as "complex adaptive systems." In short, this perspective highlights that the cluster does not necessarily develop as a whole, but that "parts of the cluster can stay at an earlier stage while others advance along the trajectory" (Menzel and Fornahl 2010, 224).

Another, more recent line of work, focuses on "the role played by spinoffs, and, more broadly, the transmission of capabilities from parent firms to independent startups" (Costa and Baptista 2015, 3), and is based on a combination of organizational heritage and agglomeration economies theories (Frenken, Cefis, and Stam 2013; Martin and Sunley 2006). These theories propose a distinct explanation for the growth of clusters over time based on the role of spinoffs linked to the advantages of regional agglomerations (Costa and Baptista 2015; Glaeser, Rosenthal, and Strange 2010). Similar to this, a group of scholars is refining the original claim that clusters are geographic concentrations of linked industries (Porter 2003), and separating related and unrelated variety. As Boschma, Minondo, and Navarro (2012, 243) note, "the related variety effect includes externalities that may come from a diversity of related industries in a region" (see also Frenken, van Oort, and Verburg 2007). They further suggest that the importance of this relatedness for regional development differs depending on the development stage or life-cycle phase the cluster is in. This means that, for example, related variety might be more important during some stages than in others.

*Cluster Evolution*

The cluster evolution strand of the literature, also called evolutionary economic geography (Berg 2015; Boschma and Frenken 2006), is linked to the life-cycle perspective through its focus on the dynamics that are connected to the emergence, growth, decline, and transformation of clusters. In this view, firms and industries move along existing (technological) trajectories at different speeds (Simmie and Martin 2010). However, "[t]his perspective does not solely analyse the path dependencies and contingencies of cluster evolution, but instead the leverage that can be used to contribute to the emergence and growth of clusters as well as to prevent their decline" (Fornahl, Hassink, and Menzel 2015, 1922). More specifically, this includes analysing the co-evolution of cluster dynamics and their institutional context, and taking on a distinct policy perspective (Avnimelech and Teubal 2008; Brenner and Schlump 2011) in response to criticism that a focus on firm-level routines has been emphasized at the expense of research on institutional actors such as the state (Martin and Coenen 2015).

In essence, the evolutionary economic geography perspective on clusters focuses on the dynamics of network formation by analysing how relationships among firms arise and develop throughout time and space (Boschma and Martin 2010). This also includes a more nuanced look at the co-evolution of technology, markets, and institutions, in combination with firm relations and proximity (e.g. MacKinnon et al. 2009). These approaches argue for policies around clusters that "take the history of the region as a starting point, and identify regional potentials and bottlenecks accordingly" (Boschma and Martin 2010, 25).

**The Institutional Layer**

Another major criticism of the cluster concept, beyond its vagueness and elasticity, is its lack of institutional underpinnings. Indeed, institutional structure was not part of the original cluster concept developed by Porter (1990; 2001). An institutional perspective, however, reveals a diversity of technology- and country-specific aspects that make clusters differ significantly in their sectoral mix, complexity, and spatial reach (Bathelt 2005). The institutional make-up of a cluster is also at times conflated with the characteristics of the national or regional innovation system (Asheim and Gertler 2005). In the innovation system literature, for example, urban regions are characterized as institutionally thick, given that they have strong universities, research institutes, companies, and an industrial structure (Amin and Thrift 1995). Institutional thickness is also associated with institutions that support knowledge exchange and learning (Grillitsch and Asheim 2015).

The idea of institutional thickness combines the stakeholders in the cluster (different types of public and private organizations) with institutions (rules that structure interactions). To avoid confusion around this aspect of clustering, I follow the differentiation proposed by Trippl, Asheim, and Miorner (2015), which sets organizational and institutional dimensions apart. Hence, an institutionally thick region is one in which the rules for interactions enable knowledge transfer and learning among the organizations in the network, while a region is organizationally thick if it has many organizations with strong capabilities (see also Grillitsch and Asheim 2015). In other words, the organizational dimension of thickness focuses on the level of competency of individual organizations, whereas the institutional one highlights the levels of localized knowledge transfer and trust.

Generally speaking, clusters are associated with locality, proximity, and different types of cooperation among institutions (Dohse 2007). Over the years, however, and in tandem with other research streams, cluster theories have moved beyond the idea of strict locality. In addition to geographical scale, global networking has become part of clustering. Further, the aspects of knowledge transfer and the policy perspective have gained importance in addressing different types, sizes, and dynamics of clusters.

**The Capacity Framework**

The capacity framework developed and applied in this book builds on the different streams of literature that contribute to our understanding of clusters. Several researchers point to the importance of capacity without making it the focal point of their study. The premise of the capacity framework is that collaboration and knowledge transfer are central elements of clusters and innovation. In economic geography terms, knowledge spillovers represent "pure externalities that produce non-compensating advantages for the receivers" (Stough, Stimson, and Nijkamp 2011, 16; see also Nijkamp and van Hemert 2009).

*Capacity, Resilience, and Adaptability*

Generally speaking, capacity can be defined as the ability of private or public organizations, and of the network as a whole, to absorb and use knowledge relevant for innovation processes. This is done through collaborative processes both inside and outside the cluster. The capacity of an organization builds, in turn, on the ability of individuals within certain structural set-ups to use knowledge (Cohen and Levinthal 1990). To further sharpen the idea of capacity, one should differentiate among capability, resilience, adaptability, and capacity.

*Capability* refers to the abilities of employees of an organization within the cluster (Liao, Fei, and Chen 2007). These abilities are largely described as individual actions, as opposed to the literature on capacity, which looks at the more cumulative effect of individual, organizational, and cluster level capacities (Menzel and Fornahl 2010). In fact, capacity and capability are used interchangeably in much of the research. A way to describe the difference would be to say that, for example, an individual is capable of being innovative but lacks the capacity, in the form of support to reach out to relevant stakeholders or funding structures, to do so.

The remaining terms – resilience, adaptability, and capacity – have been linked, especially in the economic geography literature focusing on regional industries (Hassink 2010; Simmie and Martin 2010). For example, capacity has been integrated into the idea of regional *resilience*, referring to the ability of local firms to adapt to changes and shocks in the market and to changes in technology or policy (McGlade et al. 2006; Simmie and Martin 2010). The resilience literature thereby focuses heavily on markets and, from a more evolutionary point of view, on local political structures that adapt to changing environmental conditions. These conditions can be technological as well as political (Swanstrom 2008). The regional resilience framework is presented as an alternative to the learning region idea, which focuses more heavily on the policy dimension of change (Pendall, Foster, and Cowell 2007; Swanstrom 2008).

In recent years, however, the institutional and policy dimensions have been increasingly emphasized in the discussion around regional *resilience and learning* – largely driven by the evolutionary perspective (Boschma and Martin 2010; Hassink and Klaerding 2010; Martin and Sunley 2006). Whereas the resilience framework has been presented as an alternative to the learning region, the two angles are now more often combined (Hassink 2010). This is in response to criticism of the economic perspective that the institutional context has been ignored when it comes to regional adjustment. In sum, *capacity* has been used to understand the response of individual companies, whereas *resilience* more broadly describes the ability of a region to adjust. Chapple and Lester (2007, 2) define regional resilience as "the ability to transform regional outcomes in the face of challenge."

As for the distinction between resilience and *adaptation*, Bertolini (2007) suggests that the former applies to systems that are capable of performing under unpredictable changes and the latter to systems that can adapt in the short term; resilient systems cannot change quickly, but can function in times of change. More generally, the term adaptability is linked to evolutionary studies on clusters. These look at the emergence of clusters and how they change over time (e.g. Fornahl, Henn, and Menzel 2009; Klepper 2007). Literature on cluster life cycles looks at how regional agglomerations of firms adapt, relying on frameworks of path dependence, lock-in, and path creation (Belussi and Sedita 2010; Enright 2003; Maskell and Malmberg 2007). As Wolfe (2010, 140) writes, "[t]he path-dependence approach starts from the assumption of multiple potential points of equilibrium and analyses how a particular economy gets locked into a specific pattern of growth through a cumulative series of decisions over time." This approach also includes studies on how new paths are launched and how regions shift to new industries. In this context, scholars point to "localized capabilities" (Maskell and Malmberg 1999) that stem from characteristics unique to the region, such as local infrastructure, resources, institutions, and available knowledge, and skills.

Bringing these different streams together, resilience is used as an overarching framework in which adaptability and capacity are characteristics that can be applied to individuals, organizations, and networks. Resilience scholars thus put more emphasis on the recovering of existing industrial structures than on the evolutionary perspective on the emergence of clusters (Hassink 2010). As Wolfe (2010, 142) says, "resilient regions are those in which existing clusters of firms are able to transition out of declining industries, while simultaneously exploiting the local knowledge infrastructure to cultivate new, potential growth fields." This more general definition, however, does not tackle the activities ongoing within the cluster to sustain a certain level of resilience. These activities are specifically targeted by the *capacity framework* presented in this book. They happen at the network level, since organizations collaborate and compete in a local setting that is, in turn, embedded in a larger framework of multilevel institutions and policies. Building on the definition of local capabilities by Maskell and Malmberg (1998), the capacity framework incorporates the resources, communications channels, collaborative structures, and leadership of clusters. It thus relies more heavily on the social capital and networking structures within local settings – what Putnam (1993) calls "civic involvement" – than on market structures. This approach focuses on how localized collaborations, such as cultural associations or cooperatives, enhance knowledge-sharing dynamics. Applying this to high-tech clusters, the argument remains that face-to-face collaboration to share knowledge among, for example, researchers, industry, and government stakeholders, is a relevant element of innovation.

Beyond the approach to resilience and adaptability discussed above, the existing literature also touches upon capacity by looking at the cluster as a whole as well as at individual organizations within it. This shift towards looking at possible underlying mechanisms stems from the realization that, despite examples such as Silicon Valley, clustering and collaboration have not proven to be sufficient for innovation success or for the ability to be resilient over a longer period of time (Vaz et al. 2014). The idea of capacity is largely centred on the process of knowledge transfer and learning – the ability to communicate, absorb, and learn from the knowledge pool in and beyond the cluster. As Lundvall et al. (2003, 231) phrase it, "the most important elements in the [innovation] system have to do with the learning capability of individuals, organizations and regions." Murphy, Huggins, and Thompson (2016, 1049) call these the "softer elements of innovation." Capacity also includes the context in which this learning takes place. This is linked to the ability of the cluster as a whole to attract capital, companies, and highly skilled workers from the outside, but also to connect and communicate among organizations on the inside. Trippl, Asheim, and Miorner (2015, 4) find that "a weak capacity to absorb knowledge from outside the region" leads to innovation system failures (see also Doloreux and Dionne 2008; Karlsen, Isaksen, and Spilling 2011).

Lindqvist, Ketels, and Sölvell (2013) integrate both the internal and external dimension into five major activities that firms carry out in clusters:

- general cluster networking: actors coming together to identify strengths and weaknesses by sharing information and creating communications channels, such as websites, seminars, etc.;
- human resource upgrading: attracting and retaining talent in the region and providing training for better management;
- cluster expansion: promoting inward investment into the region to increase the number of firms moving into the area;
- business development: supporting smaller and medium-sized companies in particular by sharing, for example, services or purchasing costs; and
- innovation and technology: making active networking efforts with the goal of increasing innovation – this applies to collaboration among firms as well as between industry and research.

Along the same lines, Crespo, Vicente, and Amblard (2016) speak more generally of the renewal capacities of clusters, and Schmitz (1995) points towards their capacity to adapt. Wolfe (2010) pinpoints historical capacity as one factor accounting for a region's overall resilience, having to do with strong industries that have settled in the same region over time.

Two important points need to be noted here: One is that some scholars treat capacity as something the whole network has on an aggregate level – for example, by using the number of highly skilled workers in the network as a capacity measure. Others treat capacity as a characteristic of individuals or organizations within the network. This distinction is relevant because individual or organizational-level capacity is something that can be actively supported, for example, by a cluster organization, whereas capacity at the network level requires shifts at a larger scale, through a change in government policy. A reoccurring argument in the discussion around capacity is that there are endogenous and external sources of knowledge, skills, and capital, and that a region can compensate for internal deficiencies with external sources. The institutional structure can thereby facilitate or hinder certain processes (Simmie and Martin 2010). This is closely related to parts of the literature on learning regions, which make a similar point by saying that such regions provide the environment and infrastructure for facilitating knowledge flows and, ultimately, the ability to learn (Florida 1995). The distinction between external and internal knowledge is also picked up by Belussi and Sedita (2010) in their conceptualization of local learning and global pipelines. The capacity framework follows this distinction by separating collaborative and absorptive capacity. Collaborative capacity speaks to the internal collaborative and knowledge structures, whereas absorptive capacity describes the ability to take in external knowledge.

*Collaborative Capacity*

Collaborative capacity consists of purpose, structure, communication, and resources in network relationships (Lai 2011). Purpose, as one capacity element, is defined by the presence of a leadership structure and a shared vision that focuses on collaborative efforts. Further, an (informal) structure within an organization or network "allows flexibility and adaptability for collaborators to remain open in the midst of major changes, such as changes of major goals or members" (Lai 2011, 451). Communications in general and communications channels in particular ensure information transmission and also put information in the context of solution seeking. The last element of the collaborative capacity framework is the resource category, which includes the intellectual, human, and financial capital necessary to develop and sustain collaborative efforts – predominantly knowledge, skills, and financial resources. Such resource exchanges can create interactive dependency and thus cohesion among network members (Agranoff and McGuire 2001; Pennings 1981). These aspects of building collaborative capacity all aim to enhance networking and, ultimately, to make a network or

cluster more innovative. This conceptualization is based on the premise
that proximity does not imply innovation; it is the collaborative structure among stakeholders in the cluster that facilitates knowledge transfer and, ultimately, innovation (Boschma 2005).

The various sources on local agglomerations offer different perspectives on the elements of purpose, structure, communication, and resources. *Purpose* is described in different literatures as vision or goal
setting, where key actors within the network formulate a common vision and develop and formalize collaborative relationships based on
this purpose (Wolfe 2010). The network perspective builds more generally on the idea that network members more or less work towards
a common goal, and that this drives collaboration and trust in one
another (Provan, Fish, and Sydow 2007). In this context, purpose is
closely linked to *communications*, since informal communications, in
particular, support collaborative work and strengthen common goal
setting (Saxenian 1994). Communications also rely on an opportunity
structure that allows for interactions within the network – for example,
through proximity, crossing paths with other network members during
events, or setting up channels through which regular communications
are facilitated, such as common board structures for innovation-related
organizations or regular meetings. *Structure* picks up some of the arguments made by the literature emphasizing the institutional set-up of
clusters. Specifically, it adds the institutionally thick dimension to capacity by identifying rules of interaction that enable knowledge transfer and learning among organizations in the network (Grillitsch and
Asheim 2015; Trippl, Asheim, and Miorner 2015). *Resources* encompass
a variety of elements, such as the investment structure within a cluster
or the human capital that organizations can access. The geography of
innovation literature has emphasized this aspect by looking at learning
regions and the ability of clusters to attract highly skilled individuals
in combination with a structure that allows for knowledge transfer and
innovation (Florida 1995).

The paradox that arises from this set-up is that the effort to collaborate opposes possible competitive goals among companies. A closer
look at the competition in high-tech clusters, however, reveals that there
is a distinction between price and cost competition. "For example, price
competitiveness will be said to increase in a scenario whereby outward
investment rises predicated on lower government borrowing, leading
to a decline in the value of domestic currency as export prices fall and
import prices increase in domestic currency terms" (Nallari and Griffith
2013, 34). Cost-based competitiveness is unsustainable, however, if an
increase in import prices leads to domestic inflation or if productivity

falls due to lower inward investment (Cantwell 2005; Nallari and Griffith 2013). This implies that leading firms play a crucial role in this type of set-up. The competitive advantage of a firm derives from "the cumulative and incremental learning experience of its management team" (Cantwell 2005, 560). This shows that competition in clusters is more about benchmarking performance to assess the capabilities of learning and innovation than about the mutual potential for damaging each other. Some researchers even point out that the competitive race among stakeholders stimulates collaboration and innovation. Lundvall and Christensen (2003) find that firms experiencing strong competition are more frequently involved in product innovation and organizational change. Moreover, the intensified competition was the trigger to make such changes. Overall, "at the firm level, business-to-business ... cooperation and competition are a key factor for the creation and successful development of a cluster" (Hira et al. 2013). There is, however, a caveat to fuelling such competition: it is necessary to promote organizational flexibility and innovative capability first, before competition policy can be implemented. In other words, *the capacity to collaborate has to be established before competition can bear fruit in a cluster set-up* (Lundvall and Christensen 2003).

*Absorptive Capacity*

Compared to collaborative capacity, absorptive capacity focuses on the ability of a firm, cluster, or country "to integrate the existing and exploitable resources – technological opportunities – into the production chain, and the foresight to anticipate potential and relevant techno-logical trajectories" (Narula 2004, 6). In regard to clusters, the concept highlights two interrelated aspects: the formation of linkages with extra-cluster sources of knowledge (that is, the extra-cluster knowledge base), and the structural characteristics of the intra-cluster knowledge system (Bell and Albu 1999; Giuliani 2005). The two dimensions of intra- and extra-cluster are closely related in the sense that extra-cluster knowledge needs to be transferred to intra-cluster firms by an entity with outside linkages that also has the knowledge base to pick and distribute information. The intra-cluster knowledge system consists of the learning and collaboration processes among stakeholders.

Absorptive capacity is also cumulative. By investing in and fostering capacity elements, there is a subsequent pay-off. The mechanism behind this is that the more an organization or network connects to other stakeholders and the more knowledge is gained, the better everyone can identify missing information and who can offer it. Overall, this process encompasses three components: exploratory learning, transformative learning, and exploitative learning. All three elements are part of one process, as exploratory learning describes the confrontation with new knowledge, transformative learning changes the way in which this knowledge is assimilated and combined with prior knowledge, while explorative learning describes how new knowledge is translated into action, which ideally will benefit the organization or network (Buenstorf and Murmann 2005; Harvey et al. 2010; Lane, Koka, and Pathak 2006). With a wider knowledge base, the expectation is that the network is prepared for changes and has better foresight.

However, the relationship between social capital, learning, and performance is not as straight forward. Absorptive capacity positively moderates the relationship between network-based learning and response performance, rather than posing a direct link. The "advantage accrues to entrepreneurial firms that are able to put meaning to the vast knowledge that social capital unlocks and those that effectively absorb and assimilate this knowledge into the firm's activities" (Hughes et al. 2014, 17). The same is true for clusters overall. As clusters gain the ability to pick and choose the knowledge that is needed, absorptive capacity levels are advanced and performance levels are more likely to rise.

Absorptive capacity thereby taps directly into the research on social capital, learning, and knowledge transfer. The central argument is that organizations tap into knowledge sources outside of the immediate network, and potentially can compensate for resources lacking within the cluster or pick up on new streams of knowledge that are evolving in other regions. This is also described as "global pipeline," where stakeholders learn from outside sources or substitute a lack of local learning with global knowledge transfer (Belussi and Sedita 2010). Examples of this have been observed in some up-and-coming high-tech clusters in Asia, where foreign direct investment and the general involvement of multinational companies led to knowledge gains and, ultimately, to higher innovative output in the local community (Wong 2011). Absorptive capacity further acknowledges that "a weak capacity to absorb knowledge from outside the region and a thin structure of supporting organizations" leads to innovation system failures (Trippl, Asheim, and Miorner 2015, 4; see also Doloreux and Dionne 2008; Karlsen, Isaksen, and Spilling 2011).

Both the collaborative and the absorptive capacity framework allow for the identification of activities that enhance growth and productivity within a cluster. The concepts are able to break down the capabilities into observable units, such as agreements, policy guidelines, virtual platforms, and so on. The framework also takes into account factors that are beyond the immediate cluster, such as regional and national policies. Innovation research has moved increasingly towards including policy aspects, because they play a crucial role in explaining differences in regional economic adaptability, as shown in several case studies (Hassink 2009; Tödtling and Trippl 2004; Trippl and Otto 2009). Another aspect that has gained traction in this area of research is collaborative institutions or cluster organizations that are able to connect stakeholders within the network and develop a regional strategy and vision (Wolfe 2010).

In the following chapter, I connect both elements by treating clusters as a dynamic setting where pre-existing policies and regional settings shape clusters and their ability to innovate. Cluster organizations are seen both as a tool used by governments to facilitate clusters and as something developed by network members, where a leading firm or organization is able to connect a variety of stakeholders to foster collaborative work (Dhanaraj and Parkhe 2006; Goduscheit 2014; Provan and Kenis 2007). This perspective goes back to the idea, which originates in the social capital literature, that clusters have bridging strategies to enable the better circulation of knowledge. One way to foster those bridging efforts is to rely on a central actor in the network that is well connected (Crespo, Suire, and Vicente 2014).

As for the location of capacity within the cluster, previous literature has treated it either as a network-level characteristic, such as identifying the number of highly skilled workers as a capacity measure, or as an individual- or organizational-level trait. Both levels are addressed by collaborative and absorptive capacity in that individual- or organizational-level capacity can be supported by a cluster organization through, for example, actively connecting certain stakeholders, while capacity at the network level requires larger efforts driven by, for example, policy changes to tax breaks for international personnel or companies. These levels are also linked in that the capacities of individual firms shape the dynamics of the cluster as a whole, while cluster-level characteristics shape individual- and organizational-level behaviour (Giuliani and Bell 2005; Liao, Fei, and Chen 2007).

In conclusion, whereas in this chapter I have laid out the theoretical foundation for the capacity framework and identified more concrete elements to break down the complex dynamics among stakeholders in the cluster setting, in the following chapter I look at the practical implications, with a focus on innovation and cluster policies.

# 3 Cluster Policy and Cluster Organizations

The capacity framework assumes that collaboration and knowledge exchange are at the core of innovative clusters, but these factors pose complex elements from a policy perspective. Identifying observable and potentially changeable factors opens up new opportunities for policy makers who wish to increase innovation in a specific location, but it also maps the challenges of innovation-enhancing initiatives. In this chapter, I focus on these challenges more closely for high-tech sectors.

## The Role of Government

There are different ways to conceptualize government in the cluster setting. These ideas have also shifted over time. In the early stages of copying Silicon Valley, the role of government took a backseat to the role of entrepreneurs, companies, and research institutions (Moore and Davis 2004). For example, some researchers claimed that clusters were complex, self-organizing, and composed of a broad patchwork or ecology of people and institutions, which left little room for government to steer innovation processes (Feldman and Francis 2004). Further, the literature dealing with the globalization of supply chains by focusing on multinational corporations called into question the efficacy of state policy (Hira et al. 2013).

Nowadays, much of the literature gives government policies a role in facilitating clusters. This follows work on national innovation systems (e.g. Nelson 1996) and the triple helix (Etzkowitz 2003) that shows there are complementary roles for research, government, and the private sector. An example is the "constructing regional advantage approach," which recognizes "the role of a proactive public–private partnership and the impact of the public sector and public policy support" (Asheim et al. 2017, 17; see also Isaksen and Trippl 2016; Martin and Trippl 2014). This perspective hints at a diverse set of policy instruments to promote clusters, with the spectrum ranging from correcting market failure to more interventionist measures approaching old-style industrial policy. As part of "smart specialization" in Europe, whereby a region undergoes an entrepreneurial search-and-discovery process to find out what it does best, its competitive advantages, and related innovation opportunities, the role of government is defined as "an enabler that provides incentives and encourages entrepreneurs and other organizations such as universities and research institutes to become involved in identifying the regions' specializations" (zu Köcker and Lämmer-Gamp 2017, 139).

In essence, there are two general narratives of cluster policy: First there is the laissez-faire version that emphasizes non-interventionism, and signals that the focus should be on framework conditions rather than specific sectors or technologies. Second, there is the systemic approach based on the concept of innovation systems. This perspective implies that most major policy fields need to be considered in the light of how they contribute to innovation (Hira et al. 2013). In the context of emerging clusters, this research is based on the assumption that public entities are actively involved in cluster development. Thereby, cluster policies are often pursued in parallel with other programs at different levels of government. As the discussion throughout the book will show, this can lead to uncoordinated efforts that result in ineffective cluster strategies due to initiatives being pulled in different directions.

**Innovation and Cluster Policy**

Generally speaking, innovation policy includes a variety of target areas. It covers, for example, housing policy and immigration, as affordable housing and efficient visa regulations are required to attract human capital. It further encompasses more concrete measures that target the cluster directly. In many countries, collaboration is identified as a key to innovation, leading to a wide range of policy instruments (Agranoff and McGuire 2001; Braun 2008). Thereby, cluster policies and programs have drawn from all of these research streams, such as Porter's work on clusters, learning regions and knowledge spillovers (Morgan 1997), and regional innovation systems (Asheim and Gertler 2005; Cooke 2002a; Lindqvist, Ketels, and Sölvell 2013). Implementing collaboration-enhancing measures is highly dependent on the capacity of government institutions to act as coordinators and facilitators, since local authorities become key players in the promotion of those relationships (Rodríguez-Pose and Di Cataldo 2014). According to Schneider and Ingram (1990, 517), "capacity tools provide information, training, education and resources to enable individuals, groups, or agencies to make decisions or carry out activities." This aspect has been overlooked, however, in much of the research on policy tools and implementation. Capacity initiatives are largely based on the assumption that the group being targeted will have the incentives or motivation to participate in the activity without the need for further coercion or convincing. This is a typical set-up for an innovation cluster, where the membership is voluntary, based on the notion that firms and research facilities want to improve collaboration and ultimately innovation to make themselves and the cluster a successful player in a certain field. In order to enhance collaboration levels, some of the following policy instruments or combinations of them have been implemented in clusters:

- the integration of operational institutions directly connected to the network (Braun 2008);
- the creation of new bodies for collaboration, with the goal of improving coordination and interagency relationships and lowering transaction costs (Braun 2008);
- jurisdiction-based management that addresses the locality of many high-tech networks (Agranoff and McGuire 2001;
- the promotion of collaborative spaces, such as science parks or business incubators (Agranoff and McGuire 2001);
- information-based empowerment of collaboration (Clegg and Hardy 1996);
- the provision of funding for collaborative research (Borrás 2011; OECD 2005);
- the strengthening of intermediary organizations, such as technology transfer offices (Borrás 2011; OECD 2005); and
- encouragement of the mobility of researchers between the public and private spheres (Borrás 2011; OECD 2005).

The main challenge arising from these diverse strategies is that, while reducing the barriers for the transfer of scientific and technical knowledge is at the core of enhancing collaboration, the ways to address these bottlenecks are multiple and their evaluations rather vague (Borrás 2011). The high-tech industry in particular challenges government to adapt policies to knowledge transfer processes. Such fields are moving at a fast pace, and as technologies mature, they change industry structures and supply-and-demand conditions. After a so-called fifth generation of innovation,* which was defined by a process of gradual opening up and an increase in the role of collaboration, alliances, and partnerships, stakeholders are entering the sixth phase of innovation. This marks the beginning of the inclusion of emerging economies, and thus widens the scope and scale of globalization. To a large degree, collaborative efforts and networking capabilities now determine the success of a region or even of a country (Mroczkowski 2012). High-tech industries are not only challenging due to the rapid speed of their development; they are also often described as a complex construct of related individual components (Bauer et al. 2012). This means that policy has to accommodate heterogeneous components and subsystems in which synergies exist between industries and technology in the high-, medium-, and low-tech sectors. At the same time, this has to be met with a broad spectrum of policies that go beyond a certain sector or government level. Further, policy initiatives have slowly extended to include non-governmental actors and civic institutions – adding to the number of stakeholders (Mayntz 1983). In addition, the development of high-tech products is often related to uncertainty, risk, and the challenge of drawing in new investment. Thereby, communications and collaboration among industry players to resolve and tackle these hurdles often pose a challenge in themselves for government officials.

On a larger scale, innovation policy tackles market developments. Policy designs can be situated on a continuum from creating favourable framework conditions to "picking winners." Both have their advantages and disadvantages. Creating favourable framework conditions makes countries or regions conducive to investment and relocation into the area through tax credits or basic funding schemes. Such policies, however, often do not target the needs of the high-tech industry specifically. In contrast, picking winners is a rather short-term approach that chooses a certain sector or even particular company to support, which has no immediate benefit for networks on a larger scale. Cluster policy is somewhere in between these two extremes: it picks a region or area on which to focus policy, but it is often connected to creating larger incentives that favour more players and enhance networking.

---

* Rothwell (1994) defines five shifts or generations of innovation, showing that the complexity and integration of the models increases with each subsequent generation: (1) technology push; (2) market pull; (3) coupling; (4) interactive; and (5) network. More recently, Kotsemir and Meissner (2016) have added the open innovation model by Chesbrough (2003) as the sixth.

The survey conducted for this book among companies, cluster organizations, and research institutes shows that they all see a clear role for government to remove some of the bottlenecks of innovation. According to respondents, the university system, infrastructural policy, and the education system act as incentives for cluster development. The top three policies hindering cluster development are current immigration policy (cited by 42.6 per cent of respondents), infrastructure policy (42.6 per cent) as well as a lack of tax reductions (29.8 per cent). From a government standpoint, however, making decisions based on the needs of a specific cluster regarding immigration or infrastructure policies is not always possible.

Cluster programs and innovation policy instruments have been under scrutiny due to the "blanket enthusiasm" surrounding innovation measures, paired with a lack of proper evaluation of such instruments (Duranton 2011; Martin and Sunley 2003). The surge in popularity of instruments targeting innovation and regional agglomeration is met with further difficulties in measuring their effectiveness and efficiency. Return-on-investment information is scarce, and economic growth, for which many strategies are striving, requires a mix of policy tools. Measures put in place also require long-term commitments and learning over time, which are hard to capture in evaluation cycles. In addition, there is a fair amount of disagreement about cluster policies, related to their usefulness and the vagueness of the cluster concept (Ketels 2013). Whereas the literature on cluster policy has moved away from seeing the engagement of government as a black-and-white issue towards a more holistic approach, there is scepticism around the involvement of government in the first place. The discussion largely revolves around the type of initiatives put in place and whether they should target clusters directly or indirectly. For example, Bresnahan and Gambardella (2004, 355) state that "policy implications are simple and classical: invest in education, have open market institutions, tolerate and even encourage multinationals, tolerate and even encourage the mobility of human capital." In short, they advocate for less interventionist policies directed towards the formation of clusters and more focus on creating the conditions favourable for cluster creation. Along the same lines, Wallsten (2004) argues that university R&D performance shows positive effects for employment and venture capital, but that specific government funds or research parks have had no effects or even negative ones. Lerner (2009) also cautions policy makers to put more thought into the type of initiatives being implemented. He identifies short-sighted design of cluster policies, a top-down dynamic, and black-boxing of the network dynamic as major hurdles for government support of clusters.

This implies that internal dynamics of the clusters, such as network relationships, remain unknown to government. In essence, Lerner (2009) highlights that governments need more information in order to make informed decisions on how to support clusters. Analysis of policy failures where government-driven clusters have not succeeded shows that public initiatives tried to copy the Silicon Valley example closely, rather than adjust policies to unique regional factors (Giest 2019). Findings from failed high-tech clusters in New Jersey and Texas reveal that local government prioritized the role of a university, while neglecting other dynamics, such as support for entrepreneurs and start-ups and the collaboration and networking among stakeholders. It seems decision makers were unable to balance the immediate need for skilled labour with long-term efforts and the pursuit of regional economic integration (Giest 2017).

### Evaluation Challenge

Limited learning has come from these and other failed cluster attempts, however, partially due to the challenge of conducting proper evaluations. There is hardly any coherence when it comes to evaluation criteria for clusters. One problem is that variations in governance levels lead to diverse data sets. As well, most official reports by the OECD or Eurostat focus on established clusters, such as those in Boston, San Diego, or Oxford; only recently has the focus shifted to local agglomerations in, for example, Asia. There is also no generally applied rule on what the basic measurements of cluster performance should be. In fact, the soft data, which many clusters self-report, can fall into the categories of explanatory and responsive at the same time. Further, for hard data, there is a notorious chicken-and-egg problem regarding measurements such as R&D or venture capital funding, inflow and outflow of personnel, or the sector's contribution to the region's gross domestic product (GDP). For example, did venture capital funding increase due to better performance, or was the investment an indication of the performance level itself? Has the inflow of personnel to do with the recent attraction of a big company based on high performance, or is it a product of cluster management and policy attraction initiatives, and therefore a measure in and of itself?

There is also an ongoing discussion around measurements taken regionally. For example, the OECD Scoreboard bases its performance measures on firm data: "This has the advantages of enabling presentation of data for functional cluster areas built up from municipality level rather than larger regions, enabling more timely economic analysis and providing information on financial performance not available from standard sources" (Temouri 2012, 5). These measures are prone to bias, however, due to the possible overrepresentation of some bigger companies. In comparison, the Global Innovation Index uses countrywide data for output performance, focusing on knowledge creation, impact, and diffusion, as well as intangible assets, creative goods, services, and online creativity. But national information is difficult to obtain, and is often provided with a time lag. Further, some clusters operate in several industries, which means that data collection in one sector captures only part of the network's performance. Thus, each set of indicators has its advantages and disadvantages. However, as long as there is no agreed-upon set of soft and/or hard data, no globally comparable evaluation of clusters can be done.

Overall, high-tech clusters have a data-collection problem, and thus an evaluation problem. An EU report summarizes the attempts of different countries and researchers to capture the performance levels of clusters within their jurisdictions, and the results could not be more different, ranging from focusing on the strengths and professionalism of the cluster organization to using an estimate of potential cluster growth for evaluation (zu Köcker and Rosted 2010). This is also related to an unclear conceptual basis on how cluster success comes about – with no theoretical basis to build on, the indicators become interchangeable and arbitrary at best. As Williams (2010, 26) states, "measuring effectiveness is a particularly complex challenge in collaborative settings in which outcomes are likely to be the product of a mixture of structural and agential factors." There is, moreover, a lack of clarity about what ultimately constitutes the "success" of a cluster.

There are also competing explanations for the past success of clusters. The narrative around the continued success factors of, for example, Silicon Valley changes depending on which aspects are emphasized. Scholars draw different conclusions about the key dynamics at play between a supporting (institutional) system and entrepreneurs, the exploitation or commercialization of knowledge, and low entry barriers for entrepreneurship – not only financially, but also in social and psychological terms. For example, Kenney and Patton (2006) conclude that the evolution of a strong network not only quickly attracts venture capital; it also strengthens the relationships between individuals and the institutional level. Moore and Davis (2004) point to the role of government as the driving force behind sharing findings on semiconductors (as part of an antitrust settlement) and investing in R&D. In cases that predate the semiconductor industry, Moore and Davis (2004) also see defence expenditure as important for the development of transistors and helpful to early firms' bottom lines. Another aspect of the Silicon Valley phenomenon that received attention in the literature is the role of Stanford University. Many hypothesized that the driving factor of the clusters' success was the university's role as a connector for larger and smaller companies. Professor Frederick Terman's role in Stanford's transformation and rise to prominence has been particularly emphasized: as a provost and dean of engineering, he increased ties among business and academic circles and encouraged faculty to be entrepreneurs (Moore and Davis 2004).

In this book, I focus on cluster organizations, and propose that they contribute, at least partially, to the innovative performance of clusters, because they are able to facilitate some of the processes that have been highlighted repeatedly as crucial for cluster development, such as collaboration, knowledge transfer, and common goals. These are summarized in the capacity framework. In the following section, I look at cluster organizations in more detail in order to determine how they have been framed in the past and which of their activities are capacity enhancing.

## Cluster Organizations

Cluster organizations have been given different names, depending on the focus of the research. For example, from a social capital angle they are called trust facilitators (Mesquita 2007), network brokers (Visser and Atzema 2008), or intermediaries (Baxter and Tyler 2007), whereas more management-oriented scholars describe them as managers, promoters, or leaders (Goduscheit 2014; McEvily and Zaheer 2004; Provan, Isett, and Milward 2004). Institutional and structurally oriented scholars describe them as regional development agencies or institutional thickening (Andriani et al. 2005; Seliger, Carpinetti, and Gerolamo 2008). These can be individuals or organizations, and they range from being mandated or contracted by government to acting as independent entities (Provan and Kenis 2007). Powell and Grodal (2005) further show that there are densely connected organizations that dominate the network and are key actors in collaboration within those networks.

The different literatures give cluster organizations different weight in their explanations of cluster development and innovation performance. Some see them as day-to-day managers embedded in the larger historical structures of the region and part of a multilevel policy construct. Others emphasize their ability to implement innovation-related policies and to serve as connectors for new entries to the established core of the cluster (Crespo, Suire, and Vicente 2014). This, however, is also a fragile set-up. As Grillitsch and Asheim (2015) point out, if local managers leave, it is a challenge to find equally capable and connected organizations or individuals. Another aspect is the danger of lock-in due to organizational proximity – the set of interdependencies within and between organizations "connected by a relationship of either economic or financial dependence/interdependence (between member companies of an industrial or financial group, or within a network)" (Boschma 2005, 65). Whereas cluster organizations are expected to create just the right amount of proximity in order to control uncertainty and opportunism, too much proximity can be detrimental to interactive learning due to lock-in and a lack of flexibility. This literature therefore calls for a combination of two types of relationships: official alliances – for example, based on contracts – and informal, trust-based relationships (Boschma 2005; Boschma, Minondo, and Navarro 2012; Cecil and Green 2000).

The idea of an entity facilitating or managing a cluster is not new, as the establishment of clientele or administrative units by government in the 1970s to target network mobilization and activation was similar to cluster management (Howlett 2011). Research on "network administration organizations" also provides some understanding of governing networks (Provan and Kenis 2007); the organization might be modest in scale, consisting of only a single individual, or it might be a formal entity (McEvily and Zaheer 2004; Provan, Isett, and Milward 2004). In the literature on networks, cluster organizations are captured through the idea of "a key group of nodes (organizations) within the network and their leaders" (Provan, Fish, and Sydow 2007, 502). Another strand of literature on which research on cluster organizations builds is that of "boundary spanners": actors that operate and encourage collaborative environments (Doz and Hamel 1998; Leifer and Delbecq 1976; Williams 2002, 2010). One dominant theme in this field is that of reticulist scholars who focus on certain traits that help to bridge interests, professions, and organizations (Webb 1991; Williams 2010). A managing or coordinating role in the network can also be taken by a so-called hub firm within the cluster that has the reputation as well established and well connected in the field (Dhanaraj and Parkhe 2006). Hub firms, also called "anchor firms," are further associated with attracting new investments to the cluster, providing a vision for uniting different stakeholders, and supporting local start-ups (Baglieri, Cinici, and Mangematin 2012). A similar idea exists at the individual level in the form of "star scientists": carriers of expert knowledge in certain sectors who attract the attention of other scholars, policy makers, and venture capitalists. Studies show that the star scientists themselves, rather than their potential discoveries, play a crucial role in the formation and transformation of high-tech industries (Maier, Kurka, and Trippl 2007; Zucker and Darby 2006).

Cluster organizations also exhibit different characteristics. Goduscheit (2014) offers a typology based on the foundation of their role, the formality of their appointment, and their relations with other actors, and identifies champions, gatekeepers, power, expert, process, and relationship promoters. Some emerge from within the network, others might be formally appointed. The activities these facilitators carry out vary, and are assessed differently by network members. The Global Cluster Initiative Survey (Sölvell, Lindqvist, and Ketels 2003) suggests that almost all cluster initiatives have a dedicated facilitator, and that they are initiated by government, industry, or both (Nallari and Griffith 2013). In summary, the purpose of cluster organizations is to strengthen the competitiveness of clusters, and they can be initiated by either the public or the private sector. Their structure, role, funding, and activities vary based on the context in which they operate, but they mainly involve the following tasks (European Commission 2018):

- They work to cater to different members' identified needs, and they sometimes initiate activities with a longer-term perspective and of a more radically innovative character.
- They have good networks in all these three spheres and an understanding of the culture and how these domains operate, and are skilled in bridging them.
- They initiate projects that include actors from these different spheres.
- They lobby to influence legal frameworks and standards setting to better match the needs of the cluster members.
- They arrange matchmaking and network meetings.
- They often carry out business intelligence.
- They often work internationally, arranging business opportunities and setting up international research and innovation projects.

The survey carried out for this research offers some perspective on the activities that are most valued by stakeholders in different types of clusters, and provides responses from organizations in clusters that identify as cluster facilitators, companies, government entities, or research institutes.

*Assessing Cluster Organization Activities*

Companies, government institutes, and research institutes point towards the arrangement of network meetings as the most important task performed by cluster organizations (87.9 per cent of respondents). In addition, survey respondents indicated that cluster organizations facilitate linkages among clusters, firms, and research institutions (66.7 per cent), as well as provide a communications platform (63.6 per cent), advice on funding opportunities (57.6 per cent), the creation of new projects for cooperation (78.9 per cent), and advertising the cluster on the (global) market (51.5 per cent). Further, over 90 per cent of respondents pointed out that, because of the cluster organization, there were better/stronger connections between cluster stakeholders and the indication of more meetings and more government attention. Respondents said that the work of cluster organizations led to better/stronger connections among stakeholders (84.2 per cent), to more meetings among stakeholders (78.9 per cent), more government attention (78.9 per cent), and stronger connections to other clusters (73.7 per cent).

One striking difference in the effects of cluster management is the discrepancy between the views of stakeholders and the cluster organization concerning its role of connecting the network to other clusters. Cluster organizations ranked their effect in terms of linkages to other clusters relatively high (73.7 per cent of such respondents), while less than a third (30.3 per cent) of network members saw this service as important or effective. Also, when asked about their connections to other clusters in general, 71.9 per cent of stakeholders indicated they were directly in contact with stakeholders from other regional industry clusters, but even in clusters without a cluster organization, 63.6 per cent of respondents said they had regular connections to other networks. These results suggest that cluster organizations might not play as significant a role as they think they do in connecting network members with other clusters. This has to do with the fact that more companies are becoming global and have branches around the world that they are in touch with on a regular basis. Universities also make an effort to establish collaborative research projects across borders. These connections often happen within a company or due to individual researchers who have moved from one cluster to another, and it seems the presence of a cluster organization is not necessary to create those linkages.

Based on the comparison of the self-assessment of clusters with and without cluster organizations in the survey, those with management had more connections among one another. Stakeholders who reported

Table 3.1. Comparing clusters with and without management

| Attribute | Clusters without management | Clusters with management |
|---|---|---|
| | (% of respondents) | |
| Most frequent communications channels | email (95.5) | face-to-face and email (91.9) |
| Government policy document? | yes (45.5), no (45.5) | yes (62.5), no (28.1) |
| Written agreement among stakeholders? | yes (30.0), no (60.0) | yes (45.2), no (38.7) |
| Evaluation | mostly project-based (61.9) – once a year/ every 2–3 years (both 22.7) | project-based (50.0), cluster-wide evaluation (43.3), and industry reports (33.3) – once a year (45.2) |

having a cluster organization indicated that regular (42.1 per cent) and even frequent (34.2 per cent) personal connections existed, as well as contractual links (50.0 per cent), organizational ties and third-party contact (34.2 per cent). Clusters without management reported mostly irregular links between university researchers and companies and between government officials and research institutions. The industry-government connection was portrayed as regular. The comparison between clusters with and without management further shows the two groups differed in the communications channels they used. Table 3.1 shows the difference in the networking dynamic in both types of clusters. Both types mostly communicate via email with other members, but managed clusters also have regular face-to-face contact. The personal contact supports the exchange of tacit knowledge – knowledge that cannot be explained or coded, but has to be experienced or communicated face-to-face. Regarding government policy documents targeting the industry or having a written agreement, clusters with management are at a slight advantage.

The frequency and type of evaluation also differs between facilitated and non-facilitated clusters. While clusters without management mainly rely on project-based evaluation once a year or every two to three years, facilitated clusters portray a wider variety of project-based, cluster-wide, and industry evaluation, which is done predominantly once a year. Project-based evaluation usually yields minimal results about the overall cluster, because it portrays one project, for example, between industry and university. Results are also not comparable, as projects differ in length, level of funding, goals, and size. In contrast, cluster-wide and industry evaluations give a more complete picture of what is happening in the network. Industry evaluations are usually carried out by major accounting firms to assess the cluster's performance based on external data and interviews. Cluster-wide and industry evaluation might also differ between networks, regions, and countries, although they make a variety of hard and anecdotal data available that can be used to decide on policies and give stakeholders and policy makers a better idea of where the cluster stands within a country or even internationally. The role the cluster organization plays in enabling those more comparable evaluations is to animate stakeholders to collect and combine data and make them available for possible evaluators, or use the data to understand current and future dynamics for own use. These data are also a tool in negotiations with government when talking about funding schemes for the coming years or attracting companies to the cluster by emphasizing favourable data for funding and entrepreneurial activity. Thus, the cluster organization has an interest in pursuing and supporting evaluation for two reasons: first, to advertise the cluster to investors and government officials; second, to identify gaps in funding or any related activity.

Another aspect of facilitation is the attitude of stakeholders towards accepting cluster management as a useful and helpful tool in the innovation process. In connection to the notion of social capital, without trust in the abilities of the facilitator, the support structure will not be successful. In the survey for this research, 71 per cent of stakeholders in clusters with management thought that cluster organizations made them successful. Networking among stakeholders and funding from external sources also received a majority of the responses. Interestingly, 50 per cent of the members of clusters without management indicated that they thought facilitation would make their cluster more successful. They also stated that innovative research and external funding were part of potential cluster development.

*Levels of Competitiveness*

In a second step, the question remains whether these activities have an effect on the overall performance of a cluster. As highlighted earlier, evaluating clusters is a challenge: there are competing explanations for the success of existing clusters, which could determine the factors that should be taken into account in measuring cluster performance.

The idea of identifying and ranking clusters according to their level of competitiveness has become a staple in the public policy discourse.

"Initially focused on the national level, the idea of competitiveness was quickly extended to other spatial levels" (Pessoa 2013, 101). Thereby, different groups of indicators are used to identify levels of competitiveness depending on the emphasis on certain concepts, such as social capital or proximity. To make it possible to compare and rank clusters with one another, organizations such as the OECD rely on a list of indicators to identify competitiveness – both within a region and nationally as well as internationally. For example, the OECD lists clusters according to their composite indicator, which is based on the arithmetic mean of six local indictors grouped together: "an indicator of entrepreneurialism (share of firms less than 5 years old); an employment growth indicator (average rate of employment growth); two economic growth indicators (average rate of turnover growth and average return on total assets); two financial viability indicators (average liquidity ration and average solvency ratio)" (Temouri 2012, 30).

The criticism raised earlier in the context of evaluating clusters' success factors also applies to figures 3.1 and 3.2. Well-working clusters might be more likely to agree and to support a cluster management structure and, as a consequence, use it as well. Again, the chicken-and-egg problem is that it is difficult to identify the cluster manager as the decisive factor for cluster success. What remains crucial in this context is that clusters without a cluster organization were eager to establish one in order to create better links with government and other stakeholders.

For this research, the performance measures to identify the level of competitiveness include the unemployment rate, the number of patents in the according industry within that region or state, the share of the local workforce employed in medium-, high-tech, and knowledge-intensive sectors, the number of new enterprises established, and, for some of the networks, the OECD ranking measuring the performance of local business clusters in the knowledge economy. These are based on the conceptual understanding that regions have certain characteristics that allow for business formation and, ultimately, innovation. For example, the unemployment rate offers insight into the rate of new business formation or relocation, which is aided by learning, communications, and commercialization. Spin-offs from universities and research organizations to develop an innovative product create new jobs and new venture capital investment opportunities for the whole cluster. If the unemployment rate is high, chances are that either certain types of jobs are not created or that the qualifications of the personnel do not match the jobs offered. Also, a high unemployment rate often hinders entrepreneurs who seek to create new companies in the region because, if the start-up does not work out, chances of re-employment are lower. Thus,

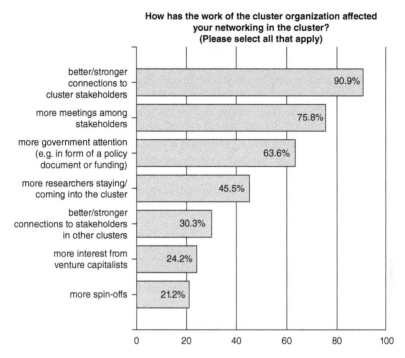

Figure 3.1. Stakeholders' self-evaluation of the impact of cluster management

Figure 3.2. Existence of cluster organizations in high-performance clusters

the unemployment number should be seen in relation to the number of new enterprises established. A similar logic applies to the share of the local workforce employed in medium-, high-tech, and knowledge-intensive sectors, which is an indication of the number of highly educated personnel in the region and the number of research institutes and firms offering these kinds of jobs – both of which are attractive features for venture capitalists and bigger firms looking to relocate. This measure, however, does not indicate innovation efficiency.

Finally, patents filed under the Patent Co-operation Treaty are often used as an indirect measure of innovation activity. Patents indicate the technological progress of firms located within the cluster. Some patents or patent applications, however, fail to be transformed into actual products, since 90 to 95 per cent lack any market relevance and 99 per cent do not bring profit (Jung, Wu, and Chow 2008; Stevens and Burley 1997). As Denti (2013, 1) notes, however, "patenting is often necessary for many firms to keep their competitive advantage so clearly patents indicate something about the innovativeness of a firm." Overall, the patent rate is a data set that is readily available and collected on a regular basis for regions, rather than at the national level, and gives at least an indication of the innovative dynamics in a sector and location. To show the results of this diverse set, I categorized the clusters examined in this research according to levels of competitiveness ranging from low performance, to nationally competitive, to high performance, with the latter two categories grouped together under "high-performance clusters" (figure 3.2). Notably, most of the clusters rated as competitive worldwide had a cluster organization in place.

Competing explanations of the success of a cluster include the presence of an entrepreneurial culture and the existence of an anchor firm and/or star scientist. Comparing low- and high-performance clusters based on these factors yields the results shown in table 3.2.

The two groups do not seem to differ based on their entrepreneurial culture, defined as one that encourages new ideas that result in new businesses. There is a slight difference between the two when it comes to anchor firms and star scientists, but cause and effect cannot be determined clearly. Because most high-performance clusters have a cluster organization, it is unclear if facilitation drew firms and scientists to the cluster or if they already existed there. Clusters with facilitation were more likely to have an anchor firm than those without (56.3 per cent and 28.6 per cent, respectively), but the two did not differ in terms of the presence of star scientists. Thus, cluster management might be connected to the existence of anchor firms, but does not seem to have an effect on the presence of star scientists. One explanation for this could be

Table 3.2. Comparing low-performance and high-performance clusters

| | Low-performance clusters | High-performance clusters |
|---|---|---|
| Attribute | (% of respondents) | |
| Entrepreneurial culture (1 – very weak to 5 – very strong) | mostly 4 (35.7) | 3 (31.9) to 4 (34.0) |
| Anchor firm? | yes (35.7); no (50.0) | yes (59.6); no (27.7) |
| Star scientists? | yes (28.6); no (57.1) | yes (55.3); no (38.3) |

that scientists are attracted by a region's structural elements, such as the education system, or national regulation in connection with high-tech industries, on which the cluster organization would have no immediate effect. The comparison also points to the larger impact of government on the relocation of star scientists than that of the cluster organization or even the cluster itself, as funding and regulation are a big part of the decision of where to situate research facilities. Anchor firms, on the other hand, are more drawn to the potential research that is happening in the cluster and the ability to access the cluster with minor adaption costs. A cluster organization can be such a point of entry, as it is able to help firms that decide to relocate.

*Capacity Building by Cluster Organizations*

These findings give a first indication of the role of cluster organizations in innovation networks and the activities to which they contribute. They further highlight the perception of network members on the work of cluster management. The goal now is to unravel how these activities play out in clusters and contribute to capacity building within the network. For this, case studies can give insights into the day-to-day activities of cluster organizations and the collaboration of companies, research institutes, and government entities among one another and with those activities. Using the capacity framework, one can categorize and identify facilitation activities within the clusters by criteria that include collaborative capacity, purpose, structure, communications, and resources. For absorptive capacity, those elements are intra- and extra-cluster knowledge systems. As highlighted earlier, these two dimensions are closely related in the sense that extra-cluster knowledge needs to be transferred to intra-cluster firms by an entity with outside linkages that also has the knowledge base to pick and distribute

Table 3.3. Collaborative capacity framework of clusters

| Dimension | Element | Operationalization |
|---|---|---|
| Purpose | Leadership | Identification of leadership role |
| | Shared vision | Mission statement/agreement |
| | Network membership | Connection to a broader functional network |
| Structure | Formal and informal procedures | Memoranda/interagency planning documents |
| | Clear roles | Agreed and informed policy guidelines |
| Communications | Information links | Formal agreements/personal connections |
| | Active communications | Communications technology |
| Resources | Knowledge and skills | Availability of human capital with relevant knowledge and skills |
| | Financing powers | Collective financial pool |

Source: Based on Lai 2011.

information. The intra-cluster knowledge system consists of the learning and collaboration processes among stakeholders.

## Collaborative Capacity Dimensions

These categories can be further refined into subcategories informed by the existing literature on innovation clusters. They bring together different aspects that have been researched up to this point but not combined into a coherent framework (table 3.3).

For the first dimension of collaborative capacity, *purpose*, the following elements are relevant:

- leadership: identification of leadership role;
- shared vision: mission statement/ agreement;
- network membership: connection to a broader functional network.

The first element, leadership, is based on its continued emphasis in the cluster literature as a factor that "can enhance or even act as a catalytic effect in endogenous regional development" (Stough, Stimson, and Nijkamp 2011, 9; see also Stimson and Stough 2009). Leadership is achieved by organizations that are well connected and have a certain level of trust among network members (Gordon and McCann 2000). Leadership can take different forms. As Orton and Weick (1990) point out, in loosely coupled settings, leadership is more subtle and, as Goduscheit (2014, 526) highlights, build "on the simultaneous provision of direction and coordination on the one hand and acknowledging the value of increased discretion on the other" (see also Boynton and Zmud 1987). In fact, many do not call it leadership but cluster management, since leadership has certain connotations of decision-making power, which do not apply for most cluster organizations. Most scholars, however, agree that leadership or management is taken on by a dedicated entity, which has a certain set of skills and competencies that enable it to connect private and public network members (Uyarra and Ramlogan 2016).

The second element, shared vision, goes back to more applied research on clusters, in which companies have identified and branded the network, as well as developed a strategy and vision for cluster and innovation activity (Lindqvist, Ketels, and Sölvell 2013). There are two underlying reasons for this. First, the branding of a cluster nationally and globally can attract talent and capital to the region; second, a common vision can create a joint goal among network members, increasing linkages and common efforts.

The final element that contributes to cluster stakeholders' having a sense of purpose is network membership. This element requires drawing clear distinctions among connection to a broader network, global pipelines, and cross-clustering. The latter is the collective action of a cluster as connected to other clusters in the same or similar sector, while global pipelines differ in the sense that they include individual firms that access knowledge from other locations, and reach out to global players (Lindqvist, Ketels, and Sölvell 2013; Normaler and Verspagen 2016). Connection to a larger network can include one within the same geographic location, which provides additional stakeholders beyond the immediate cluster. One example of this is the Chicago biotech cluster, which is both part of an agricultural "super cluster" in the Midwest and embedded in a network of hospitals within the city. This ties into the idea that a network core and periphery structure are relevant to clusters (Borgatti and Everett 1999; Crespo, Vicente, and Amblard 2016).

The second dimension of collaborative capacity is *structure*, divided into formal and informal procedures and clear roles. The former are defined as memoranda or interagency planning documents, while the latter can be described as agreed and informed policy guidelines. Regional and cluster policies play a crucial role in tying together institutional variety and a diverse set of funding instruments (Grillitsch and Asheim 2015). This is also based on the assumption that cluster policy is a form of selecting and potentially favouring certain geographical areas and industry sectors (Uyarra and Ramlogan 2016). This implies that, to best match structural components that are supported through policy with the needs of stakeholders, the policies require some form of agreement and input from those affected. Memoranda or interagency planning documents make a similar point, but link it to network members. The assumption is that inter-agency collaboration, which is agreed upon in planning documents, creates linkages that are sustainable in the innovation network.

Communications is the third dimension of collaborative capacity, broken down into two elements: information links and active communications. Both have the goal of exchanging information, but through different channels. Information links include formal agreement and personal connections within the network, whereas active communications describes communications technology through, for example, virtual platforms. Such technologies have the advantage that knowledge exchange and learning can be spatially delimited, and can provide opportunities for connections that otherwise would have not been possible (Boschma 2005). This could be because the cluster, even though locally agglomerated, is quite spread out, and technology-supported communications bridge that spatial gap. These communications links are described as "active" because they largely require conscious efforts by those involved to engage. Formal agreements and personal communications are different in that they can be based on structures that are set up to enhance correspondence – formalized, regular meetings to update investors on a project, for example. The same applies to personal communications based on regular networking events within the cluster. Taken together, all forms of communications underpin the idea that connections and collaborations benefit clusters, since "interfirm communication and interactive learning play a decisive role in explaining regional innovation and growth" (Bathelt 2005, 4; see also Cooke and Morgan 1999; Gordon and McCann 2000). The communications element is embedded in many concepts that aim to explain local agglomeration and innovation. Social capital assumes that relationships enable communications, and then relevant knowledge is exchanged (Filieri et al. 2014). Similarly, the concepts of spatial agglomeration and proximity more generally suggest that, due to proximity, communications and knowledge exchange are more likely. However, the type of information exchanged and how it affects innovative ideas down the line are difficult to measure. Therefore, the analysis of this dimension will remain somewhat superficial by looking at formal agreements, personal connections, and communications technology used within clusters.

The final dimension of the collaborative capacity framework is access to *resources* within the cluster, operationalized as knowledge, skills, and financing powers, which covers financial supplies, including funds that are available for the whole cluster. Such a financial pool gives the network the capacity to attract outside stakeholders, as membership in the network would give organizations access to those resources (Baxter and Tyler 2007). The financial pool is determined by several factors. It could be that the composition of the cluster attracts a particularly large amount of private investment that allows for collaborative projects or the employment of a star scientist. Another funding source is government; from a policy perspective, this is part of a larger discussion about whether cluster policy should target leading activities and concentrate efforts in one area or provide broader support. Put simply, the decision is a trade-off between increasing regional disparity when funding already successful clusters and diluting resources when targeting several (Hospers, Desrochers, and Sautet 2009; Uyarra and Ramlogan 2016). As a final argument linked to financial resources, monetary funds are a tangible way for stakeholders to evaluate a cluster, implying that "resource availability also strongly influences the ability to gain legitimacy and facilitate network development" (Provan, Fish, and Sydow 2007, 503). In other words, a large financial pool often breeds more funding due to these factors. Knowledge and skills are also categorized as resources into which the network can tap and, similar to finances, with a certain available pool from which organizations can benefit. To give an example, many companies desire a large amount of skilled labour, which could be maintained by universities that offer degrees in areas where companies require support, combined with urban policies that keep graduates in the geographic location.

## Absorptive Capacity Dimensions

A recurring theme in innovation research is the idea that cluster development is built on a diverse set of knowledge sources that can originate from inside and outside of the network. Another argument is that organizations can compensate for knowledge deficiencies inside the cluster by tapping into external sources. These outside connections can take shape in collaborations between clusters, also called "cross-clustering," and between the cluster and global markets (Lindqvist, Ketels, and Sölvell 2013). The following section defines these dimensions in more detail. Both belong to the theme of absorptive capacity. In the capacity framework for this research, absorptive capacity is divided into the dimensions of intra-cluster and extra-cluster knowledge systems (table 3.4). Following the logic of existing research, they cover knowledge transfer inside and beyond the cluster.

The *intra-cluster knowledge system* consists of knowledge spillovers and learning. The latter element describes social relationships, whereas knowledge spillovers account for stakeholder links within the cluster.

Table 3.4. Absorptive capacity framework of clusters

| Dimension | Element | Operationalization |
|---|---|---|
| Intra-cluster knowledge system | Knowledge spillovers | Stakeholder links |
| | Learning | Social relationships |
| Extra-cluster knowledge system | External knowledge sources | Links to external sources |
| | Interface between external and internal knowledge system | Acquiring new knowledge from extra-cluster sources and transferring knowledge to cluster firms |

This division has to do with the slightly different processes that underlie spillovers and learning. Knowledge spillovers happen when "knowledge created by one agent can be used by another either without compensation or with compensation less than the value of the knowledge" (Fischer, Scherngell, and Jansenberger 2006, 100). This is a common concept in the economic geography literature, which assumes that, through local agglomerations, companies can tap into these potentially beneficial knowledge spillovers (Audretsch and Feldman 1996). Specifically, the endogenous growth literature describes spillovers in combination with institutional arrangements as a central factor in explaining why local clustering is beneficial, since they are seen as "externalities that produce non-compensating advantages for the receivers" (Stough, Stimson, and Nijkamp 2011, 16; see also Nijkamp and van Hemert 2009). The mechanisms enabling such spillovers include stakeholders observing one another, copying ideas, iterating, and incrementally building up a knowledge stock (Feldman and Tavassoli 2014). Knowledge spillovers alone, however, are not sufficient to develop an intra-cluster knowledge system, which requires a network and relationship structure that perpetuates interaction to learn from the knowledge pool (Boschma 2005; Breschi and Lissoni 2001; Crespo, Vicente, and Amblard 2016). The collective learning processes address the ability to learn, assimilate, and use knowledge developed elsewhere (Cohen and Levinthal 1990; Fischer, Scherngell, and Jansenberger 2006). More generally, learning is described as "an interactive, socially embedded, and localized process" (Lundvall et al. 2003, 216). Learning is thereby operationalized as social relationships because, as research shows, in order to learn, trusted connections are essential. In fact, there is a whole separate set of literature on the role of trust in innovation networks and how it enables voluntary participation and the exchange of knowledge in the first place (Dasgupta 2000; Doss 2013; Giest 2019; Innes and Booher 2007; Klijn et al. 2016).

The second dimension of the absorptive capacity framework is the *extra-knowledge system*. This describes the links between the cluster and outside stakeholders and knowledge sources, as well as activities surrounding the actual transfer of knowledge into the cluster. The first element, linkages to outside clusters (cross-cluster links), plays a role in tapping into knowledge that is missing from the immediate local network or in picking up on new developments and trends occurring globally (global pipeline links) – see Normaler and Verspagen (2016). Whereas global pipelines are largely channels for individual firms, between-cluster flows include the larger network of knowledge exchange. Actual knowledge exchange, however, requires a transfer of knowledge from outside into the cluster. This transfer can be relatively passive, in the form of, for example, investments, or more active, such as in the enforcement of long-distance R&D collaborations. Actively engaging in external knowledge gain further points towards a linking mechanism in the form of an organization or forum that makes it possible for the network to identify knowledge gaps, look for relevant knowledge beyond the cluster, and decide what type of knowledge fits the network and would support innovation. Thereby, the extra-knowledge system builds on the internal one, since, without a well-working internal knowledge exchange system, external knowledge does not bring as much value if possible knowledge gaps have not been properly identified. The opposite is also true: if endogenous processes are well managed and external linkages are actively pursued based on the gaps found within the network, the network is more likely to succeed (Sammarra and Belussi 2006).

To summarize, *none of these elements of the collaborative or absorptive capacity dimensions is able to drive innovation in clusters alone.* Since the external-knowledge system depends on organizations having the relevant links to knowledge holders outside the network, as well as the ability to identify gaps and the relevant knowledge needed inside the cluster, the network can be successful only if it is set up internally in such a way that this knowledge can be communicated and if the knowledge is being used for a purpose. A well-working collaborative framework within the cluster can be halted by limited knowledge spillovers and a limited ability to source knowledge from outside the network.

*The Role of Government in Capacity Building*

Activities that support both collaborative and absorptive capacities are carried out by network members, but they can be further facilitated or hindered by cluster organizations and/or government. The survey

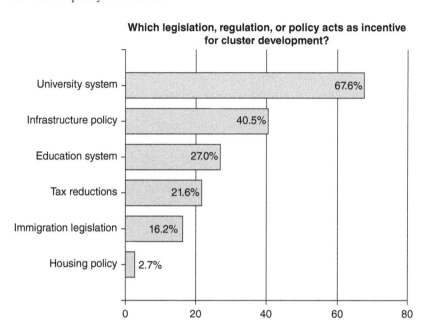

Figure 3.3. Incentives for cluster development

conducted for this book among companies, cluster organizations, and research institutes asked about the role and importance of government. According to survey respondents, government involvement is needed in many areas of cluster development, specifically for targeting framework conditions such as infrastructure, education, and tax policy (see figure 3.3). As well, government is expected to resolve regulatory bottlenecks to innovation (Anthony, Roth, and Christensen 2002).

According to survey respondents, the top three government policy areas hindering cluster development from the perspective of stakeholders were immigration (42.6 per cent of respondents), infrastructure (42.6 per cent), and taxation (29.8 per cent). As cluster and innovation policy has become more popular among governments around the world, however, some of these more fundamental framework conditions have been forgotten. When designing innovation policy, targeting firms and research institutes directly, governments have focused on the meso level (Nauwelaers and Wintjes 2008), situated between the macro and the micro levels of policy making. These meso-level decisions are restricted by larger policy preferences at the macro level while restraining micro-level tool calibrations (Atkinson and Coleman

1985; Howlett 2009). The rationale behind the meso-level approach is to enable firms to take up opportunities to collaborate with other companies or research facilities, leading to higher levels of commercialization, venture funding, and, ultimately, innovation (Boekholt and Thuriaux 1999). This is done through networking programs and public procurement as instruments of innovation policy. However, these government adjustments have created resentment among stakeholders, who increasingly look for demand-side policies, including innovation-related regulations and standards, as well as tax incentives (Aschhoff and Sofka 2008).

In recent decades policy makers have relied increasingly on collaboration to enhance innovation activity, supported by studies highlighting the benefits of collaborative structures for network performance even beyond the technological opportunities (Agranoff 2014; Powell, Koput, and Smith-Doerr 1996; Roberts and Bradley 1991; Schilling 2015). These increased interdependencies in the market are also connected to more linkages among subnational and central governments (Agranoff 2014; Skowronek 1982). In most countries, policy makers identify collaboration as key to innovation, but the definition and solution seeking remain vague and complex, leading to a wide range of policy instruments to address collaboration (Agranoff and McGuire 2001; Braun 2008). Identifying and tackling a policy problem, taking into account the constraints determined by different policy levels and the continuum and interplay of governance and government modes, complicate the classification and evaluation of such instruments (Howlett 2009). Implementing collaboration-enhancing measures is also highly dependent on the capacity of government institutions to act as coordinators and facilitators, since local authorities become key players in the promotion of those relationships (Rodríguez-Pose and Di Cataldo 2014).

*The Role of Cluster Organizations in Capacity Building*

Government is clearly an integral part in innovative networking and that regulations and policies directly affect a cluster's competitiveness. It is not always possible, however, for government to make policy decisions about, for example, immigration or infrastructure based on the needs of a specific cluster. Complex fields such as biotechnology require interministerial and interagency committees to design programs and national plans, so governments tend to focus on support systems that are easily changed, such as smaller-scale funding tools or technology transfer mechanisms. Network members, however, often demand a change in larger institutional structures and specific provisions tailored to their individual needs (Giest 2019). Here, cluster management can take on the crucial role of lobbying for the cluster, especially in regions or countries where several industry fields compete for attention.

Cluster organizations – defined in this book as those that can create favourable conditions for cooperation among industry and research stakeholders by being experts with a certain skill set (Rutter et al. 2012) – have limited impact on the capabilities of individual organizations within the network, but they can facilitate overall institutional thicknesses along the lines of collaborative and absorptive capacity building. They can, for example, promote a shared vision, provide a common communications infrastructure, and create local spaces for collaboration. The activities linked to cluster organizations vary in the literature, but their core undertakings can be linked to the dimensions defined in the capacity framework. They play a role in "managing interactions, sharing knowledge, and in providing a cognitive framework for transforming information into useful knowledge" (Carpinetti and Lima 2013, 17; see also Audretsch and Lehmann 2006; Steiner and Ploder 2008). In the literature, there is heavy emphasis on the linkages cluster organizations create among network members, with various government levels, with other clusters, and with the global market. This takes shape in, for example, establishing a communications interface, coordinating joint events and actions, or conducting strategic planning together with organizations within the cluster (Carpinetti and Lima 2013).

Further, cluster organization activities are based largely on the idea of enhancing social capital, such as "closure and brokerage" (Burt 2002). Closure affects access to information, and makes it less risky for people in the network to trust one another. Brokerage connects so-called structural holes in the system, where stakeholders on either side of a hole circulate different information. Such holes present opportunities to broker the flow of information between people and to control the projects that bring together people from opposite sides of the hole (Burt 2002). This implies that the broker in the network is able to control some of the information flow, and has a larger amount of information due to its central position among other members. More specifically, "cluster management goes beyond management of an individual organization. It implies mediating and facilitating the relationships of multiple cluster members. Each of the cluster members has their own agenda, and a key challenge for cluster managers is to make sure those agendas are united into common objectives and collective actions, that conflicting interests are resolved, and the relevant organizations see enough added value from their participation in cluster activities" (Schretlen et al. 2011, 3). As facilitators filling a central network position, cluster organizations are closely connected to the key stakeholders in a network, while keeping in touch with multiple levels of government, including local and regional, and national, or even entities such as the European Union and other global players.

**Propositions**

From the existing literature and the results of the complementary survey of cluster stakeholders, one can draw the following propositions:

- Proposition 1: Levels of collaborative and absorptive capacity contribute to overall cluster performance because capacity-building activities enable relationships among network members, make use of geographic proximity, and provide access to (extra)-cluster resources.
- Proposition 1a: Relationships among network members through enabling factors such as purpose, structure, communications, and resources result in higher levels of collaborative capacity.
- Proposition 1b: The existence of intra- and extra-cluster knowledge systems enables network members to tap into knowledge sources within and outside the cluster, raising absorptive capacity levels.
- Proposition 2: Cluster organizations facilitate collaborative and absorptive capacity activities within the network.
- Proposition 2a: The type of cluster organization depends on the extent of government involvement and its funding model.
- Proposition 3: Enhancing collaborative and absorptive capacity within the cluster depends on the ability of government institutions to act as facilitators in terms of policy decisions and on the support of local authorities.

At the core of these propositions is the idea that knowledge transfer lies at the heart of innovation and that this knowledge transfer, either among network members or from knowledge sources outside the cluster, is enhanced through relationships. These relationships are guided by enabling factors, such as purpose, structure, communications, and resources (collaborative capacity) and the establishment of an intra- and extra-cluster knowledge system (absorptive capacity). To create these enabling factors, clusters suffer from a collective-action problem, where establishing them would put a burden on one organization, but potentially would benefit the whole network. Hence, different types of cluster organizations have been established to create such elements. In addition to cluster organizations, government action also plays a role in knowledge transfer. Policy decisions, such as on immigration, housing, or taxation, affect the personnel and knowledge sources available to companies and research facilities. Local authorities can also support or hinder agglomerative efforts through the provision of, for example, meeting spaces or funding schemes.

# 4 Cluster Analysis

For a more in-depth analysis of how government can identify gaps in cluster development and implement effective policies tailored towards the cluster context, this chapter profiles four cases from the biotechnology sector that vary in terms of cluster facilitation and the degree of government involvement. To control further for context-related and nationally or regionally embedded factors, the cases were chosen from innovation-driven economies – that is, countries that have the ability to place greater emphasis on knowledge-intensive activities through, for example, high spending on the production of knowledge and high investment in information and communications technology (Cooke et al. 2007; Godin 2006; OECD 2001).

## The Biotechnology Sector

As previously noted, biotechnology encompasses different research subjects, and is summarized as the "application of science and technology to living organisms, as well as parts, products and models thereof, to alter living or non-living materials for the production of knowledge, goods and services" (OECD 2005, 9). It is a prime example of an industry based on scientific knowledge. New knowledge is usually generated by dedicated biotech firms (DBFs), which require high levels of innovative capacity. Stakeholders in the cluster that cannot absorb new knowledge from those DBFs thus face major disadvantages (Nilsson 2001). In turn, DBFs depend heavily on the financial resources of bigger companies, because the production of, for example, a new medication requires large up-front costs and long development times. This mutual interdependency, which extends to government funding and qualified personnel through universities, explains the tendency for these actors to agglomerate close to one another (Cooke 2002b; Feldman and

Francis 2004; Zeller 2001). Thus, the nature of biotechnology is that it needs well-educated and highly trained personnel, as well as capital from both the private and public sectors.

Biotechnology can further be termed a "transfer science" that has a networking character (Dunkel 2004). Networks form a knowledge-intensive cluster in terms of firms and organizations, which are embedded in a specific region and characterized by localized interactive learning. Policy interventions in the field have the opportunity to "lend these systems a more planned character through the intentional strengthening of the region's institutional infrastructure – for example, through a stronger, more developed role for regionally based R&D institutes, vocational training organizations, and other local organizations involved in firms" innovation processes" (Asheim and Gertler 2005, 302). Further, learning is seen as a necessary component for success (Lundvall 1992). Thereby, the phenomenon of clusters and biotechnology go hand-in-hand, as biotech – as a science-intensive "sunrise" industry – grew at a time when geographical clustering became more prominent. The types of links that support ties in biotechnology, can be distinguished as follows (6 et al. 2006, 200):

- Board-level links, include interlocks (overlapping board memberships for influential individuals), but also including less formal links;
- Professional-level links, including informal ties between scientists in the same sub-discipline, and more formally sanctioned links in the course of collaborations in research and development;
- And other staff-level links, including between marketing staff, account managers, project managers for joint projects, and strategic alliances.

Thus, informal and formal ties appear to be symbiotic in the biotechnology field. Government is in a position to support these ties and promote the creation of technology-based firms, typically through programs, subsidies, grants, and fiscal benefits. These efforts have paid off, as the growth of biotechnology in a number of countries can be traced back to such dedicated initiatives. Mostly, governments allocate financial support specifically to the so-called pre-seed stage of life sciences start-ups. Due to the horizontal character of biotechnology, many countries have also created cross-disciplinary government boards in support of science parks created for high-technology research (Coenen, Moodysson, and Asheim 2004). Targeted regional initiatives, such as the support of technology transfer offices, also affect the clustering process, as do the funding of universities and national-level goals for regional development. Currently, there is a trend towards emphasizing linkages beyond national boundaries and even global cluster connections, but national and regional policy inputs are still very much involved in clustering (Peck and Lloyd 2008; Wolfe 2008; Wolfe and Gertler 2004). Thus, many countries and jurisdictions have adopted the concepts of multilevel governance and place-based policy to help achieve the desired degree of cross-jurisdictional coordination (Wolfe and Creutzberg 2003).

These linkages in the multilevel framework and within the cluster – horizontally and vertically – entail helpful but also hindering dynamics for both government and stakeholders. From a governmental point of view, there is the lack of a precise definition of a cluster and how exactly to support the process of clustering. On the one hand, the concept allows for a broader definition of the initiatives implemented in a region; on the other hand, this lack of precision can lead to confusion about the focus and goal of cluster policies (Peck and Lloyd 2008). Moreover, biotechnological innovation in clusters often appears spontaneous and unpredictable, which makes it difficult to plan a systematic course of action. Adding to the problem is that governments lack "the knowhow, know-who and experiences of participants in the clusters they address" (Hospers, Desrochers, and Sautet 2009, 291).

From their perspective, stakeholders find it difficult to get their message across to policy makers. This gap can lead to less effective policy frameworks and the failure of policy to provide relevant knowledge bases for development (Borras and Tsagdis 2008). For successful clustering to happen, new channels of communications and intermediation are needed horizontally among, for example, government departments or cluster stakeholders and vertically across levels of policy making and planning. Halkier (2011, 335) calls this "a new multi-level paradigm in which promotion of indigenous growth and competitiveness is the shared goal and regional actors play a prominent role within a broad participatory framework." As Borras and Tsagdis (2008, 263) point out: "If cluster policies are to be strategic and able to tackle the actual and future problems faced by cluster firms, efforts need to be placed on creating forums and spaces where firms and policy makers can share, develop as well as revise their strategic views." In fact, cluster management efforts increasingly have been acting as such spaces.

Overall, biotechnology represents many evolving technology fields, such as nanotechnology, that have informal and ill-structured information and tacit knowledge exchanges as key components in shaping the scope and type of networks that emerge. Ideally, stakeholders in the formed cluster possess excellent information about other actors in the field, their capabilities and strategies, and about the leading edge of techniques and practices, as well as policy initiatives. In the absence of such information, key players need a central node, a facilitator, to make crucial information available to them.

The four life sciences clusters analysed below are emerging innovation networks created by a top-down motivation. The metropolitan area of Chicago is dominated by publicly traded multinationals and the federal government. Baxter International, Abbott Labs, and CVS all have offices in Chicago, and the federal government has two research sites located in that region. Similarly, Singapore houses industry leaders such as GlaxoSmithKline, Merck, and Roche, and the government heavily funds research institutes (Jones Lang LaSalle 2014). In Medicon Valley, major industry players include Novo Nordisk, Lundbeck, Leo Pharma, Alk-Abelló, Genmab, and Bavarian Nordic. There are also many small- and medium-sized companies and public research institutes (Denmark 2013). Vancouver builds on a biotech corridor of research institutes, and has relied increasingly on one big life sciences company in combination with some national and provincial support. In all four clusters, universities and hospitals support life sciences research efforts.

## Key Cluster Performance Indicators

To translate these characteristics into comparable performance measures is challenging, since data are rarely gathered at the network or cluster level due to confidentiality rules in many technology areas (Davis et al. 2006; Martin and Sunley 2003). As well, the multiple definitions of biotechnology or life sciences affect the data-gathering process. In essence, there is no standardized approach to gathering cluster data (Davis et al. 2006).[*]

---

[*]    To streamline the data-gathering process, the European Union and Pricewaterhouse-Coopers have made efforts to specify better measurements for clusters. This renewed interest, at least in Europe, stems from the fact that countries such as Hungary, Germany, and Sweden "appear to consider the quality of cluster organizations as a key indicator of future cluster performance" (zu Köcker and Rosted 2010, 15). European plans include data-gathering processes through the combination of self-reporting surveys with "hard" data. In turn, evaluation is used to adjust regional cluster activities and national government services to clusters. Another recent EU project used three interconnected indicators: employment, average real wages, and innovation. Information was further collected on current framework conditions, such as access to human capital, availability of knowledge, entrepreneurial activities, quality of public regulation, and the degree of collaboration. In comparison, an industry study by PriceWaterhouseCoopers (2011) on performance measures for biotechnology focuses on data available through various scoreboards from, for example, the OECD or the US Census Bureau. The report suggests looking at three general categories: employment, innovation, and productivity. Each indicator consists of multiple variables, including total employment, employment growth, the number of improved products, services or technologies, and wages.

For Medicon Valley, for example, it is difficult to evaluate some of the performance measures properly, as the data are often available only for Denmark or Sweden separately or with a focus on a metropolitan area such as Copenhagen, This might result in a distorted image of the region, as Sweden is strong in R&D-related activities, while Denmark performs well in firm-related actions such as patent filing. Data availability is also mixed in Singapore, having to do with the age of the cluster and the fact that the government is very aware of its outside appearance to possible investors, and presents its numbers accordingly. There is a strong focus on the government investment side of the data and the success stories of attracting multinationals and unique research labs. In the United States, the Chicago cluster shows up in performance rankings only starting in fiscal year 2005–6. Before that, Chicago was barely on the radar for life sciences; now it is consistently one of the top twenty US life sciences clusters. In Canada, the Vancouver cluster's performance (measured, in fact, for the whole of the province of British Columbia) is weaker than its counterparts in the east of the country. In addition, Canadian clusters in general perform less well on the share of patents, since many companies file them in the larger US market, particularly in pharmaceuticals and medical equipment (Brydon et al. 2014). A KPMG (2016, 24) report notes that a "slowdown in job growth may be attributed to a growing imbalance in talent supply versus demand." In short, constraints on the supply of talent and muted job growth numbers are increasingly an issue.

Singapore, Chicago, Medicon Valley, and Vancouver are all emerging clusters. This also has to do with the "winner-takes-all" feature of the current biotechnology market when it comes to, for example, venture capital investments. In fact, leading clusters in the United States receive most of the investment and the positive results following from it: in 2010, for example, of the US$25 billion raised by biotech companies in the United States, Europe, and Canada, 82.6 per cent went to US companies. The 2008–9 financial crisis also affected the have-nots more than the already successful clusters, further widening the gap between clusters such as San Diego and Boston, for example, and that of Chicago (Ernst & Young 2011). In essence, due to the dynamic borders of regional clusters and differing performance criteria, they are generally hard to compare. The following case descriptions give a more in-depth view on cluster development. The description of each case is divided into six parts: the genesis of the cluster, its current status, public initiatives supporting the cluster, cluster management, collaborative capacity, and absorptive capacity.

## Medicon Valley: The Divided Cluster

*Genesis of the Cluster*

The Medicon Valley cluster is located in the binational Øresund region, which spans greater Copenhagen in Denmark and Scania in southern Sweden, including the university town of Lund and Sweden's third-biggest city, Malmö. The establishment of the cluster builds on a larger initiative by the Øresund Science Region, an independent body that, at the time, was responsible for developing collaborative links between Denmark and Sweden. This included several network agencies with diverse responsibilities. Under this umbrella, seven regional research and innovation platforms established by universities, industries, and local authorities from both Denmark and Sweden got together. One such platform is the Medicon Valley Alliance (formerly Medicon Valley Academy), which emphasizes the commercialization of life sciences research in the region (Hansen and Serin 2008). The establishment of the Alliance was motivated by the integration challenge arising between Lund and Copenhagen universities, and was part of an EU Interreg II Project. "The rationale behind the initiative was to stimulate the formation of a cross-border life sciences region, by promoting local integration and cross-fertilization between industry and academia" (Moodysson, Coenen, and Asheim 2010, 362). The goal was also to spur development and support interaction among private companies, universities, hospitals, science parks, research institutions, and providers of knowledge-intensive services (Maskell 2004).

Both parts of Denmark and Sweden have a history of life sciences research and the existence of large pharmaceutical anchor firms such as Novo Nordisk and Lundbeck. Scania, in southern Sweden, developed a basis for life sciences through the early presence of Astra (now AstraZeneca) and Pharmacia (now owned by Pfizer), which located parts of their research activities in Lund. In Denmark, similar developments took place, which led to the decision in 1994 to stimulate binational regional development in life sciences (Moodysson, Coenen, and Asheim 2010). The construction of the Øresund Bridge in 2000 also created favourable conditions for combining the two regions into one cluster, which the Øresund committee branded as "Medicon Valley" – based on its famous predecessor, "Silicon Valley." Another favourable condition was the lack of a communications barrier between Danes and Swedes, as their languages are quite similar to each other (Streijffert 2008).

*Medicon Valley Today*

Medicon Valley currently is in a transition phase, with increased public interest in both the region and the biotechnology sector. The Danish and Swedish governments continue to facilitate life sciences research and the location of biotechnology industry in the region, and in June 2016 launched an initiative that included a special growth team for life sciences on the Danish side and so-called strategic collaborations in Sweden (MVA 2016). In 2015, the Danish government published a plan entitled "Together for the Future," in which it confirmed its support for life sciences: "The government will support a strong Danish research-performing pharmaceutical and medical industry by simplifying conditions and procedures for clinical research as well as prioritizing the improvement of procedures and waiting time for the approval of new pharmaceuticals" (MVA 2016). This push came at a time when 22 billion Danish crowns (US$3.4 billion) were being invested in the new materials research facilities MAX IV and ESS in Lund, and ESS's data management centre in Copenhagen. The relationship between the two regions has also changed. Traditionally, Sweden was a strong employer and exporter in the life sciences sector, linked to the pharmaceutical companies moving into Scania. In the past ten years, however, Danish life sciences exports and employment have surpassed Sweden's (MVA 2016). A report by the European Cluster Observatory (2016) further identified the Greater Copenhagen Region as among the top three for biopharmaceuticals, whereas southern Sweden ranked twelfth. Moreover, while the industry on the Danish side grew, the Swedish side declined (European Cluster Observatory 2016). Sweden has been especially challenged by the merger and acquisition of big Swedish pharmaceutical companies, which has led to job cuts and shrunk overall numbers for life sciences in the region (MVA 2016).

The most pressing challenge facing the cluster, according to the MVA (2016), is access to seed funding, which is especially limited on the Swedish side. Another issue is the difficulty in finding life sciences specialists for positions in the cluster. Interviewees for this research also pointed to the limited influx of qualified personnel, due to the insufficient number of life sciences graduates from Danish and Swedish universities, making international recruitment necessary:

> So recruiting or helping to recruit the attention of international [venture capitalists], also I would say, in terms of the labour market, … we are expanding our activities to, you could call it, our "nearest neighbour." So we were the initiator of what is called Baltic Development Form or ScanBelt,

and the reason for that was obviously that Novo Nordisk wanted to be able to attract talent from those places to come for summer schools and stuff like that over here, so they could get more people over here with the right skill set and experience profile. (Industry interviewee, July 2012)

The Baltic Development Forum is a recruitment group that looks beyond the immediate cluster at national factors such as visas, housing, taxes, and education. Denmark does have a special tax scheme that gives workers moving from other countries a tax break (used in 5.452 cases in 2015), but Sweden's scheme is less attractive to foreign employees' and therefore is used a lot less (994 cases in 2015, of which 715 were approved) (MVA 2016). At the same time, companies might decide not to relocate to Medicon Valley over concerns about limited qualified labour. Interviewees from the business and research sector pointed out that, due to high costs of living, immigration issues (specifically in Denmark), and better tax breaks elsewhere, many graduates leave the country after receiving their degree even if desirable jobs are available:

We've had and maybe still have some pretty tough regulations concerning whether you can be a Danish citizen and have a job permit here, and at some point they were really so ridiculous that when you completed your PhD, you only had a couple of months actually to get a job. Otherwise you would have to leave the country. Within the alliance we have the same interest ... to get our labour market accessible and attractive. (University interviewee, July 2012)

The other thing is that trying to explain to people that we are pretty high in tax, but also a lot of services are then free. So if you live here for a lifetime, it more or less balances, but if you only live here for a few years, then you ... pay a lot of tax and you only get a few benefits. (University interviewee, July 2012)

Another issue raised by both university and business interviewees was the Danish and Swedish higher education systems, both of which fully fund students for a certain number of years. Contrary to popular expectations, this kind of system does not lead to a more highly educated workforce, but rather has the unintended consequences of students frequently switching programs, high drop-out rates, and generally late entry into the workforce (OECD 2009). Interviewees pointed out that this creates an environment in which students switch among fields quite often (delaying graduation in the process), and do not necessarily study the skills that the market – in this case the biotechnology industry – needs.

*Public Initiatives Supporting the Cluster*

There is wide public support on both sides of the Øresund for the life sciences ambitions of Medicon Valley, but many obstacles to and boosts for competitiveness originate from national policies that are not necessarily linked to the cluster. The OECD has identified the following challenges: "1) national immigration and tax policy made Copenhagen less attractive to highly skilled foreign labour; 2) housing legislation has made it difficult to solve issues of housing affordability; 3) particular differences in national legislation of Sweden and Denmark have hindered the functional integration of the Øresund Region" (OECD 2009, 30). Structural reforms within the Danish government since the mid-1980s have also affected local agglomerations, with local and regional governments becoming more active in the country's economic development. "The net result [has been] a conspicuous increase in the level of sub-national initiatives and from the early 1990s all regional and the majority of local government [have been] engaged in activities aiming to stimulate indigenous economic activity, promote employment within their area, and secure a higher level of taxable income" (Halkier 2011, 332) Once the regional level established itself as a major player in spatial economic policy, the Danish government aimed for a higher degree of coordination among actors at the subnational level through permanent forums and joint regional development plans, while the number of relevant actors grew significantly.

For the Øresund region specifically, an "open house strategy" was pursued, meaning that multiple scales and different levels of institutions were brought together to form a particular place (Jensen and Richardson 2004; Tangkjær 2000). In fact, "the authority structure in the Øresund Region can be perceived as a black hole which has exercised its gravity on all kinds of political organizations and made various actors and agents rush in to fill it" (Jensen and Richardson 2004, 153; see also Berg 2000). In light of these developments, Danish local government reform has addressed the power relationship between different levels of government – from supranational bodies like the EU to the local level. The effect of this reform has been the appearance of two national centres of growth – the larger provincial towns of eastern Jutland and the metropolitan region of Copenhagen – and a reduction in Copenhagen's room for manoeuvre. Thus, a good deal of influence has remained in the hands of the central government by its rescaling the national state through giving Copenhagen a larger number of administrative obligations, while dismantling parts of the city's strategic capacity and institutions (Andersen 2008).

The Capital Region of Denmark, however, continues to play a pivotal role in organizing and planning the clustering process, and is also seen as a key player by other stakeholders. While the European and national levels give money to local initiatives – for example, INTERREG IVC, which helped establish the Øresund cross-border initiative – many of the programs launched at the national level have regional roots, and are therefore informed by regional ideas. Further, the Capital Region of Denmark sees itself as responsible for developing a strategy and identifying bottlenecks in the cluster. Together with the Growth Forum – a regionally located organization of twenty members appointed by the Regional Council and with a seat in the general Danish Growth Council – the region has created a business development strategy with six focus areas, one of which is biotechnology. The Capital Region representative who was interviewed framed the work in terms of developing a strong regional strategy to attract foreign talent, as well as looking into the living conditions of foreign researchers coming in, such as housing and education.

The variety of partners and initiatives connecting and supporting stakeholders at different government levels and also within the cluster reveal several aspects about the set-up and the role of the regional government in cluster development. First, the Capital Region is aiming for a more city-focused network based on growth strategies (Jensen and Richardson 2004). This is visible in all the initiatives targeting Copenhagen, such as "Wonderful Copenhagen," "Copenhagen Capacity," the "Copenhagen Talent Bridge," and the "Øresund Science Region." Second, the Capital Region is trying to differentiate itself from other regions in Denmark and elsewhere in Europe (Andersen 2008). The bridge to Sweden and the region's combined research in life sciences has made this easier. Advertising and branding by the national government and the idea of Medicon Valley helped to put the Øresund region on the map for life sciences in Europe and beyond. Third, the projects and forums noted above show that there is currently no need for more institutions. In fact, a 2009 OECD report on territorial reviews states that, rather than create more institutions, networks should be stimulated in the region so as to avoid the duplication of efforts.

*Cluster Management*

Several cluster initiatives and organizations in the region focus on collaboration among a specific group of stakeholders, either on the Danish or the Swedish side or in the network as a whole. Noteworthy initiatives mentioned by interviewees who work in the cluster include Invest in Skåne, Copenhagen Capacity, Biopeople, and DanskBiotek. Invest in Skåne is the official regional promotion agency facilitating inward investment in the Swedish region of Skåne, as well as promoting internationalization of the regional industry. These efforts include various sectors, among them life sciences. The organization provides free professional advice and services to companies considering Skåne for future investment and/or expansion, and helps Swedish companies find international partners. The Danish counterpart of this Swedish initiative, Copenhagen Capacity, similarly provides support for investors and business before, during, and after the move to Medicon Valley. This is done through benchmarking the region against other Scandinavian regions, market surveys, and identifying public funding schemes and incentive programs. There are also national organizations that focus on the research side of the cluster. For example, the Danish Agency for Science, Technology and Innovation co-funds BioPeople, which is located at the University of Copenhagen and hence has a sharp focus on Medicon Valley, and facilitates meeting places for public and private stakeholders, cross-disciplinary collaboration, and support of the development of professional competences (BioPeople 2017). Finally, DanskBiotek is an industry organization that collaborates with, for example, Copenhagen Capacity, BioPeople, and Medicon Valley Alliance to create favourable conditions for the biotech industry in the region. Part of the work involves raising national awareness of the conditions for the biotech industry through the media and correspondence with national governmental representatives (Dansk Biotek 2012).

Among these numerous initiatives, which are largely funded by public or research organizations, the Medicon Valley Alliance (MVA, formerly Medicon Valley Academy) has become a driving force for cluster management. It focuses specifically on the networking links on both sides of the Øresund, and has stated explicitly that it intends to take on the role of a network organization (MVA 2016). The choice of profiling the MVA as the cluster organization in this research was driven by the way it was set up structurally from the beginning to take a lead role in networking efforts among Danish and Swedish life sciences, and by the fact that all of the interviewees from this region pointed to the Alliance as having a central role in the cluster. Since its foundation, the MVA has updated its mission to include active networking and collaboration support and developing new methods to support the cluster.

In 2000, an MVA online platform supported the actual branding of "Medicon Valley," while an ambassador program was established that sends people to other clusters to learn from foreign approaches. In 2004 and 2005 – according to interviewees in the industry and at the MVA – the level of cooperation and communication at the decision-making level went up, as the MVA had earned trust and established a core node position in the cluster, involving big companies and government on a regular basis – as one interviewee noted, "the surroundings were ready to see MVA stepping up to a new role." This was a crucial step in the establishment of the MVA as a cluster organization, especially due to its competition with inward investment agencies. Also, the regularity and frequency of meetings at the MVA, including representatives from government, industry, and the universities, led to a greater appreciation and understanding among people on the board of the networking dynamics in the cluster and thus to more qualified discussions. The subsequent visibility of the cluster then led to a self-perpetuating process in which Medicon Valley became more visible, attracting more talent and investors, leading to more people working with the MVA to be part of the cluster's development. The growing size and representation function of the MVA, then, gave it the power to coordinate and advertise the cluster beyond Scandinavia.

The MVA is funded by the three regions that belong to the Øresund partnership – Capital Region of Denmark, Region Zealand, and, on the Swedish side, Skåne – as well as by universities such as the Technical University of Denmark, Copenhagen, and Lund, and by most of the (small) biotech companies. This money accounts for about 50 per cent of the MVA budget, while sponsorships and EU funding make up the other half. The constant struggle described by the Capital Region of Denmark and the MVA is that, on the one hand, it is difficult for the MVA continuously to prove its value to individual companies or to the universities, as a lot of its work involves networking support, which can hardly be measured in exact numbers or output. On the other hand, the Capital Region aims to make the MVA a self-sufficient organization in the sense that it relies on membership fees and sponsorships instead of on government funding. The region points out that this is the only way that the idea of the MVA can prove to be valuable to the cluster, and it gives the government the opportunity to evaluate the facilitation process.

Today, the Medicon Valley Alliance describes itself as a non-profit membership organization that represents the region's universities, hospitals, human life science business, regional governments, and service providers (MVA 2017). These span around 250 member organizations. During the interviews, more critical voices raised the issue that the MVA focuses more prominently on industry developments rather than on university research. This argument was presented on the basis that better-funded industry organizations would be able to articulate their preferences more prominently. The MVA itself states that it is a democratic organization, in which new initiatives are put in front of a general assembly of all the members. At the same time, however, "the members that are most active, will receive the most attention by MVA" (MVA 2017). In this context, a university interviewee points out that he sees the MVA as "more supportive of the region's commercial activities," than of research per se. In addition, the MVA is seen as "flagshipping and promoting the region to outsiders" (University interviewee, July 2012).

Beyond these more general activities, the cluster organization is mainly involved in the following initiatives:

- matching possible partners;
- "being out in the real world";
- going abroad through the ambassador program;
- evaluating framework conditions and infrastructure;
- networking activities;
- lobbying for the cluster;
- connecting companies to talent pools;
- translating regional/national strategies into action;
- synchronizing different agendas;
- keeping up the momentum; and
- keeping track of opportunities.

Other activities that stakeholders attributed to the MVA include networking possibilities through common board meetings and the MVA's connection to both stakeholders "on the ground" – meaning researchers and small firms – and internationally based players through the ambassador program, including the matchmaking of partners within and outside the cluster. The MVA itself outlines daily activities as well as strategic plans that address the pressing issue of how to stay competitive and retain key stakeholders – such as the company Novo Nordisk – within the cluster.

The MVA's day-to-day activities include creating opportunities for Danes and Swedes to become business or research partners. These meetings can take different forms – for example, scientists from the Technical University of Denmark might give a talk about new developments in a certain subfield of biotech or informal gatherings might be held where people can connect. Another important activity is lobbying politicians "based on facts and through the media." This implies assessments of cluster developments and the publication of strategic visions. One of the MVA's most important services, according to one interviewee, is to make connecting companies aware of the "talent pool within Denmark and Sweden – for example, at the universities – but also outside through the ambassador program." Another key task, as another interviewee pointed out, is the synchronization of plans within the cluster, as "it is so difficult to have all the different stakeholders, having the same agenda at the same time."

In terms of strategic planning and maintaining the attractiveness of the cluster, the MVA emphasizes the following points. First, it aims to target complex issues with an interdisciplinary approach – for example, the various universities involved offer a wide range of research that can be combined through networking activities. Second, similar to the first point, the MVA tries to converge or "bridge" different technologies for new innovative products by matching firms with other firms or researchers and companies. Third, it aims to gain a competitive advantage through "clever networking" locally and globally:

> Part of our strategy is what we call clever networking – using the entire world as our partner. Instead of concentrating on the individual things, we try to build alliances, collaborations all over the world, that's why we have these ambassador programs ... but also here in the region to try to create synergies between the different stakeholders by doing networking activities. (MVA interviewee, July 2012)

Finally, through "smart specialization," the MVA focuses on specific areas in which the cluster has an advantage. Linking these activities to capacity, the following section highlights the collaborative and absorptive elements of the cluster.

*Collaborative Capacity*

One of the main challenges the MVA faces is that different stakeholders have different agendas at different times. Thus, the goal is to bring them together in an informal networking structure in order to give the cluster direction and purpose. Since its establishment in 1997, the Alliance has worked towards defining such a purpose. The fact that big pharmaceutical companies were already in the area and the life sciences research field was strong at Swedish and Danish universities also helped to define the cluster's direction. Once stakeholders saw the MVA as a strategic leader and a membership community was established, the Alliance was able – according to one interviewee – to "lobby with decision makers and opinion leaders of government, civil servants, and so on and so forth – to get them to the right decision at any given time." The MVA also took on the role of branding the cluster. This is a long-term process, but with support from government funding and the newly branded Øresund region, the MVA was able to define Medicon Valley and its focus on pharmaceuticals.

The MVA has also developed a so-called beacon initiative, which emphasizes the cluster's strengths compared to other life sciences networks and uses them as an attractor for other entrants. As the MVA itself notes, "[a] beacon should reflect the needs of tomorrow's life science environment and thus needs to be conscious of future trends and requirements ... A beacon also is part of the regional identity and to be successful, a beacon most likely needs competences held by more than just a few organizations" (MVA 2011, 5). The beacon strategy document was developed in collaboration with the Copenhagen Business School and contributors from the Øresund region. It outlines the importance of life sciences for the global market in general and the region in particular due to increasing demand for health services. As the document points out, however, this industry will also become more competitive as the elderly market grows and attracts new entrants. In this increasingly competitive environment, the MVA's ability to access global pipelines and to identify external knowledge and the competitive advantage of internal potential becomes even more important (Wolfe and Creutzberg 2003). Clusters will compete more fiercely to attract talent as political regions see their older industries decline, and "they will invest more in the buoyant life sciences hoping to survive" (MVA 2011).

The beacon strategy will be successful, however, only if there is regional excellence in that specific area and global awareness of it by other stakeholders. This means that the excellence has to be advertised in order to attract venture capital and scientists from abroad, which is part of the success of Silicon Valley, San Diego, and Boston. Medicon Valley has identified four beacons: systems biology, structural biology, immune regulation, and drug delivery. Each of these areas is highly cross-disciplinary and builds on existing collaborations within the cluster.

The beacon strategy, which responds to the growing need to identify the network's purpose, is communicated widely both inside and outside the cluster. Respondents to the research's 2012 survey were aware of the strategy and in support of its goal. Representatives from companies and universities pointed out that, in the beacon areas, the MVA was able to make communications links among relevant stakeholders in a specific field – through, for example, meetings between stakeholders or research talks to inform industry about investment options – which led to higher levels of cooperation. Interviewees also noted that the amount of information shared among cluster members was increasing as a result of regularly scheduled meetings:

> Yes, we are in regular contact with them [the MVA] and, for example, one of the things they have initiated recently is what they call a beacon initiative. In the effort to be visible among many other fields or areas globally in medical science clusters you look at "what is actually that we can manage here, what are we able to offer?" We have been quite eager in trying to get the headlines on drug delivery systems. And we have been that, because we have good research contacts with a number of big companies – Lundbeck and Novo Nordisk – who are interested in these fields. So we ... find it a reasonable and sensible initiative for the Alliance to support such a thing. We take part in their meetings; many of our scientists give talks and so on. (University interviewee, July 2012)

New opportunities also arise from the MVA's connections to government, access to which smaller firms otherwise might not have. Interviewees pointed out that the MVA is consulted by the regional government on strategic decisions and future funding of cluster initiatives, while the MVA lobbies for the local life sciences industry at the regional and national levels on both the Danish and Swedish sides. For many stakeholders – especially industry and government – the MVA, through its ambassador program, is also the communications channel to other clusters globally.

The financing structure of the MVA also contributes to creating a close-knit network. Because all members pay a fee, there is a sense that stakeholders are more willing to support the MVA in its efforts and use its services. In 2000, however, Denmark revised its patent legislation, granting ownership of intellectual property rights by the university in which the research takes place. This has led to a point "where scientists have become reluctant to exchange knowledge" (IRIS Group 2009). As well, this change also meant that two different patent systems were in place in Denmark and Sweden, as in the latter country intellectual property rights remain the property of the inventor (Telleman and Dinnetz 2005). The new Danish legal regime thus hinders not only cooperation between firms and universities in Denmark, but also cross-border partnerships in the Øresund region. The MVA has raised the issue of patent legislation with the Danish government, but a change in the regulatory system is unlikely to occur. This highlights one of the limits to facilitation, as cluster organizations are unable to change national regulations that affect networking.

The resources of the cluster and the MVA in particular – which include financial, intellectual, and human capital – affect the network's ability to function, cooperate, and commercialize properly. Medicon Valley has far fewer such resources than have renowned clusters such as Boston or Silicon Valley, so clever networking and differentiation from those bigger clusters are part of the MVA's strategy. As well, as an interviewee from the MVA pointed out, "Novo Nordisk, Lundbeck, Leo are owned by foundations, by private foundations, so you can't buy them ... You can't make a hostile takeover" (MVA interviewee, July 201). The Novo Nordisk foundation (2013), for example, aims not only "to provide a stable basis for the commercial and research activities conducted within the Novo Group," but also to contribute to scientific, humanitarian, and social progress. According to the MVA interviewee, this results in Novo Nordisk "donating billions of euros every year to research." The 2008–9 financial crisis affected the pharmaceutical industry in the area, however, and even by 2016 pre-crisis levels had not yet been reached and overall growth had slowed down.

Another financial resource in the cluster's development has been the European Union. The Øresund region was established with European funds and, according to the Capital Region government, there is new money coming in through regional programs. But not everyone in the cluster agrees that EU funding is convenient and beneficial. One interviewee from the MVA called it a "nightmare" with "absolutely no value," pointing out that most of the money is spent on bureaucracy in Brussels and consultants who are "remote from real life." As such, although the European funding might relieve the regional government of some of its financial burden, it adds to the MVA's administrative work.

The amount of human capital in the cluster benefits from its links to both the Swedish region of Skåne and the Capital Region of Denmark. The talent pool for firms on both sides of the border is big, as it includes universities and research institutes. Although Danish immigration and housing policies have not always been in the cluster's favour, tax policy and marketing of the region have helped to attract talent. One facility that stood out during the interviews for its human capital generation and attraction was MAX IV, a large scientific facility in Lund, Sweden, that focuses on accelerator physics research and has attracted young, international talent into the region, and from which many stakeholders are hoping for spillover effects to other research institutes and companies in Medicon Valley. Policy makers have further developed several initiatives to stimulate these benefits, covering activities such as construction, maintenance, research, and research exploitation (Nauwelaers, Maguire, and Marsan 2013). One such initiative is Vaekstmotor, which is funded by the Capital Region Growth Forum and the European Regional Development Fund, and supports Danish companies in recruiting highly skilled workers. The initiative takes advantage of the location of the MAX IV lab to increase the flow of talent into the region (Vaekstmotor 2013).

*Absorptive Capacity*

To recall, absorptive capacity building is the development of interactions among different stakeholders inside and outside the cluster. This includes multilevel governance arrangements as well as formal and informal relationships within and outside the network. To tap into inner and outside knowledge sources, the MVA updates firms about research developments and contract opportunities ("match making"), and makes use of its ambassador program. According to an MVA representative, this allows the Alliance to add value to the networking relationships. Interviewees described this as a short-cut to learning about developments within the cluster, although most pointed out that they themselves were responsible for getting involved in international developments. Large pharmaceutical companies such as Novo Nordisk have a global presence, and facilities in China, the United Kingdom, and the United States beyond those in Denmark. A similar dynamic applies to universities, which collaborate with other universities and researchers around the world. Smaller companies that lack the capacity to find more globally oriented initiatives use the MVA as a link to such resources without having to find them on their own.

Through the people who are sent out to other clusters as part of its ambassador program, the MVA gains insight into management practices and programs in other countries. The program also has its own funding pool, which is separate from that of the MVA. From 2009 to 2012, the program was financed by the three regional organizations in Medicon Valley: the Capital Region of Denmark, the Skåne region in Sweden, and the Zealand region in Denmark. From 2013 to 2017, Zealand dropped out of the funding, and there has been very little information on the program ever since. As well, ambassadors acquire self-financing based on grants. The goal is to establish lasting relationships with the regions that are part of the program beyond the time the ambassador is located there and have an ongoing learning experience. This program is also a way to showcase Medicon Valley's global relationships. One project covered in the media was "Value and growth through new kinds of innovative cooperation and partnerships in Denmark," a collaboration among the Copenhagen Business School, the MVA ambassador in Boston, Torsten Jepsen, and others. The ambassador was able to connect university researchers with existing industry-research collaborations in Boston, such as Pfizer and Boston University, with the goal of having Medicon Valley network members learn about setting up and sustaining such links (Anderson 2014).

As with many of these initiatives, it is difficult to measure their impact on the overall cluster (beyond the individuals involved) and to show that the knowledge acquired from external knowledge sources actually benefited the network. Generally, interviewees spoke favourably of the ambassador program, but the immediate value and benefit seemed more unclear at the time. For the ambassador program specifically, the public funding stream, in combination with the expansion and prolonging of the program, speaks for its success. Another way to evaluate the program is based on actual output, such as business deals that were reached among businesses in Medicon Valley and companies located in clusters where MVA ambassadors have been placed. In 2012, MVA reported that 5 big pharmaceutical companies, 5 universities, and 112 small and medium-sized enterprises were actively using the program, resulting in more than 600 leads in terms of potential products or technologies (MVA 2012).

Overall, the levels of collaboration and absorptive capacity building for Medicon Valley are high, as displayed in table 4.1.

*Medicon Valley's Cluster Organization*

The cluster facilitation model that the Medicon Valley region represents is one in which government and stakeholders are both invested in the institution and therefore expect certain benefits and services. Stakeholders value the MVA's work – networking events, marketing the cluster to international and national investors, and developing long-term visions for the network through, for example, its beacon and ambassadors programs – because the institution is plugged into the multilevel governance system and able to lobby for the life sciences industry. Working with stakeholders' funds also makes the organization more vulnerable to acting in favour of a dominant group in the network, whose expectations might be linked to the money it invests. This could affect the level of trust by other stakeholders and even by government. Ultimately, the MVA has to walk a thin line: pleasing all stakeholders, providing opportunities to all groups for the cluster to thrive, and staying closely connected to government.

Table 4.1. Collaborative and absorptive capacity of the Medicon Valley cluster

| Framework | Basic elements | |
| --- | --- | --- |
| *Collaborative capacity* | | |
| Purpose | Leadership? | Yes |
| | Shared vision? | Yes |
| | Network membership? | Yes |
| Structure | Formal and informal procedures? | Yes |
| | Clear roles? | Yes |
| Communications | Information links? | Yes |
| | Active communications? | In progress |
| Resources | Knowledge and skills? | Yes |
| | Financing powers? | No |
| *Absorptive capacity* | | |
| Intra-cluster knowledge system | Knowledge spillovers? | Yes |
| | Social relations? | Yes |
| Extra-cluster knowledge system | Extra-cluster knowledge sources? | Yes |
| | Interface between the external linkages and intra-cluster knowledge system? | Yes |

## Chicago: Driver of the Midwest Super Cluster

*Genesis of the Cluster*

The Midwestern United States is generally known for its agriculture sector, leading in corn and soybean production and feed grain exports, and where widespread planting of biotech maize has taken place since 1996 (James 2010). Illinois, in particular, had a breakthrough in the biotechnology field in the 1980s when it supported what many consider to be the number one biotech company, Applied Molecular Genetics, now known as Amgen. The company's creation was based on technology from the University of Chicago and capital and management from Abbott Labs (Rosen 2009).

Chicago and the Midwest have also traditionally been seen as the "second" hub of the US pharmaceutical industry, with major companies such as Abbott Labs and Baxter International headquartered in the Chicago area. Other companies followed – for example Takeda, Astellas, Valent BioSciences, Tate & Lyle, and Hospira & Lundbeck (Illinois Innovation Network 2013). For the research component and possible spin-offs, Chicago is home to several universities and research institutions, including Northwestern University, the University of Illinois, the Illinois Institute of Technology, and the University of Chicago, all of which have dedicated biotech programs. Illinois also has federal labs and federally funded research ongoing in the Argonne National Laboratory and the Fermi National Accelerator Laboratory (Lin 2008).

To facilitate connections between the pharmaceutical and agricultural industries, organizations such as the Illinois Biotechnology Organization (iBIO) – part of a larger Biotechnology Industry Organization (BIO) headquartered in Washington – and the Chicago Biotech Network are working in the area. The latter is an umbrella organization for all biotech activity in the Chicago Metropolitan Area, established based on a grassroots initiative that held seminars on biotech developments: "At first, it was more for individuals interested in life sciences. Then companies (such as Abbott Laboratories and Baxter, two Fortune 500 pharmaceuticals located in the Chicago area), started to attend the meetings as well, and they brought different perspectives. Over time, the community came to include scientists, university deans, lawyers, venture capitalists, angel investors, city and state business development staff, and others" (Snyder and Wenger 2010, 115). This gave some of the early developments structure and drew attention to efforts linked to biotech in the area.

Another factor not directly related to the biotech industry but mentioned by all interviewees is Chicago's airport, which is the second busiest in the United States, after Atlanta's, and offers direct flights to 215 destinations. This means that going in and out of Chicago for scheduled meetings is relatively easy to do.

*Chicago Biotech Today*

Today, Illinois or, rather, the larger Chicago area is developing into a life sciences cluster integrated into a larger network of biotech collaborations in the Midwest: the so-called Mid-west Super Cluster, which now consists of clusters in Illinois, Indiana, Iowa, Kansas, Michigan, Minnesota, Missouri, Ohio, and Wisconsin. The nine-state cluster employs more than 375,000 people in nearly 17,000 establishments (iBIO 2013). It is advertised as being "the most balanced of the biotechnology regions in the United States," because it covers a variety of areas, such as agricultural feedstock and chemicals, bioscience-related distribution, drugs and pharmaceuticals, and medical-device equipment, as well as research, testing, and medical laboratories (iBIO 2013).

Illinois in particular hosts the largest concentration of biopharma companies and is a "strong driver of the industry's vitality and growth" in the region (iBIO 2013). The establishment of a University of Illinois Health Technology Research Hub for the bioscience industry also made headlines. It was financed by a $1.7 million state capital investment, matched by $1.7 million from the university. The facility hosts lab and office space, and has the goal of bringing together scientists, clinicians, engineers, and industry (Illinois Innovation Network 2013). Interviewees greatly encouraged this initiative, emphasizing that having access to often expensive equipment after leaving the university environment was crucial for further developing a product and enabled network relationships with other disciplines and larger industry stakeholders that, in turn, might then lead to further network relationships and investments.

Chicago benefits from being the second-largest pharmaceutical hub in the United States. It currently has six Schools of Medicine and the largest concentration of doctors in the country. Most of the medical institutions are in close proximity, and form the so-called Illinois Medical District (IMD), the largest urban health care, education, and technology district in the United States. The IMD started in the 1870s, when Cook County Hospital, Rush Hospital College, and the College of Physicians and Surgeons were established on the Near West Side following the great Chicago Fire of 1871. Today it houses 2,200 hospital beds, the United States' largest College of Medicine, and the biggest biotechnology and medical complex in Illinois, and provides incubation for approximately thirty emerging technology-based companies. As a collective, these institutes generate US$392 million in university research and development annually and US$34 billion in overall economic activity (IMDC 2013).

Despite these developments, Chicago faces strong competition from established clusters in San Francisco and Boston. This, according to interviewees, has to do with the share of venture capital reaching the city and the difficulty of attracting and retaining talent in Illinois. As Arafeh et al. (2016, 24) summarize: "Illinois registered less than 5% of the proportion of venture capital deals in the past decade, and even smaller in the proportion of aggregate value in venture capital deals. In comparison, California leads the pack with over 40% and 50% in those categories respectively followed by New York and Massachusetts at over 10% each." A similar trend applies to human capital. Whereas Chicago has one of the most highly educated workforces (41 per cent of the population holds a bachelor's degree), significant brain drain limits the pool of employees and entrepreneurs in the biotechnology field (Arafeh et al. 2016). According to interviewees, the combination of limited venture capital and incubation space constrains human capital in Chicago, making the East and West coasts very attractive to recent graduates.

*Public Initiatives Supporting the Cluster*

The US government has invested heavily in agriculture – an estimated US$277.3 billion over the 1995–2011 period alone (Environmental Working Group 2012) – and, as Heinemann et al. (2014) describe, these subsidies have favoured monocultures because they are based on the acreage of the crop; thereby, "the larger and more uniform the crop, the more amenable it is to cost reductions through planting and harvesting mechanization and simplified pest control ... one of the primary drivers of GM [genetic modification] traits in the staple crops" (Heinemann et al. 2014, 78). This has created a fruitful basis for biotechnology developments, especially in the Midwest, where most of the agriculture is located, and has led some states, including Illinois, Michigan, and Wisconsin, to earmark funds specifically for the biotech industry and start-ups in the life sciences sector. The Michigan Life Sciences Corridor, for example, aims to create biotech developments from Detroit to the Grand Rapids area. Similarly, Wisconsin has branded itself as the "BioBelt," and developed government programs to support the industry (JETRO 2003).

In line with states that are deploying programs for biotech, the Illinois Department of Commerce and Economic Opportunity launched the Office of Entrepreneurship, Innovation & Technology. The office was established with the help of a biotech entrepreneur who shaped it according to the needs of the cluster and in line with what the Commerce Department could offer. Currently, the office is able to invest directly in some companies and up to a certain amount while offering assistance in a variety of areas, such as business planning, marketing and product development, training, business assessment, counselling, and networking, as well as contracting and international trade.

In Illinois, the primary goal of these initiatives is to provide so-called gap funding for smaller businesses that have difficulty attracting venture funding. Among these programs are tax credits for firms that invest in one of the state's qualified new business ventures or venture capital funds, such as the Invest Illinois Venture Fund, which aims to accelerate investments for small innovative companies (iBIO 2013). Specific programs launched by the Office of Entrepreneurship, Innovation & Technology include:

- establishing Small Business Development Centers to provide one-on-one counselling for new and existing small businesses;
- creating Procurement Technical Assistance Centers for companies interested in selling products to government agencies;

- creating International Trade Centers to offer counselling and training to companies interested in international trade and exporting;
- establishing Manufacturing Extension Centers to help companies improve their performance; and
- setting up a Small Business Environmental Assistance Program to help businesses that have to comply with state and federal air pollution regulations.

Overall, the office helps to service smaller companies in their quest to become part of the Illinois life sciences community while complying with state rules and finding funding opportunities.

The Invest Illinois Venture Fund, which is financed through federal means and implemented by the state of Illinois, supports young companies and start-ups that show potential for creating high-paying professional jobs in Illinois. The State Small Business Credit Initiative of the Small Business Jobs Act (2010) invested US$78 million to support such companies (Illinois 2013).

The city of Chicago has also been engaged in the establishment of the Illinois Medical District (IMD), governed by a seven-member commission charged with operating, assembling, and redeveloping land to enhance the district. Members are appointed by the governor, Cook County president, and mayor of Chicago. The administrative structure includes a director, accounting, facility management, and a legal department, as well as marketing and medical sciences outreach. As a political subdivision and unit of local government, the commission is charged by the Illinois Medical District Act to "maintain the proper surroundings for a medical center and a related technology center in order to attract, stabilize, and retain hospitals, clinics, research facilities, educational facilities," and to oversee the creation and expansion of the district.

In 2013, the IMD had expansion plans to include four West Side hospitals in the heart of the district. The project was part of a strategy that outlined hiring a private firm to increase the efficiency of clinical research trials, and establishing a fibre-optic network to support the analysis of huge amounts of clinical data by providing connectivity at speeds ten to one hundred times faster than commercial broadband (Dudek 2013). Reports suggest that health care improvements have resulted from the district's pact with private research firm Quintiles, of Research Triangle Park, North Carolina, to improve clinical trial results by improving patient recruitment, data analytics, and clinical trial management (Guy 2013). The upgrade also included a flagship biotech "validation centre" called the Health, Technology and Innovation Center, where biotech start-ups can convert their technologies into products and validate their products' market viability (Guy 2013). The center was made possible by a US$1.7 million capital grant from the Department of Commerce and Economic Opportunity, matched by $1.7 million in university funds.

*Cluster Management*

Several initiatives are under way in the Chicago cluster to facilitate connections among different stakeholders. This section reflects on those that were mentioned by interviewees from industry, government, and research fields.

At the centre of many of these initiatives is the life sciences industry association iBIO, composed of small and medium-sized companies and international firms in the agricultural and human health sector, entrepreneurial leaders of start-ups and spin-offs, scientists and technology transfer specialists, venture capitalists, seasoned government people, service providers from major law, accounting, financial, and research firms, and a variety of business professionals. Apart from industry leadership, there is also public policy input through the "iBIO government affairs committee" on human health, food, and agriculture. Committee members meet with various government officials and their staff to gain information, offer insight and advice. iBIO has two target areas: agriculture and pharmaceuticals in the biotech field, and is also looking into a third area related to medical devices. Another indication of iBIO's expanding activities is its ability to initiate advocacy in the Illinois state legislature to promote an environment attractive to firms and research. This is no small mandate, as Illinois lags behind other clusters in venture and angel capital, the major fuel for start-ups (Rosen 2009). Its mission, as iBIO puts it, is to "make Illinois and the surrounding Midwest one of the world's top life science centers by promoting sound public policy at the local, state and federal levels, improving Illinois' and the Midwest's ability to create, attract and retain businesses, and through the iBIO institute, deliver education, training for students, biotech professionals and the general public" (iBIO 2013).

iBIO also has a program called PROPEL established in 2007, that aims to increase the number and success rate of start-ups, and helps guide the development of formation-stage and early-stage life sciences companies by offering entrepreneurs access to specialized resources and expertise, such as coaching, business plan presentation panels, technical assistance, educational programs, and business plan competitions (PROPEL 2013). Along with the iBIO Institute and iBIO support staff, PROPEL depends on the time and expertise of the life sciences community who serve as coaches, technical experts, subject matter experts, and panelists. The chief executive officer of a biotech start-up company underlined the importance of these institutions in underpinning network relationships by stating: "iBIO, Chicago Innovation Mentors, the Women in Biotechnology organization are very active, so there are several organizations that are constantly gathering together expertise from throughout the community and finding a way to bring people together."

One initiative the CEO mentioned, Chicago Innovation Mentors, supports university-based and local technology innovation ventures through the use of mentor teams. Its board of governors comprises representatives from three universities (University of Chicago, University of Illinois, and Northwestern University) and from the Argonne National Laboratory and iBIO/PROPEL. As a representative from the technology transfer office at an Illinois university pointed out:

> We've been running a program with Northwestern University of Chicago and iBIO. We all started a program called Chicago Innovation Mentors and that has been a catalyst for us, one to work closer with the other universities as well as iBIO, and then our mentor pool is people in industry. Through all that, it has been an opportunity to enhance the community a little bit. So it is easier for me now to talk to someone from Northwestern, because I see them at least once a month, and I am on the phone with them almost every week in helping run that program. (Technology Transfer Office interviewee, March 2013)

Still another platform for collaboration is the Illinois Science & Technology Coalition, which provides networking opportunities in different kinds of technology areas – including life sciences. The coalition manages the Illinois Innovation Network, which is a platform allowing connections among start-ups, enterprises, service providers, and research and academic institutions. The goal is a mixture of providing services to entrepreneurs while also showcasing successful examples and outlining "who does what" in the network (Illinois Innovation Network 2017).

Illinois also has two science parks with spaces for life sciences companies. The Illinois Science + Technology Park is located in Skokie, in the former headquarters of the pharmaceutical company G.D. Searle. The facility offers access to Northwestern University and the Midwest technology and life sciences business environment. One industry interviewee from this location emphasized its structure, which gives small companies opportunities to access expensive equipment and to attend networking meetings and presentations organized on site. The other science park is University Technology Park, at the Illinois Institute of Technology. The site offers flexible lab and office space for start-ups and established technology companies linked to a technology business centre and an incubator. The facility is located ten minutes south of downtown Chicago, with access to two airports (University Technology Park 2011).

Finally, similar to the science parks, the 1871 project – a digital start-up hub located on the twelfth floor of Chicago's famous Merchandise Mart and operated by the non-profit Chicagoland Entrepreneurial Center – has the goal of being an incubator in the heart of the city to bring together venture capital, universities, and start-ups. The space started with stakeholders from the digital sector, but life sciences entrepreneurs have increasingly taken interest in the project.

*Collaborative Capacity*

The Chicago cluster mainly focuses on two leading organizations: the Office of Entrepreneurship, Innovation & Technology and iBIO. One strategic element for greater competitiveness in the Midwest is the attraction and support of the annual Chicago BIO convention, which showcases the region for potential investors. To make it accessible for everyone in the network, iBIO offers grants to smaller companies to cover attendance fees. Organizers also set up special events for entrepreneurs to meet with bigger companies, as well as an entrepreneur "boot camp." The event draws thousands of attendees from industry, government, and academia from scores of countries.

To organize a yearly event of this scale, iBIO can tap into the network of its parent Biotechnology Industry Organization, which "represents more than 1,100 bio-technology companies, academic institutions, state biotechnology centres and related organizations across the United States and in more than 30 other nations" (BIO 2013). Members are involved in different areas, such as health care, agriculture, and industrial and environmental biotechnology. Beyond the BIO convention in Chicago, the organization also hosts other events, such as biotech conferences in China, Montreal, and Washington, DC.

Beyond the Midwest connection and the BIO convention, there is no formal strategy guiding Illinois or the city of Chicago in relation to biotech, but there was solid political commitment in the early 2010s on the part of then governor Pat Quinn, who created the Illinois Innovation Council to promote and attract innovation-driven entrepreneurs to the state. For his work of increasing Illinois' economic, scientific, and technological output, Quinn was named the 2011 Governor of the Year by BIO. According to stakeholders, the Quinn administration was the third state government in a row to support biotechnology consistently in Illinois, an engagement that has been a catalyst for increased National Institutes of Health and Food and Drug Administration funding. According to interviewees, stakeholders were looking for sustainable long-term development with continued funding opportunities. As one university interviewee pointed out, "there is a lot of interest and excitement about what we are doing, a lot of momentum right now, but can it be sustained?" (March 2013). An industry interviewee (March 2013) also said: "I'd rather have a moderate strong investment and a government organization and community that was committed for a longer time frame than a giant first investment." From 2015 to 2019, Bruce Rauner was Illinois governor. The election of Rauner led to a budget stalemate between the Republican Senate and the Democratic-held Legislature. This resulted in budget uncertainties and budget cuts for universities and funding programs, including in the life sciences sector (Bosman and Davey 2017). Jay Robert Pritzker became governor in January 2019, and has promised to expand the Chicago biotech ecosystem.

Stakeholders in Chicago have developed strong communications ties, often originating from a core group updating one another on current developments within the cluster. This group crosses paths in the same organizations, creates new organizations, and even recruits one another in the process. And along with iBIO and smaller groups such as PROPEL and Chicago Innovation Mentors, there are direct linkages among individuals, either based on common employment in one of the organizations or more personal linkages. As I note in an earlier study, "[o]verall, the Chicago innovation network in the field of life sciences displays a variety of personal relationships that are based on repeated interactions outside and inside the network. Positions essential for the network were distributed and redistributed among a small number of individuals. In addition, organizations established and sustained by those key individuals serve as entities that now connect actors within the network" (Giest 2019, 337).

For any communications beyond the core group, the cluster has several mechanisms in place. First, because there is no marketing budget for the major organizations, iBIO and the Office of Entrepreneurship, Innovation & Technology call, email, and meet network members to get the word out on new funding opportunities and events. Many stakeholders have also taken on more active roles in the cluster by reaching out to other members. For example, the technology transfer offices at the universities increasingly are talking to industry and government.

Technology parks around the city also organize gatherings, and provide the physical space needed for networking events. Another program is "entrepreneur speed-dating," where faculty members and serial entrepreneurs get together, and researchers pitch their ideas in a five-to-ten-minute talk.

Communications opportunities are also available through the structural set-up. Communications-enhancing elements are primarily connected to the Office or iBIO, including the Chicago Innovation Mentors, on-campus innovation and technology transfer offices, the science parks, the medical district, and incubator facilities. In connection to those incubator spaces, in particular project 71 in downtown Chicago, one interviewee said: "I was so excited about project 71, the name of the facility downtown, because it is a permanent space and they [government] invested enough to give it a great shot at being self-sustaining, self-funding, self-justifying" (Industry interviewee, March 2013). The various components all contribute to the ecosystem and help foster formal and informal relationships. They also each have a defined role: while organizations such as iBIO and the Office have the bigger picture in mind when connecting and fostering some of these structures, the two major technology parks offer custom space to both multinational companies and start-up companies. The science park in Skokie has developed a model building on the competitive advantage of local universities, leading it to define itself as an intersection between biotechnology and nanotechnology. For companies coming from outside the United States, the technology parks also offer an entry point into the North American market in general and the cluster in particular.

In addition, the on-campus innovation centres and technology transfer offices as well as lab space offer opportunities for researchers to interact with entrepreneurs. In the innovation labs, they can learn about patent laws, costing a project, and how to sell it. In recent years, the technology transfer offices have pursued a more active role. The University of Illinois, for example, added economic development to its mission statement, which reads: "The University of Illinois is among the preeminent public universities of the nation and strives constantly to sustain and enhance its quality in teaching, research, public service and economic development." According to a university official, the economic development component implies a focus on technology management and technology transfer offices in creating procedures for the university to be aware of how to commercialize intellectual property and generally have closer ties to industry. The expectation is that enabling researchers to create spin-off companies and gain investment from industry creates jobs and contributes to the economic development of

Illinois. These changes are part of a growing movement towards commercialization in the region. In connection to these developments, one interviewee pointed out:

> They are active in seeking out disclosure, seeking out interaction with potential investors and company founders within their community, transforming that into protectable intellectual property when it is possible and giving them some connections and some guidance to the broader university community and the community in general around Chicago, and it gets them financing, expertise and potential partners." (Technology transfer office interviewee, March 2013)

The University of Illinois is also a landlord in that it offers small wet labs to start-ups. These spaces give new companies the opportunity to have their own office. Renting or owning lab space is in turn needed to receive federal funding, which requires companies to have "a place of business" (Small Business Innovation Research 2013). Another resource available to companies in terms of financial support is the Invest Illinois Venture Fund, which provides young, innovative firms and start-ups money received through the federal Small Business Jobs Act (Illinois 2013). From the total amount of US$78 million, US$20 million went into the venture fund, which supports small businesses during the time they need funding, but are not yet eligible for a credit. Then-governor Rauner renewed support for this funding scheme, and committed US$220 million in venture funds focused on emerging local technology companies. A 2015 assessment revealed that the state had received nearly US$27 million in capital gains and dividends through the program and that an estimated 3,900 jobs had been created (Elahi 2016). The fund is unique because it is distributed by the government office itself, not contracted out. The process to receive funding includes an online application, followed by an evaluation through five or six members of a forty-strong due diligence committee that includes iBIO. The committee ranks individual companies and, based on that score, entrepreneurs are invited to in-person interviews with committee members.

Spin-off companies also have an opportunity to receive proof-of-concept funding from technology transfer offices. These are rather small amounts of money – US$10,000–$20,000 per company – but they help to attract more funding from government or venture capitalists. As well, companies from outside Illinois can take advantage of tax incentives offered by the Office of Entrepreneurship, Innovation & Technology. As one government interviewee pointed out:

We can give them various tax deals on their property taxes, we can off-set income tax liability depending if they have one, we can try and give them subsidized space for some period of time. If they have infrastructure needs, we can do investments and some kind of retrofitting of an existing space. Or, if they are going to build, we can give them money towards building. (Government interviewee, March 2013)

The Office is relatively flexible in the way it offers tax cuts and cus-tom tailors financial incentives for firms. However, Illinois needs more venture capital investments and therefore more aggressive tax breaks for angel investors. Looking at the distribution of venture capital in the United States, it becomes clear that most of the money goes to the East and West coasts. According to the Martin Prosperity Institute, the top five spots in 2016 for investments were San Francisco, New York, San Jose, Boston-Cambridge, and Los Angeles. San Francisco made up more than a third of the national total, with US$23 billion. Compared to Silicon Valley's dominance, Chicago ranked ninth, with US$1.2 billion in investments and accounting for just around 2 per cent of venture capital investments (Florida 2017). A similar picture emerges when it comes to human capital resources in the area. As one interviewee put it, "it is not so much that you need to get the capital, you need to get the people that the capital is willing to invest in. So we either need to attract people from the outside, or we need to better prepare people here" (Technology park interviewee, March 2013).

There are, moreover, general hurdles to overcome in the Chicago region. For one, graduates and entrepreneurs still tend to want to relocate to the life sciences clusters in Massachusetts and California. The regional network is losing more members than it is attracting – according to census data, the state of Illinois had an estimated net migration loss of 6.5 people for every 1,000 residents and considerably lags in attracting new residents. Chicago mirrors this trend, and the data show out-migration largely affects younger residents (Reyes and O'Connell 2019). As well, US immigration laws hinder Chicago's abil-ity to retain highly skilled human capital. As one industry interviewee pointed out, even with the support of companies and universities, it is sometimes difficult to get visa extensions and green cards approved, which means that entrepreneurs take their ideas back to their home country and essentially start creating jobs somewhere else. Although 40 per cent of students graduating with a master's or doctorate degree in science, technology, engineering, and mathematics are temporary immigrant residents, many specialists in areas such as engineering and biomedicine (2,700 in 2011 alone) were unable to obtain longer-term work visas after graduating from Illinois institutions (Illinois Innovation Network 2013).

*Absorptive Capacity*

Opportunities for knowledge spillovers, as part of the cluster's absorptive capacity, exist in hubs around town. These include the shared lab spaces on campus at the different universities, in the Illinois Medical District, and as part of the 1871 project. There are also plans for a tech incubator similar to 1871 for life sciences. External sources also shape the cluster's absorptive capacity. Elements of Chicago's entrepreneurial support structure mimic longer-established clusters. The mentoring service, for example, is modelled after that at the Massachusetts Institute of Technology, while the iBIO PROPEL approach is based on activities in San Diego. Table 4.2 summarizes collaborative and absorptive capacity building in Chicago.

*Standing Out in the Crowd*

Chicago is one of the emerging life sciences clusters in the United States trying to overcome latecomer disadvantages. The Chicago area is home to several top research universities and institutes, and has had success attracting some of the big names in Pharma, but the region still struggles against competition from the coasts. There is concern that Chicago's educational institutions train scholars who then relocate to more prestigious clusters in Massachusetts or California, although interviewees indicated their hope that entrepreneurs drawn to the coasts would come back eventually or at least uphold ties to stakeholders in the Illinois area.

Among Chicago's advantages, network members cited the area's lower cost of living, resulting in affordable lab space and flexibility in offering these spaces. Geographically, Chicago is well connected to North American markets, and awareness of Chicago as a hub is growing, especially as the annual BIO convention is held there. In strategic terms, Illinois makes use of the bigger biotech community in the Midwest to compensate for the greater knowledge accumulation in leading clusters; this includes a holistic regional approach, rather than state by state, with respect to, say, tax breaks. Government is further targeting the start-up community with federal funds and attracting bigger companies to the area with "soft landing" packages. All plans target job creation and learning, as foreign firms create spillovers for local stakeholders, and hubs encourage collaboration (Feldman and Florida 1994; Kuemmerle 1996; Serapio and Dalton 1999).

Table 4.2. Collaborative and absorptive capacity of the Chicago cluster

| Framework | Basic elements | |
|---|---|---|
| *Collaborative capacity* | | |
| Purpose | Leadership? | Yes |
| | Shared vision? | Yes |
| | Network membership? | Yes |
| Structure | Formal and informal procedures? | No |
| | Clear roles? | Yes |
| Communications | Information links? | No |
| | Active communications? | Yes |
| Resources | Knowledge and skills? | Yes |
| | Financing powers? | No |
| *Absorptive capacity* | | |
| Intra-cluster knowledge system | Knowledge spillovers? | Yes |
| | Social relations? | Yes |
| Extra-cluster knowledge system | Extra-cluster knowledge sources? | Yes |
| | Interface between the external linkages and the intra-cluster knowledge system? | Yes |

These efforts have born fruit: by 2012, Illinois had "a large, diverse and well-concentrated industry base in the biosciences with nearly 80,000 jobs that span 3,424 individual business establishments" (BIO 2012, 72). Furthermore, employment in the state increasingly is concentrated in drugs and pharmaceuticals, agriculture feedstock, and bioscience-related distribution. Illinois ranks fifth among US states in drugs and pharmaceutical manufacturing, behind California, New Jersey, Pennsylvania, and North Carolina. Retaining start-ups and smaller companies will continue to be a major challenge for the region, however, as other clusters, particularly on the East and West coasts, rethink their own competitiveness.

*Chicago's Cluster Organization*

The Chicago case represents a facilitator model that is independent. It is heavily funded by industry, and officials have no regulatory power over the organization. As informal as they might be, however, ties with government are strong. iBIO, the organization interviewees identified as the facilitator, is a life sciences industry association composed of international and small- and medium-sized companies in the agricultural and human health sectors, entrepreneurial leaders of start-ups and spin-offs, scientists and technology transfer specialists, venture capitalists, seasoned government people, service providers from major law, accounting, financial, and research firms, as well as a variety of business professionals. This mix of people helps to accommodate the various needs of stakeholders. Former entrepreneurs and life sciences experts also bring experience from more-established clusters, leading to the adoption of current mentoring and funding services. Another feature of this model is that iBIO is part of an umbrella organization, BIO, which offers access to additional services, funds, and networking with other parts of the country.

iBIO has a government counterpart in Illinois' Office of Entrepreneurship, Innovation & Technology, which makes government accessible for cluster needs and helps maintain a strong link between cluster and government officials. iBIO has also been able to establish smaller subdivisions for more specialized services, such as PROPEL. In this way, concerns of network members are addressed by experts and subsequently answered with potential funding programs and government support. Overall, iBIO has gained trust by being part of a bigger, already established organization and having people involved who are well known in the industry. Links to government are pursued through personal relationships in the rather small life sciences community, and strengthened by the government's having something to offer through such a specialized office. This accessibility might be harder in states where governments do not have such offices and where trust might be harder to establish if the facilitator is not part of a larger organization or lacks experienced personnel for support.

### Singapore: The Government-Driven Cluster

*Genesis of the Cluster*

The Singaporean life sciences industry started in 2000, when the government announced that the sector would become the main driver of the city-state's twenty-first-century economy (Wong 2006a). With this move, Singapore began to build on the rapidly expanding pharmaceutical manufacturing output that started in the 1990s, and seized on what some call the "second-mover advantage," where uncertainties of first-order technological innovation have been managed elsewhere and late-entry countries such as South Korea, Taiwan, and Singapore upgrade to already "mature technologies" (Wong 2011). The timing also had to do with declining numbers in manufacturing and to compensate for the lack of natural resources. Glaxo, a large pharmaceutical company, had already relocated to Singapore in 1982 following efforts by government to get biotechnology off the ground (Arnold 2003). "The plan was to turn Singapore into Asia's premier hub for biomedical sciences, with world-class capabilities across the entire value chain, from scientific discovery to technology commercialization and production" (Wong 2006b, 232). This makes Singapore a young cluster, far behind established clusters in the coastal areas of the United States, because drug development usually takes around ten years before commercialization. However, the financial power behind its establishment, in combination with foreign investment and the attraction of international talent, gave Singaporean life sciences a boost and the opportunity to leapfrog in the field. Already in 2004, the pharmaceutical sector contributed 19 per cent of total manufacturing output, a steep increase from 5 per cent in 1990 (Wong 2006a).

The financial incentives were mirrored in both organizational and physical structure. For the latter, the Singaporean government built two state-of-the-art biomedical research parks in 2003 and 2008. "Biopolis," an SGD$300 million (1 Singapore dollar equals around C$0.98 or US $0.73) project with 190 hectares of buildings, is home to public as well as corporate research laboratories. The technology centre brings together over two thousand scientists, researchers, technicians, and administrators (A*STAR 2009; Finegold, Wong, and Cheah 2004). Among its anchor tenants are GlaxoSmithKline and Proctor & Gamble. The second complex built to house research institutes is called "Fusionopolis." Together, Biopolis and Fusionopolis are strategically co-located at "one-north" – an area of Singapore where many research institutes and universities agglomerate. Beyond these two government-created hubs, many firms have also settled into a separate Science Park located along Singapore's Technology corridor and in close proximity to research and tertiary institutions such as the National University of Singapore, the National University Hospital, and one-north. The organizational change to fuel life sciences developments was the creation in 1991 of the Agency for Science, Technology and Research (A*STAR), the goal of which is to foster innovation by bridging the gap between research and industry and act as a focal point for government entities and stakeholders involved in innovation.

Parallel to these government efforts, in the late 1990s, the National University of Singapore moved towards emphasizing technological commercialization beyond its educational mission. According to Wong (2006b), this was further facilitated by the appointment of a university president in 2000 who had trained in the United States and had both industrial and university research administration experience.

*Singapore Biotech Today*

The Economic Development Board of Singapore (EDB) has separated biotech development in the city-state into four phases. The current phase, phase four, focuses on five therapeutic areas: diabetes, infectious diseases, cancer, sensory and neurological disorders, and cardiovascular diseases (EDB 2016). Previous phases encompassed setting up the core scientific capabilities (phase 1), moving towards translational and clinical research (phase 2), and integrating those capabilities and establishing industry partnerships (phase 3). The pharmaceutical sector contributes around 3 per cent of the country's GDP and generated SGD$16 billion worth of products in 2017 (EDB 2019). As of 2018, there were more than three hundred biotechnology and medical technology companies in Singapore, employing around 18,000 people in the sector (EDB 2016, 2019). Overall, in 2017, although biomedical manufacturing cluster output decreased by 8.3 per cent from the previous year, subsectors such as medical technologies grew by 17.7 per cent due to the export of medical devices (EDB 2017b). R&D expenditures (including capital expenditures) in the sector in 2015 was roughly equally distributed among higher education (SGD$482.4 million) and public research institutes (SGD$471.8 million). The private sector saw expenditures of SGD$606.7, while SGD$262.9 million went to the government sector (Statistics Singapore 2017).

Highly ranked research universities and hospitals further support biomedical sciences in Singapore. According to the National Research Foundation: "Singapore's universities have steadily risen up in global rankings and improved their research influence internationally. In 2015, the annual World University Rankings placed the National University of Singapore ... and the Nanyang Technological University ... in the 12th and 13th positions respectively, up from 22nd and 39th the previous year" (Singapore 2017, 3). Hospitals and other health care providers further deliver translational clinical research. Through a government-established joint program office, the Health and Wellness Program Office, health care stakeholders work with industry partners from various industries, such as medical equipment and pharmaceuticals (EDB 2017a).

Another development is the tightening of work visa approvals in Singapore. Under the Fair Consideration Framework, the government increased the minimum salary for eligibility to apply for a work visa, and there have been reports of withholding decisions on work permit applications for Indian companies (Alawadhi 2017). In addition, jobs have to be advertised locally before work permit applications for an opening can be submitted. Companies must also show that they are contributing to the Singaporean economy and society. The Ministry of Manpower has noted that the goal is to regain a Singaporean core in the overall workforce (Chuan 2016). These changes have resulted in the rejection of hundreds of applications from employers and the creation of a watchlist of companies for failure to possess and build a Singaporean core in their workforce (Chia 2017). These changes have affected the biomedical sector, which, as an emerging market, relies heavily on foreign skilled workers and on international companies moving their workforce to the city-state (Deloitte 2016).

*Public Initiatives Supporting the Cluster*

Government is the main driver of the Singaporean cluster, and both financial and structural support mechanisms have boosted the biomedical sector. Starting around the Asian economic crisis (1997–98), the Singaporean government shifted towards market liberalization, policy deregulation, and the privatization of government-linked companies (Yeung 2010). Officials established a Life-Science Ministerial Committee to oversee long-term strategy formulation, followed by instituting a highly coordinated implementation approach involving the EDB, A*STAR, and the ministries of Education, Manpower, and Health (Finegold, Wong, and Cheah 2004). To boost the sector further, the government capitalized on the ban on new stem cell lines in the United States, and allowed the establishment of such research in Singapore (Chang 2001; Wong 2006a). This was coupled with efforts to attract high-profile scientists to Singapore, which, in turn, would serve as a magnet to attract other young researchers (Wong 2006a; Zucker and Darby 1996).

As government worked out a growth strategy for the country, it turned towards a tripartite arrangement with trade unions, the business community, and the public sector. "Co-option of the parties was seen as the pragmatic way of addressing the challenging problem facing the new city-state" (Kumar and Siddique 2010, 7). This laid the groundwork for a still-present mantra of an investment-led and export-driven ethos in Singapore.

Fuelling this approach is the strength of the Economic Development Board, which has the goal of attracting foreign investments, and has become an integral actor in the science and technology development strategy. The EDB's functions include formulating and implementing economic and industrial development strategies to transform Singapore into a global hub. Its board members are a mix of private and public sector leaders. The latter, however, largely come from the EDB, the Ministry of Trade and Industry, and the National Trade Union

Congress, which leads to a "bias towards a larger private sector component" (Kumar and Siddique 2010, 18). Hence, the board structure resembles the tripartite approach to planning.

In tandem with the EDB, A*STAR – the former National Science & Technology Board and a statuary board under the Ministry of Trade and Industry – focuses on the support of biomedical sciences. It is both an R&D funding body and crucial R&D performer because of the many research institutes under its lead, and A*STAR guides the cluster and structures relationships among stakeholders. After the launch of the Biomedical Science (BMS) initiative in 2000, A*STAR further developed key capabilities to develop this sector as the fourth pillar of Singapore's economy, alongside electronics, engineering, and chemicals (A*STAR 2011).

Financial support for the biomedical sector in Singapore is high compared to that in other countries, and government support is growing. The Research Innovation Enterprise 2020 Plan (RIE 2020) committed SDG$19 billion to support R&D over the 2016–20 period, compared with SDG$16 billion in the RIE 2015 scheme (Fai and Kek 2016), with spending emphasis on advanced manufacturing and engineering, health and biomedical sciences, services and the digital economy, and urban solutions and sustainability (Singapore 2017). Of the total amount in the RIE 2020 plan, SDG$4 billion (21 per cent) was earmarked for health and biomedical sciences. These investments translated into about 1 per cent of Singapore's GDP (Fai and Kek 2016).

*Cluster Management*

Several entities, largely government led, focus on bringing stakeholders in the Singapore cluster together and facilitating biomedical developments. Interviewees highlighted several connected to their specific perspectives from government, research, or industry domains.

A*STAR, the EDB, and the National Medical Research Council together formed the Singapore Biomedical Sciences Industry Partnership Office (BMS IPO) in order to provide a one-stop coordinating office for the various research agencies and performers in Singapore (A*STAR 2012). The Standards, Productivity and Innovation Board (SPRING) was set up by the Ministry of Trade and Industry to help small- and medium-sized enterprises to grow in terms of productivity and innovation, standards and quality (Wee 2017). This encompasses businesses beyond the biomedical sector, however, due to the national focus on this particular field through the Biomedical initiative, and financial and other efforts that have been channelled towards this field. In addition, the Research, Innovation and Enterprise Council and the National Research Foundation were created in 2006 under the Prime Minister's Office to coordinate various agencies linked to the national R&D agenda (A*STAR 2011).

All interviewees mentioned not just A*STAR itself but also its subdivisions as playing a pivotal role in fostering scientific research and talent. A*STAR's management structure consists of an operational group and a corporate group (A*STAR 2017). The operations group consists of:

- the Biomedical Research Council, which oversees and coordinates public sector biomedical research and development activities;
- the Science and Engineering Research Council, which supports and oversees public sector research and development in physical sciences and engineering;
- the A*STAR Graduate Academy, which develops human capital through scholarships, fellowships, and collaborative programs with universities and other partners; and
- Exploit Technologies Pte Ltd, the commercialization arm of A*STAR, which is geared towards new companies, and services the industry-research interface where teams of technology transfer professionals harness new technologies, increase the value of intellectual property, and incubate business ventures to create commercial impact.

The A*STAR corporate group is largely responsible for communications, administration, and human-resource-related tasks. According to government interviewees, A*STAR's goal is to engage proactively with industry at various stages of the research and commercialization phase and facilitate technology transfer. A*STAR further provides more specialized programs that focus on particular issues linked to the commercialization chain, such as scholarships for Singaporean students and that were successful in recruiting renowned scientists to lead research institutes in the past. Some of the famous names include Professor Sir David Lane (co-discoverer of the p53 gene and founder of Cyclacel), Professor Sir George Radda (pioneer of nuclear magnetic resonance imaging and former chief executive of the UK Medical Research Council), Professor Edison Lin (former director, Division of Clinical Sciences, National Cancer Institute, National Institutes of Health), and Professor Jackie Ying (former professor of chemical engineering, Massachusetts Institute of Technology) (A*STAR 2011, 24). A*STAR further supports entrepreneurial activities through gap and seed funding, technology incubators, and mentorship and role models – through the

A*STAR-MOE-SPRING-GET-up program. The Industry Development Group helps A*STAR researchers with moving early-stage discoveries towards commercial outcomes (BMS Institute 2010). To pursue these activities, A*STAR received SDG$6.39 billion through the 2011–15 funding cycle (A*STAR 2011). Overall, A*STAR describes itself as closely aligned with industry needs through five mechanisms: (1) engaging industry; (2) facilitating the use of intellectual property; (3) securing gap funding; (4) encouraging entrepreneurship and commercialization; and (5) spurring new growth through open innovation (A*STAR 2011).

Singapore's general vision focuses on industry inclusion and greater involvement of all stakeholders in the life sciences field. The government points out that the BMS initiative is working towards greater integration across various players of the BMS ecosystem to facilitate the translation of research into applications for better economic value, and across the entire value chain from basic, translational and clinical research, process R&D to manufacturing (A*STAR 2011). Thereby, according to interviewees, A*STAR is an integral part of managing and structuring that ecosystem, while being entrenched in research and commercialization activities itself through its numerous research institutes. In this, it differs from other cluster managers in the sense that the agency combines government and research while connecting other players in the network.

This complex structure of government departments and branches as well as programs and joint ventures is simplified by the management of one core group, made easier by the fact that Singapore has had just one dominant party in power from the day it separated from Malaysia. "A political party that has been in power for so long and which has integrated the public sector decision-making capabilities to its own enables public servants to also act in unison with decisions made by the political hierarchy" (Kumar and Siddique 2010, 13). Further, all agencies have allowed civil servants – individuals with already-established relationships to cabinet members – to take up government positions. Many civil servants go through the same scholarship program and form a bond before they enter office. In biomedical science, A*STAR was created under the guidance of the former head of the EDB, Philip Yeo, who had been instrumental in restructuring the manufacturing sector in earlier years. "The trust that ensues from such working environment then provides the glue with which critical agencies are managed from the center" (Kumar and Siddique 2010, 13). Thus, the Singapore network has a top-down model for cluster management, which is also very centralized and uniform. This, in turn, affects the cluster's collaborative and absorptive capacity-building activities.

*Collaborative Capacity*

In the process of creating a strategy for the cluster, the Singaporean government launched the Biomedical Science initiative in 2000 with the goal of making life sciences the fourth pillar of Singapore's economy. Officials also linked the establishment of A*STAR to this step by renaming the National Science and Technology Board in 2002 to "highlight Singapore's emphasis on the creation and exploitation of intellectual capital and the training of research manpower in its transition to a knowledge-based economy" (A*STAR 2011, 13). This makes A*STAR the lead agency for all things connected to biomedical science. A*STAR's leadership position is further fostered by continuity in personnel, which creates trust among stakeholders.

A*STAR is also part of all the processes ongoing in the cluster. The agency identifies and develops R&D agendas and strategies for the biomedical field. It engages industry at various stages of research and commercialization and carries out government plans. It manages the overall development budget for research and administration, and it monitors the programs being pursued by the institutes. As part of the current strategy (RIE2020, 20160–2020), the government committed to invest SGD$19 billion in research, innovation, and enterprise. This is an increase from SGD$16 billion in the 2015 plan and SGD$13.5 billion in the 2010 plan. Health and Biomedical Sciences specifically received SGD$4 billion (21 per cent) of the overall budget (NRF 2019).

The biotech portfolio has progressed from the general target area of biomedical into five key areas in which Singapore is expected to thrive: (1) drug discovery; (2) bio-imaging; (3) stem cells; (4) cohort studies; and (5) biomarkers. These rather translational programs then interface with basic biomedical core capabilities (Singapore 2012). The presence of leading pharmaceutical companies such as GlaxoSmithKline, Genentech, Roche, Lonza, Baxter, and Novartis has also fuelled the program, which has trickled down to researchers working in the labs: "In the past it was quite broad, in the past we did agriculture in Singapore, there are still institutes that focus more on the clinical side, more on health care. So the trend is more going towards translational medicine, where your research is really put into use for patients with needs" (Research institute interviewee, February 2013).

As a visible commitment to the life sciences industry, the Singaporean government's two biomedical research parks, Biopolis and Fusionopolis, tie in with structural aspects that characterize the cluster, including formal and informal procedures as well as the roles ascribed to players in the network. The short distances in the city-state are an advantage for meeting collaborators in a more informal manner. The set-up of Biopolis also enhances informal communications, although critics point out that the costs of renting space in these buildings and long-term contracts with landlords prevent others from moving in.

Another structural element is changes in funding, which have led to higher levels of collaboration among stakeholders, in line with A*STAR's mission to enhance the ecosystem in BMS. Funding for some research institutes used to come directly from A*STAR in five-year chunks. Thus, when meeting performance targets, new and often more funding would be provided. Today, for institutes such as the Singapore Immunology Network (SIgN), 75 per cent of the funding is provided by A*STAR, while 25 per cent has to be attracted through collaborative projects with other institutes or, preferably, with industry. According to interviewees, this encouraged some institutes to sell equipment that existed in duplicate during the time when more funding was available. By sharing lab equipment, more people came into contact with one another and found common ground to collaborate or exchange knowledge and, ultimately, to prepare researchers to compete for grants inside and outside the country. This aggressive shift in funding has been a challenge for some, as Singapore is still a growing cluster compared to other life sciences hubs and "heavily driven by risk-averse academics and government-funded scientists" (Lee 2012). Here, researchers and government are at odds over the speed of commercialization and academic output. The new funding structure reflects the general attitude of not doing R&D for R&D's sake, but having a clear plan about outcomes, as this statement from one official shows: "It is one thing if you get good journal articles and peer review, but we really get excited if the industry is interested in what you are doing. Until that happens, it is just having fun on our account" (Government interviewee, February 2012). At the same time, however, Singapore is able – through a wealth of funding – to offer long-term grants that make it easier to attract researchers, as they do not have to live on a project-to-project basis. Also, as the grants run longer, researchers work together over longer periods of time, and are able to build relationships and trust.

Favourable networking conditions are also linked to the government set-up. A*STAR can tap into a wide network of well-known CEOs and scientists. Also, since A*STAR monitors the whole commercialization process, funding gaps can be identified more quickly and filled through department branches such as Exploit Technologies. In fact, the Singaporean government in general, and A*STAR in particular, has a business-like structure: "The unique difference between this environment and other countries is the government basically operates like a business – they are very strategic and very smart about it. Other governments work more towards a constituency base and are more preoccupied by politics and less about where the country is going" (Biotechnology company interviewee, February 2013).

Other Singapore industry stakeholders, however, paint a more cautious picture. Because A*STAR acts as a business partner to companies, interviewees said that funding cuts send a signal that might scare off investors and endanger links to industry. Overall, Singapore has profited from the government-driven structure of the BMS initiative, while the relationship between the EDB and A*STAR has been changing, and is less structured. After working in tandem with the EDB, A*STAR has been taking a more obvious lead in the sector's development through the establishment of its own Biomedical Research Council and partnerships with public and private stakeholders (Kumar and Siddique 2010; A*STAR 2020).

The Singaporean cluster shows limited signs of communications among network members. There are formal communications, such as board meetings, but rarely any informal networking events such as those in Medicon Valley or Chicago. A*STAR made an attempt to increase informal collaboration through funding cuts, which, as noted, led some institutes to share equipment, but although stakeholders are better informed about ongoing research in other labs, there is little evidence that information is being translated into regular communications or joint projects. Regular communications further seem to be limited to government circles and the technology-push side of the cluster. For the latter, this means that most communications are concerned with translating research into products, with research institutes talking to officials and subdivisions about transforming their findings into products. This usually includes A*STAR, Exploit Technologies, and a small group of researchers involved in the project. After that, communications with possible angel investors or companies begin. This suggests there is a lot of vertical communication within the network, but limited horizontal relationships among scientists.

In government circles, many officials are part of the same recruitment pool or know one another from earlier cooperation in other departments, which creates a culture of bonding and networking among government employees (Kumar and Siddique 2010). To carry this culture forward and enhance stakeholder connections, especially across disciplines, A*STAR announced plans to implement virtual joint councils: "The virtual network will make use of a hub-and-spoke model of resource allocation, compromising a hub of a core group of researchers working in a centralized location in the host [research institute], supported by distributed sub-groups located in each collaborating [research institute]" (A*STAR 2011, 80). Virtual joint councils, however, have yet to take on a prominent role in the cluster.

In various aspects, resources are a hot topic in Singapore, having to do not only with funding changes, but also with an ongoing discussion around immigration. In a nutshell, as one interviewee pointed out, "Singapore researchers have the money to buy expensive equipment and open programs, however, they still need the people to operate the equipment and that supply is limited." This means that, although the long-term funding structure might work in the city-state's favour, Singapore lacks skilled people to fill positions, and ultimately needs to "import" human capital. In other words, one major challenge for the life sciences sector is the lack of qualified personnel. In order to be attractive globally, Singapore offers tax reductions to researchers, for whom rising costs of living are a disincentive to relocate. For company employees, many bigger firms in Singapore pay rental fees and moving costs. Further, Singapore offers a secure, English-speaking environment with many highly ranked international schools and a good infrastructure.

Many describe the human capital issue as still in "catch-up" mode, with programs such as the scholarships A*STAR offers to prepare students for careers in science and to prevent brain drain. Under this program, the government covers tuition fees and living expenses at universities in North America and Europe upon the condition that candidates return to Singapore and contribute to local research institutions for three to six years. Education programs also happen in collaboration with pharmaceutical companies such as Merck Millipore. As one consultant connected to the training program explained:

> There are different programs, there is one program where some students can join a company and then go out of Singapore to the parent company – this could be in the US or Europe – work there for a certain period and come back. The other approach is where they certify certain training organizations in Singapore who can provide quick trainings in diverse areas that cater towards biopharmaceuticals. (Biotechnology company interviewee, February 2013)

With respect to building a life sciences workforce, local company leaders voiced concern that many Singaporeans do not stay with one company over a longer period, which means they are trained by their employer and then leave. Also, many high-ranking positions within international companies in Singapore are occupied by foreigners, who build up the branch over time by attracting human capital from other parts of the world, rather than training local people to fill these positions. Changing attitudes and a changing political climate towards the influx of foreigners led in 2013 to the release of a "population white paper" that claimed Singapore could not allow an unlimited number of foreign workers into the country: "We do not want to be overwhelmed by more foreign workers than we can absorb, or to expand our total population beyond what our island is able to accommodate" (Singapore 2013, 5). In controlling its immigration rate and making eligibility changes for work visas, Singapore hopes to have a steady permanent resident population of between 500,000 and 600,000 and a citizen population of between 3.6 and 3.8 million by 2030. The National Population and Talent Division has also pushed for a shift in the division of work whereby Singaporeans upgrade themselves into higher-paid, more highly skilled professional, managerial, executive, and technical jobs, while more of the lower-skilled jobs are done by foreigners. Singapore, however, still needs a flow of highly qualified people from elsewhere, as star scientists – researchers known in their field and able to mentor and guide Singaporean talent and attract foreign researchers and investors into the country – tend not to stay. As one interviewee noted:

> Big names really drive research and innovation, but because of this funding change those people are leaving now, and I think the risk they face is going to be the same risk that they are going to face on the commercial side – the for-profit organizations, where the people driving the people having the vision aren't the Singaporeans. Unless they get the Singaporeans up to speed quickly on thinking that way, there is not going to be the talent here to drive it for them. (Research institute interviewee, February 2013)

The Singaporean government is committed to training Singaporeans to fill high-ranking positions as well as to staying attractive for big names. There is, however, underlying doubt in many research institutes about Singapore's entrepreneurial culture. They point out that hierarchical thinking and the notion of job security, rather than uncertainties connected to spin-offs and start-ups, might prevent at least the current generation of researchers to thrive in the life sciences. The government hopes to change this by training students outside the country and portraying entrepreneurs and investment risk takers as role models.

*Absorptive Capacity*

Another capacity crucial for the development of the cluster, facilitated by A*STAR, is the ability to absorb knowledge from other networks, identify knowledge gaps within the cluster, and react to change (Giuliani 2005; Narula 2004). Generally speaking, the Singapore model is a combination of best practices from around the world, and the city-state tries to connect with successful networks elsewhere at either the research or the political level. Singapore's openness to foreign workers and investment early on led to a "tacit acceptance that there are lessons from elsewhere that can be adapted for Singapore" (Kumar and Siddique 2010, 4). The learning process is ongoing, as multinational corporations complement local knowledge and create knowledge spillovers, including managerial and technical competencies and information on international markets (Belussi and Sammarra 2010).

Inspired by Porter's cluster theories, different agencies have borrowed ideas for the Science Park and Biopolis from the North Carolina Research Triangle, the Boston Science Belt, and Silicon Valley (Kumar and Siddique 2010). A*STAR also operates research platforms where Singaporean scientists collaborate with foreign researchers to exchange knowledge. For example, in 2009, A*STAR announced a collaboration with the Center for Integration of Medicine and Innovation Technology, a consortium of Boston-based hospitals and engineering schools. The goal was to create "greater opportunities for impactful innovations in the areas of medical technology", and, more importantly, provide "an environment conducive to training innovators for the growing medtech industry in Singapore" (A*STAR 2011, 58). Early on, Singapore profited from researchers who were part of the Silicon Valley wave and then moved back to Singapore, bringing tacit knowledge of cluster evolution and networking with them. The process continues, as stakeholders go to successful US clusters and then return to Singapore, all the while keeping in touch with the network (Yeung 2010).

Complementing A*STAR's work, the EDB's goal is to develop Singapore "into a global city with total business capabilities by attracting foreign investments, developing local enterprises as well as implementing, strategic overseas projects with significant linkages to Singapore" (Kumar and Siddique 2010, 17). This is done through offices in key locations around the world, including in China, France, Germany, Sweden, the United Kingdom, and the United States. This forms a communications and knowledge channel to other clusters, and enhances Singapore's absorptive capacity in terms of knowledge inflow. As early as the 1980s, the EDB established a venture capital office in the United

Table 4.3. Collaborative and absorptive capacity of the Singapore cluster

| Framework | Basic elements | |
|---|---|---|
| *Collaborative capacity* | | |
| Purpose | Leadership? | Yes |
| | Shared vision? | Yes |
| | Network membership? | Yes |
| Structure | Formal and informal procedures? | Yes |
| | Clear roles? | Yes |
| Communications | Information links? | In progress |
| | Active communications? | In progress |
| Resources | Knowledge and skills? | In progress |
| | Financing powers? | No |
| *Absorptive capacity* | | |
| Intra-cluster knowledge system | Knowledge spillovers? | No |
| | Social relations? | No |
| Extra-cluster knowledge system | Extra-cluster knowledge sources? | Yes |
| | Interface between the external linkages and the intra-cluster knowledge system? | In progress |

States to invest in dedicated biotech firms, establish networks, and create global visibility for Singapore among US venture capitalists. As Finegold, Wong, and Cheah (2004, 923) note: "The primary objective at that stage was to use venture funding, and the access it provided, to some of the leading first-generation DBFs so as to learn about the bio-medical science industry, rather than to attract companies to Singapore. It was only from the late-1990s that EDB began selectively to invest in DBFs that were willing to bring key new technologies and generate higher value-added research jobs in Singapore."

Table 4.3 summarizes the collaborative and absorptive capacity features of the Singapore cluster.

*The Human Capital Challenge*

Singapore is in the process of identifying and facilitating its competitive advantage – especially in light of evolving regions in China and India. Singapore is competitive because it is well placed, well connected, and language is not a barrier. It has qualified people and a strong academic and industrial base. This locational benefit is paired with a second-mover advantage and strong commitment by the government (Wong 2011). Another competitive feature, according to interviewees working in Singapore, is that the government "works like a business," "gets things done," and "does what it promises." In fact, some government agencies mirror company organization, and civil servants have the same professional background as decision makers in firms. Singapore offers a secure, English-speaking environment, and research facilities carry all the Asian phenotypes that companies need to test their drugs while offering a Western-style working environment.

As A*STAR itself has noted, however, Singapore is still in the early stages of commercializing, and has yet to develop a breakthrough drug. Also, "the current technology-push approach is not sufficient to attract increased adoption rates from small and medium enterprises" (A*STAR 2011, 62). This has been reflected in innovation rankings: in 2012, for example, Singapore was ranked the most innovative country in Asia, and also placed first for its innovation capabilities, based on a well-trained workforce, a robust research community and sophisticated financial markets. Globally, Singapore ranked just below Switzerland and Sweden in the 2012 Global Innovation Index, and seventh in the 2017 rankings. Singapore has done well in terms of innovation inputs, which include institutions, human capital, and research, infrastructure, market and business sophistication. In terms of output measures – knowledge and technology and creative outputs such as intangible assets and knowledge diffusion – Singapore's rankings have also improved considerably in recent years. Interviewees noted, however, that firms had not relocated their R&D operations to Singapore at a pace or in scope that the government originally had envisioned. Another issue was temporal uncertainty connected to the life sciences field as people were becoming increasingly frustrated with the slow pace of commercial growth, and some were beginning to question the extensive investments in biotechnology (Wong 2011). To compensate, the government has manufactured "successes" by overinvesting in certain endeavours – some would classify Biopolis as such an overinvestment, as local firms were reluctant to move in and networking among tenants was rather limited.

*Singapore's Cluster Management Model*

As a cluster manager, A*STAR differs from those in North America and Europe. As in many Asian regions, Singapore has not developed the kind of institutional thickness enjoyed by clusters elsewhere (Amin and Thrift 1995; Yeung 2010). To change this, Singapore built a mix of institutions and programs that make navigating the life sciences field rather complex, although efforts have been made to simplify the system, at least for incoming investors and firms. A*STAR, the EDB, and the Ministry of Health have set up the Singapore Biomedical Sciences Industry Partnership Office to serve as a "one-stop" coordination office for multinational corporations seeking collaborations and investment opportunities (RIE Secretariat 2011). In this, A*STAR has combined several functions under one roof by being a government branch, host to key research institutes, and facilitator to the overall cluster in terms of managerial guidance and funding.

The core group of the cluster is thus well connected due to established relationships and trust among stakeholders. However, this tightly knit community includes only a few individuals, which could hamper the ability of outside companies to secure government funding or connect with other stakeholders (Finegold, Wong, and Cheah 2004). This means that, if A*STAR struggles in one or more of its roles as government agency, research coordinator, or facilitator, there is the danger of disconnecting from a wider group of network members. The challenge for A*STAR is thus to remain true to its role as an advocate for the whole network, although some stakeholders closer to the basic research side of the biomedical field already see A*STAR as being too applied and as pushing too hard the commercial side of research.

Heavy public investment in biotechnology has increased political pressure on the Singaporean government. The ruling government's legitimacy is linked to economic performance, and with uncertain success a retreat of the state might be in Singapore's future. The weaknesses of the current model further extend to the lack of informal communications and networking on the ground, as most links are generated or facilitated from the government-side. And finally, far-sighted public policy plans only work with the according scientific manpower base and business capabilities (Finegold, Wong, and Cheah 2004). There is a lack of attention to fostering the development of local biotechnology start-ups and, more generally, the generation of informal ties among stakeholders.

Singapore's facilitator model differs from that of Medicon Valley or Chicago in that the responsibility for network management lies with government – A*STAR is a government department and reports to the Ministry of Trade and Industry. Because the facilitator is part of government, Singapore took a very proactive approach towards engaging industry and establishing itself as the channel through which to gain access to government funding and larger developments in the life sciences sector. The advantages of this approach are obvious: as part of government, the facilitator can develop coherent funding programs, and gaps in the cluster can be met with policy initiatives more quickly. The facilitator is able to coordinate physical space with cluster needs, such as creating a science park close to a university, as Singapore did with Biopolis. A*STAR has also created trusting relationships among stakeholders by building personal links over many years with the department, and taps into a wide network of well-known CEOs and scientists through its own or other government employees. This makes A*STAR credible when talking to stakeholders.

Some of the models' disadvantages include closeness to government, with the risk that A*STAR might be seen not as independent, but as acting in favour of government plans, thus possibly limiting the facilitator's reach in terms of industry connections. The Singaporean model has even been described as "overbearing" by stakeholders outside the immediate government network. This implies that entering the cluster and being able to establish informal relationships is more difficult.

## Vancouver: Finding the Competitive Edge

*Genesis of the Cluster*

The Vancouver biotech industry is built on a strong research tradition of life sciences research at several British Columbia institutes, such as the University of British Columbia (UBC), the BC Cancer Agency, and Vancouver General Hospital. Biotech activity began in 1982, and attracted human and financial capital to the province. A pioneer in these early years was QLT, spun out of a university lab; by 1999, shares of the company had already topped $127 (Hon 2008). Following this example, several other life sciences companies moved to Vancouver, including Amgen Inc. and Stemcell Technologies Inc. The development of the UBC-Broadway Corridor, running from the Downtown core to the UBC campus, spurred the location of research facilities and companies in one area. Another hub developed in the suburb of Burnaby, where the British Columbia Institute of Technology attracts technology professionals focusing on microbiology and immunology, and where pharmaceutical companies such as Amgen and Xenon Pharmaceuticals have located (Jones Lang LaSalle 2014).

Over the years, the Vancouver biotech network has been increasingly dominated by firms in the health care sector and closely watched by provincial and national governments (Bogomolny et al. 2004). In 2000, Genome BC, a non-profit research organization focusing on genomics innovation, was founded. Both the provincial government and the federal government invest in the company, which has a Canada-wide counterpart, Genome Canada. In 2007 the provincial government invested $200 million in Genome BC. In the same year, the government-financed BC Renaissance Capital Fund was established with $90 million to support biotech firms and other high-tech companies (Hun 2008). By then, however, Vancouver had become increasingly dependent on one company, QLT, which generated 87 per cent of the cluster's revenue (Gertler and Quach 2005). In 2008, the company lost significant revenue, laying off half its staff and selling its headquarters for additional cash flow (Hun 2008), and overall market activity slowed down in the sector, leaving buildings in the UBC-Broadway Corridor vacant that had once hosted life sciences companies (Jones Lang LaSalle 2014).

Among the reasons for the hub's difficulties at that time – as identified by Holbrook et al. (2003), Gertler and Quach (2005), and Casper (2007) – were:

- little horizontal or vertical integration of life sciences activities;
- challenges finding and retaining qualified employees due to substantial competition from the United States and eastern Canada, as well as high housing costs;
- lack of "robustness to failure" – the risk of joining a biotechnology firm that might eventually fail was not offset by other job opportunities in the region;
- Vancouver's becoming a hub for intellectual property "vendors" – firms that do not manufacture or market a product in the region, but sell intellectual property to larger multinational companies in the United States; and
- the attraction of the US market, with its greater specialization in high-tech, R&D-intensive industries, ability to profile itself more prominently for investors, and attract graduates with degrees in science and engineering.

*Vancouver Biotech Today*

Today, Vancouver has a large, young biotech community linked to the university focus on life sciences and research hospitals. Around 300 companies are established in the region, and about 50 research centres focus on biotech. Key areas include biotechnology and pharmaceutical, medical devices, and medical technology. In 2017, about 14,000 people were employed in the sector (British Columbia 2017b). Mid- to large-sized companies are present only in low numbers, however, as they often move to the US west coast or to eastern Canada due to the limited capital available locally to make the transition from a start-up to the next scale (Siren 2017). The availability of human capital is another issue: "The BC workforce will need to continue to develop its set of core competencies to maintain or increase the pace of innovation over the next few decades and beyond" (Jothen 2017, 15). The province trails the Canadian average in the number of degrees linked to disciplines such as engineering and life sciences, while the retention of qualified workers is linked to housing and accommodation costs in Metro Vancouver.

Quark Venture Inc., a Canadian-based venture capital company, and GF Securities Company Limited, a leading investment bank in China, have invested US$500 million in Vancouver-based biotech companies. These funds are seen as a potential catalyst for the expansion of mid- to large-sized companies in the region (Siren 2017). Venture capital investments in British Columbia's biotech industry are on the rise: "In 2019, British Columbia obtained the third largest share of total VC in Canada with $1.3 billion, closely behind Quebec ($1.6 billion)" (British Columbia 2020, 28). Provincial tax credits, a stable banking system, and a highly qualified workforce are among the factors that attract investment to the region. Life sciences remains relatively small in comparison to British Columbia's natural resources sector, and ranks third in size after Ontario and Quebec in terms of employment, wages, and GDP. The sector did, however, make $5.4 billion in revenue in 2018 and produced $1.6 billion in GDP (British Columbia 2020).

*Public Initiatives Supporting the Cluster*

The province of British Columbia has several incentivizing schemes to attract companies and capital to the region. They include (British Columbia 2017b):

- the Small Business Venture Capital Act, through which investors of venture capital funds receive a 30 per cent tax credit;
- International Business Activity, where executives recruited to work in the province and qualified life sciences companies receive a refund of provincial income tax and tax refunds on patent-related revenue, respectively;
- the Canadian Scientific Research and Experimental Development tax credit, whereby Canadian-controlled private corporations receive a tax credit of up to 35 per cent of qualified expenses for work carried out in Canada; other corporations receive up to 15 per cent;
- the British Columbia Scientific Research and Experimental Development tax credit, whereby corporations conducting scientific research and experimental development in the province receive a tax credit of up to 10 per cent for expenses related to these activities; and
- the National Research Council's Industrial Research Assistance Program (IRAP), under which small- and medium-sized companies

focused on the development and commercialization of innovative, technology-driven products, services, or processes in Canada receive financial assistance on a case-by-case basis.

In addition, the BC government has invested heavily in R&D in recent years (British Columbia 2020). The province and the federal government also committed to a Western Economic Partnership Agreement, towards which the two governments each contributed $25 million over the 2009–13 period to support long-term economic growth and competitiveness in British Columbia, including strengthening knowledge-based businesses and technological innovation. Specifically targeting emerging technology companies, a BC Tech Fund was also launched to invest around $100 million in venture capital. Other government resources include Technology Transfer Offices; the Institutional Programs Office; IRAP; the Centre for Drug Research and Development (CDRD); and the Natural Sciences and Engineering Research Council (NSERC).

Technology Transfer Offices are the primary point of contact for companies and other entities that wish to acquire technologies and make use of the resources of the government-led Communications Research Centre. They also represent an opportunity for small- and medium-sized enterprises to establish intellectual property rights through the Centre's laboratory infrastructure, and support successful cooperation between firms through intermediation (Brenner et al. 2011). Technology Transfer Offices are largely government financed: UBC's University-Industry Liaison Office, for example, is supported by the British Columbia Innovation Council, which is a provincial Crown agency. At Simon Fraser University, the Innovation Office receives ongoing support for its activities and programs from a program by the federal granting councils, Western Economic Diversification Canada, and IRAP. The BC Ministry of Advanced Education also offers operational support through the British Columbia Innovation Council.

The Institutional Programs Office provides administrative and strategic support for researchers pursuing major federal, provincial, and regional infrastructure awards. In British Columbia, these awards are offered by the British Columbia Knowledge Development Fund and by Western Economic Diversification Canada. The Office also offers services such as internal reviews of funding applications and post-award workshops. IRAP, in contrast, funds individual small- and medium-sized enterprises, and does not necessarily link up with universities, but rather focuses predominantly on the industry side of the biotechnology network.

The CDRD is a national, not-for-profit public-private organization headquartered in Vancouver that provides drug development expertise and infrastructure to enable researchers from leading academic and health research institutions to advance promising, early-stage drug candidates. Genome BC works closely with the CDRD because of its platform of drug discovery and antibody development for drugs.

Finally, the NSERC supports university students in their advanced studies, promotes and supports discovery research, and facilitates innovation by encouraging Canadian companies to participate and invest in post-secondary research projects. Thus, the NSERC uses federal funding to support collaboration between industry and academia. This funding is located at the national level, which means the amount allotted to British Columbia varies.

Core institutions through which the federal and BC governments support biotechnology are Genome Canada and Genome BC. Genome BC is a non-profit research organization that "leads genomics innovation on Canada's West Coast and facilitates the integration of genomics into society" (Genome British Columbia 2017b). The main investors are the province of British Columbia and the federal government through Genome Canada and Western Economic Diversification Canada. Genome Canada is funded by Industry Canada, and conducts large-scale projects and technology platform competitions in which Genome BC competes. Western Economic Diversification Canada is a department of the federal government with the goal of strengthening innovation, entrepreneurship, and community economic development in the Western provinces. Genome BC carries out initiatives on behalf of Western Economic Diversification Canada (Genome British Columbia 2015). Partnerships with funding organizations, both public and private, complement these funds. In its 2017 Technology Strategy, British Columbia committed $20 million to health projects conducted by Genome BC, this was on top of the $221.5 million that had flowed into Genome BC since 2001 (British Columbia 2017c).

*Cluster Management*

Genome BC also plays a crucial role in initiating and channelling biotechnology developments in Vancouver. It has a portfolio of activities it supports in the region and different programs catering to various stakeholders. It is said to have contributed $1.4 billion to British Columbia's GDP and 21,149 jobs between 2001 and 2014 (Genome British Columbia 2015). In its 2015–20 plan, Genome BC laid out the following cornerstones for supporting biotech developments in the region (Genome British Columbia 2015, 2):

- Enhance BC's recognition as a bio economy leader, attracting top talent and new investments;
- Support innovation and sustainability in BC's key socio-economic sectors through the translation of research;
- Promote and support world-class genomics research;
- Develop a vibrant life sciences cluster; and
- Enhance recognition of the value of genomics, while addressing societal concerns.

The portfolio of programs supporting these pillars includes, for example, the User Partnership Program, the Strategic Opportunities Fund for Industry, the Research Leadership Awards, and the Entrepreneurship Partnership Program. The Industry Innovation ($I^2$) Program provides commercialization support for companies that develop life science technologies with a focus on biological challenges in the agriculture, energy, mining, or environmental fields. The program also facilitates the development of digital health technologies for precision medicine. As Genome BC (2017a) notes: "Funding from the $I^2$ program is allocated to promising technologies (products, processes or services) at the early stages of commercial development. The program aims to provide risk capital that is concurrently matched by other public or private funding sources."

The amount of funding can vary between $100,000 and $1 million per company. According to a recipient of such an investment, Augurex Life Sciences Corp., Genome BC stepped in when other funding streams dried up. As CEO Norma K. Biln noted, "Often at this point, it is harder for companies to access government funding and that is why the Genome BC program comes at such a pivotal time for Augurex" (T-Net 2017). This applies to companies that are no longer considered start-ups because they have exceeded a certain size or profit margin but still require outside funding to push innovative technologies further.

Thereby, Genome BC sees itself in a position to "lead academia, government and industry in the growth of a world-class genomics R&D cluster" and to support "genomics discovery research; applications development; and translation" (Genome British Columbia 2015, 8). Its focus is on supporting entrepreneurial activities to increase the number of small and medium-sized enterprises – and, in turn, employment – in the sector. This translates into an emphasis on translation and commercialization activities. In addition, Genome BC wants to be an "honest broker" in providing input on government strategies linked to biotech and in branding the region as a "life sciences province" (Genome British Columbia 2015).

Interviewees also pointed to LifeSciences BC, a not-for-profit, non-government industry association that represents a diverse set of stakeholders from the region's human life sciences community. Among its activities to encourage collaboration among and beyond the membership organizations are: organizing events, programs, and projects in support of the sector; public policy initiatives in collaboration with the federal and BC governments; and formal discussion rounds between government and the LifeSciences BC constituency (LifeSciences BC 2017b). LifeSciences BC relies on sponsors: mainly big pharmaceutical companies such as GlaxoSmithKline and Pfizer, as well as Genome BC and the Simon Fraser University Sauder School of Business (LifeSciences BC 2017a). The members come from academia, research institutions (such as the BC Cancer Agency, UBC, and Genome BC), associations (for example, the Vancouver Board of Trade), as well as companies from subsectors such as bioinformatics, biopharmaceuticals, and medical technology. Public institutions such as the BC Ministry of International Trade and the National Research Council of Canada are also members (LifeSciences BC 2015, 2017a).

*Collaborative Capacity*

According to several interviewees, the Vancouver life sciences sector is split into smaller groups, none of which is big enough to pursue a common biotech agenda for industry and lobby public office holders. As one interviewee pointed out, "the sector is diversifying ... Of these industry associations, some are government-funded, some are government subsidized, some of them are industry dues" (Non-governmental organization [NGO] interviewee, March 2012). A life sciences industry organization interviewee added: "Life science is increasingly a broad spectrum ... one of the [key elements] should be to bring some consolidation. It's not about having ten different voices; it's about having one voice. For government, this raises the question where best to put your government money? What gives you the best banking back as a tax payer?" (NGO interviewee, March 2012). One research institute interviewee (A, March 2012) concluded that, "everyone needs to work together more, but when everyone is raising funds independently and everyone has ultimately different stakeholders, it doesn't mean that always everyone's programs are going to fit together."

In 1991, the establishment of the BC Biotech Alliance Society (now LifeSciences BC) was an attempt to unite industry players. LifeSciences BC is thus described as a steward of industry partnerships. By unifying some of the biotech stakeholders, LifeSciences BC facilitates collaboration among them and devotes resources to managing the image of the sector (Ansell and Gash 2012). The organization also lowers transaction costs for single firms and serves as an umbrella organization for smaller entities in the network. For researchers, the non-profit Genome BC is a uniting element in the network, connecting stakeholders of genomics projects. Neither organization, however, has been able to overcome sector fragmentation. Interviewees pointed to the fact that some stakeholders remained in the background because they were not connected to either one of the bigger organizations or they could not afford membership. This created a challenge for uniting forces to identify key players and encourage relationships among all network members. In response to this, some stakeholders saw the need for government to step in: "Government should not fund life sciences. Government should come up with – and I keep coming back to this – this idea of some sort of industrial strategy that they are going to focus on" (Life sciences industry organization interviewee, April 2012).

Currently, the sector is largely geared towards health-related products. Here, government and stakeholders face trade-offs in terms of cost control versus innovation, because R&D takes a long time and is heavily dependent on high levels of funding. According to industry representatives, a strategy to resolve this bottleneck could involve both sides agreeing on future goals and investments that follow along these lines.

These challenges spill over into the challenge of working with a social health care system. Interviewees pointed to two issues in particular: First, there was limited incentive to make changes to the current system because health care is a politically charged topic with patterns of costs and benefits for providers, consumers, and funders that are difficult to alter. Second, from an industry perspective, it is a mostly inaccessible system. British Columbia's provincial legislation reinforces the Canada Health Act, which forbids extra billing for facilities or materials and places a cap on what can be charged for services by doctors who opt out. Thus, the health care system is trapped in a series of segregated budget functions. LifeSciences BC sums up the problem from an industry perspective: "The development of British Columbia's biopharmaceutical, medical device industry and all related academic and industrial institutions who feed the life science industry, are directly and negatively impacted by our present healthcare system, and in particular, by BC's Pharmacare policies. We believe there is a better way forward – one that recognizes the interests and value of industry while advancing the public interest and delivering appropriate patient outcomes" (LifeSciences BC 2007, 4).

Looking at similar health care systems in France, Norway, and the United Kingdom, a report by LifeSciences BC (2015, 15), points to co-ordinated strategic plans that other countries are putting forward to manage health care in general, and that thereby have a positive effect on the life sciences industry: "many developed nations with socialized healthcare systems have announced or are delivering on significant coordinated strategic plans to prioritize, develop and grow their life science sectors." On the positive side, Canada's health care system of-fers an existing infrastructure and network based on the single-payer system. A database for providers and firms in the sector is in place, which could be extended based on genomics components and other innovative aspects. This, according to interviewees, could also facilitate post-marketing and surveillance studies.

To establish common ground on this issue, the life sciences network in British Columbia has some informal linkages and communications mechanisms, but no formal structure. Both LifeSciences BC and Ge-nome BC have procedures in place to communicate within their organ-izations and between each other. Within Genome BC, the cooperation mechanisms in place are sector consultations, taskforce networks, and connections developed by research project managers. Sector consulta-tions are industry-led task forces – including champions and decision makers, experts in the field, industry, government, and academia – that occasionally come together to identify research priorities and current challenges. They also emphasize possible areas where genomics can ad-dress such challenges and make the network competitive. This involves much dialogue and consultation to outline which activities might be useful in the future.

In British Columbia, the set-up of taskforces was a one-time initia-tive led by industry in 2006. The taskforces ran for about two years, and gave advice on how to design research programs and make smart investments. Although they have not been active formally since, many of the same people are now directly involved in Genome BC projects either as co-funders, advisors, or researchers. They provide materials or locations for research or are called when a new project is launched in order to get ideas on how to collaborate and which stakeholders to involve.

The third mechanism within Genome BC is the existence of a re-search project managers' (RPMs) network. Project managers are crucial to the development and realization of research projects because they get to know their six to twelve projects very well and are able to communicate with key stakeholders in the field. RPMs also draw together a specific group of researchers for each project, who are able to exchange knowledge from the science to the social science side and back. Thus, project managers are able to foster knowledge transfer not only within one specific group, but also beyond disciplinary boundaries. One example of this dynamic is a Genome BC water project where RPMs were able to add expertise for starting a scientific team, which got national recognition. In this role, RPMs can be seen as acting as a catalyst in the network by going beyond organizing or administration and engaging in the substantive content of negotiations with the goal of "identifying and exploiting opportunities for productivity value" (Ansell and Gash 2012). They bridge the work of different stakeholders and disciplines by communicating who has the expertise and which people should connect to create a successful new research project.

Further, British Columbia's increasingly accessible project funding structure and the role of Industry Technology Advisors (ITAs) in IRAP contribute to positive developments in the cluster. The latter program, a cornerstone of the province's innovation policy, also provides advisory services through ITAs and funding support for high-risk R&D projects. IRAP also helps non-profit and post-secondary institutions provide technical and commercialization advice to small and medium-sized enterprises, thus creating an informal structure for knowledge transfer, consultation, and advice within the network. IRAP generally seems to be a successful program, although it falls short of supporting British Columbia on a larger scale. The main criticism is that it not only disappears between other programs due to its size, but its funds are also exhausted early in the fiscal year. Smaller firms complain about the difficult first-time application process and the length of time between application and decision (Jenkins et al. 2011). In connection to accessibility, some interviewees pointed out that the BC R&D ecosystem had become more open in terms of programs being less rigid in their definition of where the funding comes from and who participates, which makes interagency cooperation easier.

Intellectual property rights pose another challenge for biotech stakeholders. Canadian regulation is not on par with other innovation-intensive nations. For example, unlike the United States and the European Union, Canada does not provide an extra period of patent protection as compensation for time lost during regulatory approval delays. And because pharmaceutical industries rely so heavily on patents, the life sciences industry is especially dependent on an enhanced legal environment to create profit and investments (Lybecker 2012). Some life sciences companies are also reluctant to work with universities due to the uncertainty of academic programs' ability to support long-term, large-scale projects and to adjust to the rapid pace of research. For the network to be successful, these impasses need to be communicated among stakeholders for potential restructuring. The successful government component of IRAP also shows that agreed-upon and informed policy guidelines are needed not only regarding the contents and goals of BC biotechnology, but also the structural elements of communications and cooperation. Overcoming these problems, in turn, is related to the availability of resources for biotechnology work.

In the BC biotech network, stakeholders struggle with the way government provides some of the funding and also with the lack of opportunities to attract human capital. There is a variety of governmental support, but not all of it is effective. Genome BC, for example, is a major investor focused on the tools of genomics for biotechnology; about a quarter of its funding comes from the province and half from the federal government. But genomics is only a small part of an increasingly broad spectrum of life sciences. Further, government-funded programs are subject to restrictions: the funding has to stay in the province, and includes a cap on how much one project can receive. The funding regulations sometimes even specify program participants. In short, there is a complex mix of resources at the national, provincial, and regional levels, which poses a challenge to stakeholders as navigating the initiatives becomes increasingly difficult. Some interviewees suggested the development of an online platform for all funding programs or even a "match-making" service for firms and the appropriate funding. Also, the "stacking" of incentives "may result in subsidies that are higher than needed to achieve policy objectives" (Jenkins et al. 2011, 42), but without a coordinated strategy to facilitate specific initiatives.

*Absorptive Capacity*

Vancouver is at a disadvantage in absorptive capacity building due to its geographic location. Despite its large population, there are limited development opportunities for an "inland hinterland" (O'Connor & Scott 1992), which makes Vancouver dependent on its transportation and communications links. At the same time, the city is a "pivot point" between North America and Asia, which is an advantage to other high-tech clusters in Canada and the United States. However, "its major continental competition is in California, which has similar geographical attributes" (Wixted and Holbrook 2011, 21). This means

Table 4.4. Collaborative and absorptive capacity of the Vancouver cluster

| Framework | Basic elements | |
|---|---|---|
| *Collaborative capacity* | | |
| Purpose | Leadership? | No |
| | Shared vision? | No |
| | Network membership? | No |
| Structure | Formal and informal procedures? | Yes |
| | Clear roles? | No |
| Communications | Information links? | Yes |
| | Active communications? | No |
| Resources | Knowledge and skills? | No |
| | Financing powers? | No |
| *Absorptive capacity* | | |
| Intra-cluster knowledge system | Knowledge spillovers? | Yes |
| | Social relations? | No |
| Extra-cluster knowledge system | Extra-cluster knowledge sources? | No |
| | Interface between the external linkages and the intra-cluster knowledge system? | No |

that, in the immediate area, Vancouver is missing a critical mass of other networks to connect to, especially when they are located farther south. Hence, a strong connection to the Asian market would be important, but, as the Singapore case study has shown, Singapore has been successful in employing scientists of their own from North America and in making themselves attractive to foreign researchers. Vancouver's location thus could be a barrier to its development beyond a certain size (Wixted and Holbrook 2011). Overall, as several interviewees pointed out, there is limited knowledge exchange due to weak links within the cluster and the low critical mass and distance from mega-regions for outside ties.

Table 4.4 shows that the Vancouver cluster lacks key elements of cluster-based commercialization activity. Stakeholders were generally aware of the strengths and weaknesses of the cluster, but also disenchanted by the facts. The cluster has a strong research component, and there are ad hoc cooperation mechanisms and resources in place, but with a largely informal structure and little purpose or communications activity.

*Concluding Remarks*

Several life sciences stakeholders in Vancouver said that the cluster required "coordinating on several fronts" and that "everyone needs to work together more" (Research Institute interviewee A, March 2012). In addition, "networking is a critical element" (Research Institute interviewee B, March 2012). Interviewees further stated that they would profit from building a strong network, as many capabilities remained untapped due to weak linkages among academia, industry, and government. Some of the disadvantages, such as Vancouver's location or funding schemes, could be offset by gaining value through collective links (Raines 2003). According to an industry representative interviewed for this book, "government shouldn't fund life sciences ... government should come up with this idea of some sort of industrial strategy that they are going to focus on" (Life sciences industry organization interviewee, April 2012). In short, it is no longer enough for the provincial and federal governments to support the university and research structure in British Columbia: government should target directly behaviour and networking within the cluster. A report by the Council of Canadian Academies (2013, 31) makes a similar assumption, and points out that, in the years to come, Canadian companies will develop strategies that focus on innovation, and firms will create a much more powerful "business-pull." In light of these developments, governments "must continue to provide the support needed to sustain Canada's research excellence as the demand for leading-edge skills and ideas rises to meet the supply." Further, enhancing coherence within the cluster in terms of purpose, communications, and structure could go a long way towards improving the competitiveness of life sciences research in the province – health-related life sciences are especially mobile, moving to wherever they can access money and human capital. Thus, the most important competitive advantage for British Columbia will be the quality of the network and the management of networking processes.

### Summary

Comparing the four clusters based on their collaborative and absorptive dimensions elements (see table 4.5), Medicon Valley and Chicago inherit ten of thirteen elements specified, while Vancouver and Singapore are not as consistent. Vancouver is missing many of the elements connected to purpose and resources, and is working on its absorptive capacity. Singapore does possess a clearly defined purpose, but has mixed results on the remaining categories, as it is progressing in its extra-knowledge system while lacking significant knowledge spillovers or social relations among stakeholders. In terms of addressing these gaps through cluster policy and cluster management, the cases further show that policy and management need to be intertwined either

Table 4.5. Collaborative and absorptive capacity of the four clusters: A summary

| Framework | Basic elements | Cluster | | | |
|---|---|---|---|---|---|
| | | Medicon Valley | Chicago | Singapore | Vancouver |
| *Collaborative capacity* | | | | | |
| Purpose | Leadership? | Yes | Yes | Yes | No |
| | Shared vision? | Yes | Yes | Yes | No |
| | Network membership? | Yes | Yes | Yes | No |
| Structure | Formal and informal procedures? | Yes | No | Yes | Yes |
| | Clear roles? | Yes | Yes | Yes | No |
| Communications | Information links? | Yes | Yes | In progress | Yes |
| | Active communications? | In progress | No | In progress | No |
| Resources | Knowledge and skills? | Yes | Yes | No | No |
| | Financing powers? | No | No | No | No |
| *Absorptive capacity* | | | | | |
| Intra-cluster knowledge system | Knowledge spillovers? | Yes | Yes | No | Yes |
| | Social relations? | Yes | Yes | No | In progress |
| Extra-cluster knowledge system | Extra-cluster knowledge sources? | Yes | Yes | Yes | In progress |
| | Interface between the external linkages and the intra-cluster knowledge system? | Yes | Yes | In progress | In progress |

structurally (public funding, for example) and/or organizationally (regular meetings/communications).

Several overarching themes can be drawn from these cases linked to the challenge government faces to create cluster policy that is in sync with a potential cluster management structure as well as capacity gaps. All four cases show that there are layers to cluster development that include overarching structures, such as geographic location and long-term (funding) decisions, as well as short-term goals. Policy has to be aware of both short-term needs and the larger structures in place that can facilitate or hinder public initiatives. Cluster organization is thus a key part of the relationship between stakeholders and government and the task of creating collaborative and absorptive capacity by managing the network and ultimately enhancing performance. The cases further show that cluster organizations facilitate capacity-relevant aspects, such as enabling networking and support structures that are in tune with the needs of different stakeholder groups within the cluster.

Chapter 5 further elaborates on these mechanisms, taking into account how cluster policy, cluster organizations, and capacity-enhancing activities are embedded in a larger structural setting of regional and local dynamics.

# 5 The Innovation Context for Cluster Management

The cases examined in the previous chapter show that cluster development has both somewhat stable and more dynamic elements that vary in the ways they can be combined. Stable elements are related to the geographic location, institutional set-up, and industrial history of the region. More dynamic elements include network-related factors such as collaborative and absorptive capacity building and the type of cluster management.

Clusters in Asia, Europe, and North America rely on substantial research facilities and existing universities. There are, however, more world-class universities than biotechnology clusters, and many regions have not developed sizable life sciences networks (Casper 2007). Those that have been successful were able to build on existing structures or even historical legacies formed by previous industries (Feldman and Florida 1994). Even if the previous industry was unrelated to the high-tech or biotechnology field, innovation depends on a set of underlying factors that make up a technological infrastructure for generating new ideas and bringing them to the market. The US Midwest, for example, has a history of manufacturing infrastructure in steel, automotive, appliance, and consumer durable production, which paved the way for today's biotech developments (Feldman and Florida 1994). Singapore was open to foreign investors early on as the government actively promoted bilateral free trade agreements in order to maintain locational attractiveness in regional production networks. This led world-class electronics companies such as Hewlett-Packard, Philips, and Toshiba to locate their high-value activities in Singapore (Yeung 2010). Thus, the city-state already had an infrastructure for hosting R&D and manufacturing facilities. In the late 1990s, following the same strategy of cluster development previously applied to electronics and chemicals, Singapore developed the Tuas Biomedical Park, a

183-hectare world-class manufacturing hub that attracted names such as MSD, Novartis, and GlaxoSmithKline Biologicals (Medrisch 2008). In fact, "Singapore's first foray into the biomedical sciences sector was through the establishment of the Institute of Molecular and Cellular Biology ... in 1987 at the National University of Singapore" (Finegold, Wong, and Cheah 2004, 922), and other research institutes followed between 1996 and 2000, including the Bioinformatics Centre, the Genome Institute of Singapore, the Bioprocessing Technology Centre, and the Institute of Bioengineering and Nano-technology. This does not take away from the importance of cluster management, but rather emphasizes the relevance of the preconditions for the success of a network in connection with facilitation.

Three of the clusters – Singapore, Chicago, and Vancouver – struggle with the lack of knowledge spillover opportunities in connection with location. Due to their geography, these cases are at a disadvantage compared to Boston, San Diego, and even Medicon Valley. They are farther away from other research hubs, and have greater difficulty connecting to other knowledge sources. Singapore has partly solved this problem by "importing" knowledge through multinational corporations and absorbing as much of the foreign experiences as possible. Illinois, on the other hand, has laid out plans to collaborate more closely with neighbouring states. This issue, however, is mostly tackled by cluster management in cooperation with government, which is the reason Vancouver has been unable to tap into the evolving life sciences hub in Seattle and connections with Asia.

Framework conditions further impact cluster development. These include market developments in the sector and possible first- or second-mover advantages compared to other clusters. Another question is how economic downturns affect the ability of countries and multinational companies to invest in innovation: investors might be willing to provide funding, "but it is being doled out in smaller increments and it comes with more strings attached and more risk 'sharing' (which typically means that more of the risk ends up being borne by smaller biotech companies)" (Ernst & Young 2011, 2). Clusters are further embedded in the innovation system of a country or region, including economic, social, political, organizational, and institutional factors that affect cluster development. This relates to the importance of location in terms of a region's unique institutional endowment, which can act to support and reinforce local advantage, for example. National and regional innovation systems can be thought of as institutional infrastructure that coordinates the production function of the cluster and even possesses a "culture" that influences the practices of firms in a certain area, which in turn is the product of commonly experienced institutional forces (Asheim and Gertler 2005).

## Cluster Organization Characteristics

To manoeuvre around these conditions, this book argues that the organization of the cluster and its capacity levels matter if it is to thrive economically. The cluster organization holds a central position in the relationship between stakeholders and government and in the task of creating collaborative and absorptive capacity by managing the network and ultimately enhancing performance. Variations of the management model in Chicago, Medicon Valley, and Singapore show that there is not one way to manage a cluster and that the role of government differs. Often the model adopted is based on existing structures that emerged from earlier industries. And government action is restricted by the political system and power constellation – depending on the jurisdiction and funding opportunities. The cluster management process itself, however, portrays common characteristics, including the following:

- those who deal directly with cluster stakeholders are knowledgeable in the biotech field;
- there are connections among government, research, and industry;
- an organization by or at arm's length of government is managing the cluster;
- a conscious decision was made to focus on biotech/life sciences; and
- cluster managers support elements of collaborative and absorptive capacity.

In addition, the structural set-up of cluster organizations differs depending on the level of government involvement and the funding sources. Table 5.1 highlights the variations in cluster facilitation, and compares them according to characteristics that build on the dimensions highlighted in previous research, in combination with what the survey and cases revealed. The cluster organization types address the different versions of setting up such an organization, which can be a collaborative effort by public and private entities, a public initiative, or something put in place independently by a group of stakeholders. At the same time, cluster organizations have different relationships with the network. Being partly or fully publicly funded obviously leads to high levels of government recognition, but lower recognition by

Table 5.1. Cluster organization characteristics

| | Relationship with the cluster | | |
| --- | --- | --- | --- |
| Cluster organization type | Stakeholder recognition | Government recognition | Positive impact on the network |
| Chicago (independent) | High | High to medium | High |
| Singapore (part of government) | Medium to low | High | Medium to low |
| Medicon Valley (government- and stakeholder-financed) | Medium | High | High |
| Vancouver (in development) | Medium to low | Medium | Low |

stakeholders. Leverage over the whole of the network increases when the cluster organization is already being supported by both public and private parties or has been set up from the bottom up by stakeholders. Depending on the willingness of stakeholders to have government involved, public funding can be a good or bad thing for the network.

The fact that the independent facilitator has more impact on the network and is more widely recognized than a government manager or partly publicly financed entity might seem counterintuitive. This has to do with the US example, where government involvement is not welcomed as much as in other countries. The independent facilitator, as described in the Chicago case, can be successful only if the institution is able to gain trust and legitimacy among cluster stakeholders and government officials. This is done through having specialized knowledge in the specific industry and connecting to and communicating with cluster participants. Ideally, the facilitator enters into a recognition cycle: the more connected the manager is to industry and academia, the more legitimate the facilitation process is in the eyes of government officials. This also works the other way around: the more lobbying power and information on government funding the manager has, the more trustworthy facilitation becomes in the eyes of network members. Ultimately, the cluster facilitator then has a highly positive impact on the overall network. If the cluster facilitator is unable to establish trust with any of these groups, however, the impact diminishes. This distinguishes the independent facilitator from the other two models. While the independent manager has barely any impact without the trust and legitimacy of government and stakeholders, facilitators gain automatic legitimacy on account of their connection to government, and thus can at least partially impact the network even with lower levels of recognition.

This is what happened in the Singapore example, where the manager is part of government. Even though not everyone agreed on the legitimacy of A*STAR as a facilitator, the government agency was still able to pool competencies and funding opportunities and thus impact the network. The closeness to government, however, harms A*STAR"s image, as the institution is not seen as independent but rather as acting in favour of government plans. This also limits its reach in terms of industry connections. Generally speaking, having a government-operated facilitator in Singapore is not as problematic as it would be in the United States, where government is run and seen differently. Government involvement further contributes to an institution's legitimacy. This might not be transferrable to other countries, which then have to pay special attention to their stakeholders' connections if deciding on a government-run management for clusters.

In the final category, government- and stakeholder-financed facilitation, Medicon Valley shows that network members welcome facilitation, but that a funding commitment involves expectations. Because stakeholders are paying to take advantage of the cluster organization, they look for (measurable) results. But facilitation output is not easily measurable, and members then get frustrated. There is also a fine line as to how much the cluster facilitator can charge given that the goal is to involve as many stakeholders as possible – including small and medium-sized enterprises and start-ups with smaller capital. This is where the government funding portion can cover some costs for smaller stakeholders. In the Øresund example, however, government was in the process of phasing out public funding, putting pressure on the facilitator, the Medicon Valley Alliance, to prove its use for the region. This poses the question of whether being involved in finding funds to pursue capacity-enhancing activities ultimately diminishes the facilitator's effectiveness. Early-on public funding gives the cluster management a platform to connect with more stakeholders; once the use of that facilitation and the trust are established, stakeholders might be more willing to pay for some of the services offered. Overall, this facilitation model has a high impact on the network because it engages stakeholders and government alike through funding commitments. In the Medicon Valley example, it started out with European funding, then national government funding (mostly from the Danish side), and ultimately incorporated stakeholders.

In Vancouver, management activities are either split between Genome BC and LifeSciences BC or they are not taken up at all. This makes it difficult to assign a more general model to current developments, and Vancouver is now labelled as "in development." The structure suggests, however, that the biotech network in British Columbia is moving towards a combined stakeholder- and government-funded model due to the funding structure underlying Genome BC. In addition, stake-holders that share a similar focus as Genome BC and LifeSciences BC recognize those organizations as key stakeholders in the cluster; how-ever, those that fall outside of this do not. Government is aware of both, and has invested in Genome BC through Genome Canada. Finally, lim-ited recognition and the complex structure that exists in the province limit the impact both organizations have on the local network.

## The Capacity Mechanism

To summarize, there are different types of cluster organizations, but all contribute to the collaborative and absorptive capacity levels of clusters. As the cases in this book highlight, cluster organizations facil-itate capacity-relevant aspects such as enabling networking and sup-port structures that are in tune with the needs of different stakeholder groups within the cluster. As many researchers have pointed out, there is no one-size-fits-all approach to clusters or innovation (Bathelt 2005; Tödtling and Trippl 2004; Vaz et al. 2014). Framing cluster dynamics in terms of capacity provides the opportunity of establishing differ-ent dimensions that can be targeted by cluster organizations and/or government. Capacity is thereby a form of resilience to changes that might be happening in the larger framework of economic prosperity or national-level policies. It further helps to pinpoint starting points for initiatives.

One reason capacity has not been the focal point of cluster strategies is that it incorporates the softer targets of innovation – things that can-not be directly measured but that affect knowledge transfer and learn-ing. It also sheds light on the smaller initiatives that could make a big difference for individual networks, such as a common local space to meet and work or affordable lab space for start-ups that is close to re-search hospitals or universities. This might make an unpopular policy target at times, as it does not have big appeal and also no immediate effect. Over time, however, it creates the resilience a cluster requires to adjust and absorb new developments in the ever-changing environ-ment of innovation.

This resilience, in the form of capacity levels, is a composition of dif-ferent elements that fall under either the collaborative or the absorptive label. Depending on the characteristics of the region and actors, then, the weight given to individual elements might change. For example, a region that has knowledge spillover due to its location and a net-work that extends beyond the cluster will focus more on collaborative elements inside the cluster, such as creating a strategy or vision for network members and making sure communications channels are established. The same applies to a cluster with a clear strategy and vision in a network that is well connected, but where the location prevents some external spillovers, necessitating additional links.

## The Outlook for Biotech Clusters

Life sciences are becoming more complex and competitive (Birch 2017; Halkier 2011; Wolfe and Creutzberg 2003). An increasingly aging population attracts new competitors into the growing field. The drugs and pharmaceuticals subsector faces considerable competitive challenges posed by the rise of generics, the slow pace of regulatory approval for new drugs and biopharmaceuticals, and the continued fast pace of mergers and acquisitions as firms seek long-term profitability (BIO 2013). Raising capital has also become more difficult in the aftermath of the financial crisis. That drives firms to seek capital on a broader basis, tapping into government funding programs, and thus looking for regions that offer grants and funding schemes. Networking is also rising in importance among different stakeholder groups. An example is the relationship between big pharmaceutical companies and small spin-offs: small biotech companies are often brimming with innovative new technologies and product candidates, they are short of capital, while big pharma companies have cash, but are hungry for new product ideas and scientific breakthroughs (Ernst & Young 2011). The link between government and biotech stakeholders is also becoming increasingly relevant. Companies need "to work with policy makers and other stakeholders to develop solutions to boost investor returns to levels more commensurate with the risk they are currently taking" (Ernst & Young 2011, 21). Accumulated knowledge in the area has also exploded: there are "more areas of potential use, more competing technologies, more pathways for product development and growing complexity as regard to proof of concept" (IRIS Group 2009, 63). Investors have become more demanding in terms of commercial insight and market perspective and reluctant to invest in early-stage biotech projects. These developments call for a focus on those things that can be altered in the cluster, which include networking support mechanisms.

Increasingly, evaluations point to the "cluster ecosystem" – the concerted effort of government, industry, and research institutions to foster innovation through knowledge exchange – as a main driver of innovation and economic performance (KPMG 2016). The characteristics of this ecosystem are what the capacity framework aims to break down into more clearly defined activities that can be carried out by cluster organizations and/or facilitated by government entities. The goal is to dive deeper into the underlying soft skills that might prevent clusters from reaching their innovation goals, such as formulating a vision or creating formal and informal communications channels that allow for networking to happen. The increasing emphasis on networking dynamics also shows that governments are realizing that, although funding-related incentives can remove some of the bottlenecks in clusters, they cannot address a range of other obstacles to the establishment of innovation networks.

# 6 Concluding Remarks: Capacity Building in Biotech Clusters

This concluding chapter revisits some of the challenging elements of innovation and cluster policy to show how cluster management and capacity building can help meet these challenges. Cluster management is helping governments and stakeholders agree on the right mix of policy tools for clusters. Many policy makers still work with an oversimplified view of the innovation process, for many reasons. One is that few have links to industry and, therefore, a limited understanding of local networks. Governments are well aware of the importance of innovation, but they often treat the process as linear. A linear understanding of innovation, however, addresses "inputs in the process rather than the functioning of the system, and providing support to firms in isolation rather than to networks of actors" (Nauwelaers 2001, 102–3).

In addition, governments have difficulty finding a balance between a laissez-faire and a systemic approach to clusters. This means that decision makers either step in if there is obvious market failure, based on the neoclassical understanding of industrial policy, or include all major policy fields in an attempt to redesign linkages between parts of the system. The latter, however, requires specific insights not only into institutional characteristics of the national system, but also into the types of technologies and sectors being addressed. Both approaches have advantages and disadvantages, but the second perspective, more so than the first, needs the input of stakeholders active in the relevant sector. Overall, researchers and practitioners agree that a balance between the two is necessary to support innovative capacity (Edquist, Hommen, and Tsipouri 2000; Ibata-Arens 2003; Pack and Saggi 2006). The cases reveal that facilitators help to make such linkages by building relationships among cluster members, with government, multinationals, and investors. Cluster organizations also have an important role in connecting with a region's historical legacy and the opportunities it creates. Conceptually, the activities following from this position can be categorized as supporting either collaborative or absorptive capacity.

### Summary of the Findings

Three major findings come from the research and analysis in this book. First, seeing cluster development through the lens of capacity and understanding the capacity-enabling and capacity-reducing traits of cluster management as well as more stable and dynamic elements of networks help to unravel cluster dynamics linked to performance. The capacity framework adds to our policy understanding of clusters by breaking down the idea of collaboration and exchanging knowledge inside and outside the cluster. In doing so, the framework builds on the idea that knowledge exchange is at the core of innovation and that proximity in the cluster setting is only the starting point for more structured activities, such as defining a strategy and a vision for network members and creating communications channels among them. Cluster management plays a central role because collective action dynamics within such competitive networks often prevent concerted activity. A cluster organization can overcome this tendency by acting as a link among stakeholders as well as to government while carrying out or facilitating activities that fall under collaborative and absorptive capacity building.

The elements of *collaborative capacity* are as follows:

- Purpose:
  - taking on a leadership position or identifying a leader within the cluster;
  - identifying and formulating, together with stakeholders, a shared vision; and
  - potentially connecting the cluster to a broader network with additional resources.
- Structure:
  - developing formal and informal procedures for regular collaboration and support; and
  - identifying services and roles of institutions that can support cluster development.
- Communications:
  - establishing links among stakeholders for regular information exchange – either through personal connections or formal agreements; and
  - facilitating active communications through events or communications technology.

- Resources:
  - supporting the availability of human capital with relevant knowledge and skills; and
  - establishing financing powers by attracting different types of funding and potentially creating a collective financial pool.

*Absorptive capacity* contains two main elements:

- An intra-cluster knowledge system:
  - creating opportunities for knowledge spillovers and learning through connecting individuals among each other and developing informal spaces for collaboration.
- An extra-cluster knowledge system:
  - linking the cluster to external networks and acquiring knowledge from them as well as transferring it to relevant stakeholders within the network.

Not all of these activities can be driven solely by a cluster organization. Although they obviously need the support of network members, some dimensions also require political support, such as backing a vision or helping to attract human capital through, for example, tax breaks. In addition, the activities overlap and might happen at the same time or with a delay. Together, however, they take advantage of the soft skills needed in local agglomerations to drive innovation. As the four cases presented in this book show, each of these elements has several layers. One is the spatial dimension, in terms of having local space in which to house start-ups or networking events that are well connected to relevant stakeholders and readily accessible. Then there is the policy layer at local, regional, national, or even supranational levels, which can affect collaborative and absorptive capacity building through legislation connected to taxes, housing, immigration, technology, or patenting. Finally, there are the global biotechnology market, the dynamics of large venture capital investments, and the movement of multinational companies, all of which affect capacity building in clusters, and is reflected in the competition among clusters in the same sector. A reoccurring theme among interviewees for this study was the worry that promising start-ups and individuals might prefer more established clusters such as Boston or San Diego than those surveyed here. Singapore's investment strategy also raised concerns about attracting star scientists to the city-state or having large companies look elsewhere in Asia for new investment opportunities.

A second finding of the book is that, although cluster management appears in many different clusters, its positioning within the network depends on the role government plays and how the cluster organization is funded. From the geographically diverse cases in this book, three cluster management models emerge: those financed by government and stakeholders; those that are part of government; and those that are independent. Each model has different effects in terms of recognition by stakeholders, government, and the overall network. Based on conversations with stakeholders in the four cluster cases, an independent cluster organization with a high profile in the sector gains legitimacy quickly. In the Chicago case, individuals in the cluster organization were known to many network members and had already established themselves in the US Midwest biotech sector. Further, since the organization was embedded in the network, recognition by local government came more easily, and allowed public officials to gain a better understanding of the challenges and opportunities arising in the city. Finally, many cluster successes were traced back to services offered by cluster organizations, such as matching start-ups with investors or creating spaces where stakeholders could connect. In Singapore, the cluster organization was on the opposite end of the spectrum in being both part of government and also receiving funding from public sources. This meant almost automatically high levels of government recognition. Stakeholders, however, saw the cluster organization as the right hand of government: although it offered a variety of services and funding instruments, obligations linked to such support ultimately could be enforced by government. It also created quite a closed system for those trying to enter the cluster. The government- and stakeholder-financed model is the one found in Medicon Valley, where such funding has created high levels of commitment by both actors. Network members did express concern, however, over the weight large companies had in strategic decisions making due to their access to larger funds. Nonetheless, here the cluster organization's impact on the network has been high due to its continuing work to identify the cluster's competitive advantage, reach out to high-profile clusters around the world, and facilitate links between Denmark and Sweden.

The third and final conclusion drawn from this research is that government policy matters for cluster development, and in several ways. This finding follows from the layers of each of the capacity-building elements. The cases show that larger policy decisions that on the surface are unrelated to clusters or innovation affect local agglomerations: "While globalization may call into question the applicability of early 20th century industrial policy, by no means does it obliterate location, geographic advantage, or uneven gains resulting from such advantage" (Hira et al. 2013, 32–3). Instead, globalization has forced governments and industry to identify the competitive advantage of places at an international level – an advantage rooted not only in output performance, but also in the effectiveness of networking, knowledge exchange and links between local and global players. In fact, as a result of globalization, there is a convergence of the competitiveness of the company and that of the place. Against this background, cluster policy is at a crossroads. Scholars have been successful in persuading policy makers of the importance of clustering, but the role of government remains unclear. There has been a shift in the status of innovation from a means to achieve other economic objectives to becoming a policy goal in itself (Perren and Sapsed 2013). Because empirical evidence targeting the effectiveness of certain policy tools is scarce, however, most governments still rely on imitating successful examples, such as Silicon Valley, which often results in failure due to tensions between regional capabilities and policy initiatives.

Governments increasingly rely upon collaboration to enhance innovation activity. This is supported by studies that emphasize the benefits of collaborative structures for network performance even beyond the technological opportunities (Agranoff 2014; Powell, Koput, and Smith-Doerr 1996; Roberts and Bradley 1991; Schilling 2015). The rationale behind higher levels of collaboration among companies or research institutes is that they lead to more commercialization, venture funding, and, ultimately, innovation (Boekholt and Thuriaux 1999). This is done through networking programs and public procurement as instruments of innovation policy. These adjustments, however, are in contrast to wishes of stakeholders who increasingly look for demand-side policies, including innovation-related regulations and standards as well as tax incentives (Aschhoff and Sofka 2008). In most countries, policy makers identify collaboration as key to innovation, but the definition and solution seeking remain vague and complex, leading to the use of a wide range of policy instruments to address collaboration (Agranoff and McGuire 2001; Braun 2008).

In contrast to this emphasis on collaboration are statements by some stakeholders in the clusters under study in this book. Representatives from industry and research facilities saw collaboration as something that is either in their own hands or could be facilitated through cluster organizations. They further pointed towards the preconditions that would enable collaboration. The main issues they raised were as follows (Giest 2017):

- attracting and retaining global talent through, for example, tax breaks for individual researchers, immigration policy, and housing policy;

- consistency and stability in government goals and support for cluster through, for example, increased competitiveness and making the cluster attractive to outside investors; and
- creating a strong, but flexible network.

The cases show that stakeholders are demanding more capacity-enhancing initiatives for collaboration, including resources for exchanging knowledge and the financial power to pursue projects. Further, network members are looking for and using the services of cluster organizations that can create structure and vision for the cluster in a specific field. Players also rely on government to create a stable and consistent environment for innovation. This mainly concerns the promise of continued funding and the inclusion of sector-specific goals in policy documents (Giest 2019).

*Cluster Management*

Researchers increasingly are recommending that clusters contain institutions that play the role of a channel or bridge for companies and other institutions to government stakeholders (Martin 2012). Such cluster managers, facilitators, or connectors are largely service oriented and knowledge based as they implement government-funded initiatives based on stakeholders' needs, including providing networking programs and training, setting up platforms and technology centres, and targeting the integration of start-up companies and researchers.

The four cases in this book reveal that facilitators also help to make linkages outside local agglomerations by building relationships with multinationals and investors. Conceptually, these activities are categorized as supporting either collaborative or absorptive capacity; in practice, they blend into one another, as networking events for local stakeholders might include out-of-town companies and investors or outside stakeholders who inspire a strategic vision for the cluster. By contributing to the network in this way, facilitators can prevent some of the common pitfalls in cluster policy. Analysis also shows that policy needs to identify system deficiencies before regional and local agglomerations can be successful, as structural weaknesses can affect innovation by creating "lock in," or hinder network dynamics in the form of bottlenecks (Rosenberg 1982).

In addition, the implementation and development of cluster facilitation is more efficient when existing opportunities are exploited, rather than when new avenues are explored (Lundvall 2001). This means that policy makers have a higher success rate when tackling regions that already have a certain level of agglomeration in one industry or field, and uniting those competencies with university research and companies. This can then become the basis on which cluster management can be built (Feldman and Florida 1994). Chicago, Medicon Valley, Singapore, and Vancouver all had prior structural set-ups connected to a low-tech or medium-tech industry that could be used and developed to facilitate the creation of a high-tech cluster. Thus, when evaluating the potential success of a region, policy makers have to think not only about present and future competitiveness, but also about past set-ups that enable cluster development. As well, cumulative investments are important over longer periods – these can include the development of a technological infrastructure with agglomerations of manufacturing firms in related industries and the concentration of industrial and university R&D, which then create the regional "stock" of innovative capabilities. A more radical version of this argument would suggest that "cluster development is path dependent or heavily influenced by chance historical events" (Feldman and Francis 2004, 132; see also Kenney and von Burg 1999).

Overall, many of the advantages of clusters arise from face-to-face interaction. And although government might be guilty of "black boxing" stakeholders in the network, the same is true for industry players and researchers towards government (Flanagan, Uyarra, and Laranja 2011). Interaction between the two groups could solve this problem, perhaps simply through regular meetings facilitated by a manager. Stakeholders and governments, of course, must be willing to talk to each other. Here, prejudgments about the involvement of government sometimes get in the way.

## Advancing Innovation and Cluster Theory

Different strands of the literature have attempted to find generalizable patterns that work for different clusters within an industry as well as across sectors. These analyses also can be observed through different lenses, such as individual or company relationships within and beyond the cluster as well as within a larger network or region. The distinct policy perspective of this book is to offer insights into the collaborative and absorptive activities of clusters in combination with their management. These insights provide a more detailed perspective than do other studies of the vertical, multilevel, and horizontal dynamics of clusters and how they are managed. This is in line with the call of Fornahl, Hassink, and Menzel (2015) for research to disentangle what is happening inside and outside the cluster. The development of the collaborative and absorptive capacity framework is new in the literature in that it further defines capacity by making it a focal point of the empirical analysis. Several scholars have mentioned capacity – as a trait of individuals, companies, and regional networks –in passing, but such a framework has been lacking so far in the discussion at the intersection of cluster research and policy making.

The policy literature on innovation and cluster policy has widened its scope by including framework conditions for high-tech clusters to flourish and by moving away from meso-level initiatives. Lacking, however, has been a focus on underlying mechanisms that then yield a diverse set of policy initiatives. Indeed, some scholars have criticized "the strong emphasis placed on firm-level routines at the expense of institutions and other actors, for example the state" (Martin and Coenen 2015, 2010). The research presented in this book suggests that at the core of clusters are versions of knowledge transfer that include relationships within and outside the cluster. This is also in response to the need Strambach (2010) has identified for scientific work to take on a more holistic perspective regarding the co-evolution of institutions and technology. These relationships are guided by enabling factors such as purpose, structure, communications, and resources (collaborative capacity) and the establishment of an intra- and extra-cluster knowledge system (absorptive capacity). These aspects, rooted in relational dynamics, are often overlooked when working backwards from performance indicators, since their effects are largely indirect, and the literature so far has not linked them.

In addition to highlighting these capacity-building features, cluster stakeholders and policy makers need a way to communicate about them. Cluster management thus becomes a central component of this research, but there is limited discussion of it in the literature, which tends to focus on leadership (e.g. Stough, Stimson, and Nijkamp 2011), boundary spanners (e.g. Williams 2010), or so-called anchor firms (e.g. Baglieri, Cinici, and Mangematin 2012). In addition, few studies have gathered data that uncover when cluster management makes sense or how to design and implement it (6 et al. 2006). The literature on cluster management also has limited linkages with the literature on cluster economics and policy making, which is largely treated as a separate phenomenon. As this research shows, however, cluster management can be a tool of access and communication for both government and cluster stakeholders. Cluster management should also be considered in the theoretical debate around government capacity and the establishment of support systems that enhance government's implementation and delivery capabilities (El-Taliawi and Van der Wal 2019; Painter and Pierre 2005).

As Wu, Ramesch, and Howlett (2015) argue, organizational-operational capacity can be enhanced by coordinating among government, non-governmental, and private organizations. This research stream also highlights the role of "hybrid" institutional arrangements (UNDP 2011) as relevant for government to achieve its policy goals. Thus, cluster management can be categorized as a flexible arrangement in the form of a (non-)governmental or private entity that helps increase capacity through creating coherence throughout government programs as well as a responsive feedback mechanism among cluster stakeholders and public officials.

### Limitations and Future Research Questions

For future studies, a critical assessment of the approach presented here reveals several limitations. First, the comparative analysis focuses on a narrow set of clusters in place of more in-depth analysis. This applies to the cases selected along the continuum of government involvement and visibility of cluster management, as well as their geographic location and industry context. For the latter, the research bases its findings on emerging clusters in the biotechnology sector located in the Western hemisphere and Asia. This neglects a large group of developing and emerging economies that potentially bring a new set of challenges when it comes to cluster policy and funding. This does not mean that the capacity framework is not applicable in those cases – only that such a conclusion cannot be drawn from this study. Further, the cases are taken from the biotechnology sector, which is especially demanding in terms of networking. One could argue that this is why cluster management is needed more in this area, but clustering is happening in other areas as well, including in high-, medium-, and low-tech industries. The survey shows that activities within the cluster and links to both cluster management and government involvement go beyond biotechnology, as respondents also came from the energy, food production, and oil and gas sectors. More in-depth research is required in other fields to determine if these theoretical dimensions hold in other industries.

Another aspect the research does not account for, but should be the subject of further exploration, is that of the development over time of cluster management and policy support linked to capacity building. This study has provided insights into these dimensions at a particular point in time, but clusters evolve and cluster management might become more effective over time. In addition, throughout these dynamic developments, government might undertake several smaller policy initiatives, from which lessons might be learned about how to move forward. This raises several questions for further research on the process by which government and cluster management become more effective over time in boosting a cluster's capacity-enhancing activities, as well as which capacity dimensions remain stable and which ones decline or increase over time and how this affects performance.

## Policy Recommendations

There is wide-ranging agreement that supporting and sustaining innovation through policy initiatives is a complex undertaking. The cluster setting is one innovation outlet that limits these efforts geographically, and has led to a hype around the idea of clusters as economic quick fixes. The cluster concept is regarded as essential to interpret the structure of economies and to provide insights into effective policy making. It also has the ability to channel policy discussions towards geographic concentration and specialization in terms of sectors. Policy documents promise major improvements through the support and creation of such high-tech networks. Even these regionally limited efforts, however, are part of a larger, multilevel context, both economically and governmentally. This exposes a paradox inherent to clusters: *Although clusters help to focus policy efforts, they are also exposed to synergies that reach far beyond their location.* The policy recommendations drawn from this research try to address this paradox by breaking down cluster dynamics into elements that can be targeted individually or in conjunction with one another without being necessarily time dependent. *Looking at cluster policy from the perspective of absorptive and collaborative capacity can help policy makers identify underlying mechanisms that add up to a more robust innovation development.* Underlying the following policy recommendations is not to present a shopping list of factors that can be crossed off, but rather a process in which underlying and often invisible interlinked elements can be supported sustainably. Much of the literature fits cluster dynamics into a life-cycle model, which helps to track economic evolution but is of limited help to policy makers, since policy is not flexible enough to adjust to a cluster's different phases or even to predict a change. Assuming that factors are more fluid and dynamic, this raises the question of how to support policy making in an uncertain and dynamic environment. This book has shown that breaking the dynamics down into individual elements helps to reduce complexity and allows one to disconnect partially from the current cluster narrative in order to focus on capacity-building mechanisms.

The current cluster narrative is based on several assumptions that are linked to the idea that they occur naturally and that stakeholders are in proximity to one another and specialize in a competitive market field, which can then drive the region's overall economic performance. The narrative further builds on inherent attributes, such as geographic concentration and specialization, that can focus the discussion at the policy level. As a result, governments often create support systems such as smaller-scale funding tools or technology transfer mechanisms. This has been framed as "meso-level support" in the form of innovation policy design that targets firms and research institutes directly (Nauwelaers and Wintjes 2008). The rationale behind the meso-level approach is to enable firms to take up opportunities to collaborate with other companies or research facilities, based on the idea that spatially confined, industry-specific innovation efforts thrive on good relationships between industry and research.

*Changing the "Cluster Narrative"*

There are other versions of the cluster narrative, depending on which success factors are being emphasized. Scholars point to the supporting (institutional) system and entrepreneurs, the commercialization of knowledge, and low entry barriers to entry – not only financially, but also in sociological and psychological terms. *The cluster narrative matters because it simplifies innovation processes for policy making; if oversimplified, however, it can lead to gaps in funding and fail to create the capacities needed for networking and knowledge exchange.* Hence, what this book has attempted to show is that the spatially confined, industry-specific policy perspective is only a small part of the dynamic environment required in order to have the capacity to innovate. The following sections highlight some of the most prominent cluster narratives and how they can lead to misconceptions on the policy side.

*Beyond Locality*

The focus on locality in the context of clusters is a false pretence for facilitating innovation. Innovation relies heavily on the formation of linkages beyond the cluster setting (extra-cluster sources of knowledge). The central argument of the absorptive capacity framework is that organizations can compensate for resources lacking within the cluster by tapping into knowledge sources elsewhere. In order to facilitate these connections, policy makers need to think beyond the local setting and look at strategies such as fostering the inflow of human capital or encouraging long-distance R&D collaborations. In short, although local and spatial characteristics matter for cluster development, for capacity creation policy has to keep a broader perspective on the ecosystem in which clusters are situated. This ecosystem might include seemingly unrelated things, such as the quality of schools and housing prices. This also means scrutinizing all policies from a multilevel, multi-actor view in order to identify bottlenecks. In this setting, broader regulatory frameworks, such as taxes, that cannot be changed easily might have been compensated for by several smaller incentives targeting collaborative and absorptive capacity elements. To summarize, the narrative needs to change from clusters as local networks to clusters as complex adaptive systems (Martin and Sunley 2010).

*Beyond Life Cycles*

The cluster life-cycle idea has served as a discussion template among government officials in order to identify development steps or stages. The life-cycle approach, however, oversimplifies some cluster dynamics. First, the life-cycle stages might not fit all clusters, or they might identify development stages incorrectly (Martin and Sunley 2011). Second, clusters do not always develop evenly and as a whole – some parts might remain at an earlier stage while others advance (Menzel and Fornahl 2010). Finally, "the movement of the cluster through the life cycle is not performed by the cluster, which is only a concept, but is the result of the activities and the evolution of its elements" (Menzel and Fornahl 2010, 212). In other words, while the life-cycle concept simplifies the language around clusters, it might give a faulty idea of what is going on in them. It might, for example, suggest that there are specific policy instruments fit for specific stages. Martin and Sunley (2011, 1303) point out that "explanations of cluster development continue to be hamstrung by recourse to underexplained 'ageing' analogies and 'life-course' metaphors," and that the life-cycle idea needs a rethink. They suggest that change is unpredictable, as, for example, product diversification disrupts an industry trajectory and external forces come into play. In essence, the cluster is in constant mutation, a phenomenon that is difficult to tackle when developing policy plans and initiatives into the future.

This book has argued that the life-cycle model of cluster evolution might not be useful in grasping the dynamics of cluster development. The argument has two bases. First, the suggestion that clusters go through phases is appealing, but can lead to wrong classifications and ultimately ill-fitting policy initiatives. Second, the temporality element is difficult to keep up with from a policy perspective. Policies are often layered and hard to change, which means that updating a policy based on cluster life cycles is difficult to achieve, and might take longer than the defined phase of development. To overcome these issues, I have suggested stripping down cluster dynamics to their core elements by looking at clusters' collaborative and absorptive capacity mechanisms. Such an approach would help policy to refocus efforts on capacity-building aspects within the cluster, rather than on its developmental stages.

*Beyond One Industry*

Although the findings in this book build on research in the biotechnology industry, the goal was to identify mechanisms that work beyond a specific industry, and to show potential linkages to institutional structures and regional settings that might outlive or help transform regional industries from one industry focus to another. For the first point, this means disconnecting some policies from an industry-driven approach and looking instead at the characteristics of the cluster. This reveals a constant struggle, where policies try to tackle specific issues relating to one industry or one location, while being broad enough to apply elsewhere. Most cluster policies are designed to reinforce regional strongholds and to encourage further specialization in the context of existing industries (Asheim et al. 2017). In the context of collaborative and absorptive capacity, however, the research in this book shows that policy requires a broader and more comprehensive understanding of innovation – one that looks at the capacity-building mechanisms underlying local successes in order to answer two questions. First, *what drives performance differences within the same industry?* Second, *what drives performance similarities across different industries?*

I suggest that the answer to both questions is that there are processes specific to clusters and their context that are not necessarily related to an industry, but rather to the support and facilitation of the collaborative and absorptive capacity of a cluster. Across geographic locations, policy initiatives that pick up on soft skills, such as supporting the creation of a vision for the cluster, in combination with a multilevel approach to the cluster's spatial dimension, facilitate capacity building.

*Varieties of Cluster Management*

Although the above tasks are complex and require a level of oversight, both governments and stakeholders have only limited ability to address them. As Boschma and Frenken (2011) point out, relationships in cluster settings often suffer due to a lack of institutional proximity, in that university, industry, and government do not work together and/or operate in different institutional regimes. Active cluster management is one solution, because cluster organizations can enhance the collaborative and absorptive capacities of the cluster while creating links between government and stakeholders. Instead of a "best practice" model, the cases presented in this book show that the model of cluster management – whether financed by government and stakeholders, part of government, or independent – can account for local characteristics and different forms of the political system.

The implementation of a cluster management mechanism in the realm of science and technology policy is also a public management innovation in itself. Such structural changes challenge government to rethink current working ethics and, more important, enter a state where they are conducive to learning. The implementation of cluster facilitation is not easy, since it changes the dynamics of longstanding structural and institutional frameworks in mostly nested, multilevel political systems. Also, it enters an arrangement in which instruments and goals have been added to existing ones – the process of layering – which often leads to incoherence among policy ends and means (Howlett 2011). Thus, the network management tool might not always be successful in redesigning or replacing existing elements, but must find a compromise arrangement with current policy tools, which might reduce its capacity-enhancing abilities. Overall, the success of cluster management depends on a variety of factors, including structural and organizational preconditions, current policy frameworks, and the coherence of policy instruments. It challenges existing set-ups for science and technology policy; over time, it makes innovation policy more coherent and knowledgeable about on-the-ground needs and helps to navigate the complexity of innovative activity within networks.

*Policy Adaptability and the Capacity to Innovate*

Given the dynamic setting of clusters, policy needs to be sufficiently flexible both to set a frame in which clusters can flourish and to support individual elements. In other words, policy faces the challenge of having to take into account its influence on a comprehensive range of issues, while also being adaptable to an ever-changing and uncertain context. The idea of adaptive policy making has been around for quite some time (see e.g., Holling 1978; Lee 1993), but has been revived in recent years given the dynamic settings not only of innovation, but also of climate change, health care and international developments (Bizikova et al. 2018; Swanson et al. 2010). The core idea is that, for policies to be effective, they must be able to adapt to conditions that cannot be anticipated. This comes with a shift in the understanding of the policy target in that it shifts from achieving a single goal or performance indicator to an integrated view of maintaining ecosystem resilience by looking at the network of relationships and interactions (Glouberman et al. 2003; Swanson et al. 2010).

The continuous adaptation of policies is especially challenging, however, given the lack or limited evaluation of cluster performance. As highlighted throughout this book, there is hardly any coherence when it comes to evaluation criteria for clusters. Much of the soft data are self-reported, and hard data are linked to discussions around how measurements are acquired and have potential inherent bias (Temouri 2012). By introducing cluster management styles and breaking down some of the dynamic elements of a cluster, this book has aimed to contribute to the discussion about which policy options should be pursued and in what combination, and how they should be adjusted based on how cluster development unfolds. The strength of the collaborative and absorptive capacity framework is that it pays attention to the smaller elements (such as vision formulation for the cluster), as well as to the larger framework settings (such as a region's infrastructure). One question in the adaptive policy literature is how to trigger adjustments once a misfit is identified; here, cluster management can play a role in that it is both a communications channel and a facilitation mechanism. Depending on the management style, integration with government differs, but the mechanism still provides access to inner cluster dynamics and a way to implement initiatives that target regional and cluster dynamics. In other words, cluster management becomes a "built-in policy adjustment mechanism" that helps policy makers to respond to ongoing changes (Swanson et al. 2010).

Additional implications for policy include the need to acknowledge pre-existing traditions of interaction and the establishment of infrastructure and other goods that the market fails to provide. For government to match the existing set-up, there needs to be communication between entrepreneurs and officials, as government often focuses attention on "relocating firms, offering one-off special deals and other incentives, rather than understanding the needs of existing firms and providing solutions" (Feldman and Francis 2004, 134). Cluster organizations therefore become an important link not only among stakeholders, but also in connecting with the region's historical legacies and the opportunities they create. Beyond the acknowledgement of historical legacies, the network manager can further adjust trajectories towards knowledge-intensive activities, since deep knowledge of the region is needed to renew and reposition local production systems (Bailey et al. 2010). Repositioning can take place based on three mechanisms: first, by entering and securing high-value-added market segments by moving away from mass production and price competition; second, by using cross-fertilization and searching for market opportunities beyond the usual final customer; and, finally, by repositioning the region in the global value chain, creating a shift in its core competencies (Bailey et al. 2010). The cluster organization can play a role in all three adjustments, and inform and guide the process based on its knowledge of the region, stakeholders, and connection to government.

# References

Acemoglu, D., and J. Robinson. 2012. *Why Nations Fail: The Origins of Power, Prosperity and Poverty*. London: Profile Books.

Agranoff, R. 2014. "Reconstructing Bureaucracy for Service: Innovation in the Governance Era." In *Public Innovation through Collaboration and Design*, ed. C.K. Ansell and J. Torfing, 41–69. London: Routledge.

Agranoff, R., and M. McGuire. 2001. "Big Questions in Public Network Management Research." *Journal of Public Administration Research and Theory* 11 (3): 295–396. https://doi.org/10.1093/oxfordjournals.jpart.a003504.

Alawadhi, N. 2017. "Singapore blocks visas for Indian IT professionals." *Economic Times*, 4 April. Online at https://economictimes.indiatimes.com /nri/visa-and-immigration/singapore-blocks-visas-for-indian-it -professionals/articleshow/57983557.cms.

Amin, A., and N. Thrift. 1995. *Globalization, Institutions, and Regional Development in Europe*. Oxford: Oxford University Press.

Andersen, H. 2008. "The Emerging Danish Government Reform – Centralised Decentralisation." *Urban Research & Practice* 1 (1): 3–17. https://doi.org /10.1080/17535060701795298

Anderson, M. 2014. "MVA Ambassador contributes to CBS report about pharmaceutical public-private partnering." *Nordic Life Science News*, 21 January. Online at http://nordiclifescience.org/mva-ambassador -contributes-to-cbs-report-about-pharmaceutical-public-private-partnering/.

Andriani, P., C. Jones, M. Perkmann, L. Propris, V. Sena, R. Delbridge, K.M. Möslein, and A. Neely. 2005. "Challenging Clusters – The Prospects and Pitfalls of Clustering for Innovation and Economic Development." Summary Report from an AIM Management Research Forum in Cooperation with the Welsh Economy Research Unit, Advanced Institute of Management Research, June.

Anheier, H.K., and J. Kendall. 2002. "Interpersonal Trust and Voluntary Association: Examining Three Approaches." *British Journal of Sociology* 53 (3): 343–62. https://doi.org/10.1080/0007131022000000545.

Ansell, C., and A. Gash. 2012. "Stewards, Mediators and Catalysts: Toward a Model of Collaborative Leadership." *Innovation Journal* 17 (2), article 7.

Anthony, S.D., E.A. Roth, and C.M. Christensen. 2002. "The Policymaker's Dilemma: The Impact of Government Intervention on Innovation in the Telecommunications Industry." Harvard Business School Working Paper 02–075. April.

Arafeh, L., M., Bruce, N., Hurst, B., Williams, D. Yoon, and J.C. Zapata. 2016. "Chicago Biotech: A Cluster Analysis. Microeconomics of Competitiveness." Online at http://www.isc.hbs.edu/resources/courses/moc-course-at-harvard/Documents/pdf/student-projects/Chicago%20Biotech%202016.pdf.

Arnold, W. 2003. "Singapore goes for biotech." *New York Times*, 26 August. Online at http://www.nytimes.com/2003/08/26/business/singapore-goes-for-biotech.html.

Aschhoff, B., and W. Sofka. 2008. "Innovation on Demand – Can Public Procurement Drive Market Success of Innovations?" *Research Policy* 38 (8): 1235–47. https://doi.org/10.1016/j.respol.2009.06.011.

Asheim, B.T., and M.S. Gertler. 2005. "The Geography of Innovation: Regional Innovation Systems." In *The Oxford Handbook of Innovation*, ed. F. Fagerberg, D.C. Mowery, and R.R. Nelson, 291–318. New York: Oxford University Press.

Asheim, B.T., A. Isaksen, R. Martin, and M. Trippl. 2017. "The Role of Clusters and Public Policy in New Regional Economic Path Development. In *The Life Cycle of Clusters: A Policy Perspective*, ed. D. Fornahl and R. Hassink, 13–34. Cheltenham, UK: Edward Elgar.

Asheim, B.T., and J. Moodysson. 2008." The Öresund Region: A Dynamic Region in Europe Due to Inter-regional Collaboration." Working Papers On Line (WPOL), Institut Universitari d'Estudis Europeus. Online at http://www.iuee.eu/pdf-publicacio/151/YvmnA8XR5Bcmz6FzGWMG.PDF.

A*STAR (Agency for Science, Technology and Research). 2009. "Growing Enterprises through Technology Upgrade (GET-Up)." Online at http://www.a-star.edu.sg/Industry/ProgrammesforSMEs/GETUpProgramme/tabid/220/Default.aspx.

A*STAR (Agency for Science, Technology and Research). 2011. "STEP 2015, Science, Technology & Enterprise Plan 2015." Online at http://www.a-star.edu.sg/portals/0/media/otherpubs/step2015_1jun.pdf.

A*STAR (Agency for Science, Technology and Research). 2012. "The Biomedical Sciences Initiative." Online at http://www.a-star.edu.sg/AboutASTAR/BiomedicalResearchCouncil/BMSInitiative/tabid/108/Default.aspx.

A*STAR (Agency for Science, Technology and Research). 2017. "Organisation Structure." Online at https://www.a-star.edu.sg/About-A-STAR/Corporate-Profile/Organisation-Structure.aspx.

A\*STAR (Agency for Science, Technology and Research). 2020. "Biomedical Research Council." Online at https://www.a-star.edu.sg/About-A-STAR /biomedical-research-council.

Atkinson, M.M., and W.D. Coleman. 1985. *Corporatism and Industrial Policy: Organized Interests and the State.* London: SAGE.

Audretsch, D., and E. Lehmann. 2006. "The Role of Clusters in Knowledge Creation and Diffusion: An Institutional Perspective. In *Clusters and Regional Development: Critical Reflections and Explorations,* ed. B. Asheim, P. Cooke, and R. Martin, 188–98. Abingdon, UK: Routledge.

Audretsch, D.B., and M.P. Feldman. 1996. "R&D Spillovers and the Geography of Innovation and Production." *American Economic Review* 86 (3): 630–40.

Avnimelech, G., and M. Teubal. 2008. "Evolutionary Targeting." *Journal of Evolutionary Economics* 18 (2): 151–66. https://doi.org/10.1007 /s00191-007-0080-6.

Aylward, D., and T. Turpin. 2003. "New Wine in Old Bottles: A Case Study of Innovation Territories in 'New World' Wine Production." *International Journal of Innovation Management* 7 (4): 501–25. https://doi.org/10.1142 /S1363919603000891.

Baglieri, D., M.C. Cinici, and V. Mangematin. 2012. "Rejuvenating Clusters with 'Sleeping Anchors': The Case of Nanoclusters." *Technovation* 32: 245–56. https://doi.org/10.1016/j.technovation.2011.09.003.

Bailey, D., M., Bellandi, A. Caloffi, and L. De Propris. 2010. "Place-Renewing Leadership: Trajectories of Change for Mature Manufacturing Regions in Europe." *Policy Studies* 31 (4): 457–74. https://doi.org/10.1080 /01442871003723408.

Baily, M., and N. Montalbano. 2017. "Clusters and Innovation Districts: Lessons from the United States Experience." Economic Studies at Brookings. Washington, D.C.: Brookings Institution. Online at https:// www.brookings.edu/wp-content/uploads/2017/12/es_20171208 _bailyclustersandinnovation.pdf.

Bathelt, H. 2005. "Cluster Relations in the Media Industry: Exploring the 'Distanced Neighbour' Paradox in Leipzig." *Regional Studies* 39: 105–27. https://doi.org/10.1080/0034340052000320860.

Bauer, J.M., A. Lang, and V. Schneider. 2012. *Innovation Policies and Governance in High-Technology Industries: The Complexity of Coordination.* Berlin: Springer.

Baxter, C., and P. Tyler. 2007. "Facilitating Enterprising Places: The Role of Intermediaries in the United States and United Kingdom." In *The Economic Geography of Innovation,* ed. K.R. Polenske, 30–59. New York: Cambridge University Press.

Becattini, G. 1979. "Dal Settore Industriale al Distretto Industriale: Alla Ricerca Dell'unita` D'analisi Dell'economia Industriale, Rivista di Economia e Politica Industriale" [Sectors and/or districts: Some remarks on the conceptual foundations of industrial economics]. In *Small Firms and Industrial Districts in Italy*, ed. E. Goodman, J. Bamford, and P. Saynor, 123–35. London: Routledge.

Bell, M., and M. Albu. 1999. "Knowledge Systems and Technological Dynamism in Industrial Clusters in Developing Countries." *World Development* 27 (9): 1715–33. https://doi.org/10.1016/S0305-750X(99)00073-X.

Belussi, F., and A. Sammarra. 2010. "The International Fragmentation of the Industrial Districts Value Chain between Relocation and Global Integration. In *Business Networks in Clusters and Industrial Districts: The Governance of the Global Value Chain*, ed. F. Belussi and A. Sammarra, 3–24. London: Routledge.

Belussi, F., and S. Sedita. 2010. "The Evolution of the District: 'Reverse Relocation' and the Case of the Leather-Tanning District of Arzignano." *European Review of Industrial Economics and Policy* 1. Online at http://testrevel.unice.fr/erie/index.html/id=3067.

Berg, P.O. 2000. "Dreaming Up a Region? Strategic Management as Invocation." In *Invoking a Transnational Metropolis. The Making of the Øresund Region*, ed. P.O. Berg, A. Linde-Laursen, and O. Löfgren, 55–94. Lund, Sweden: Studentlitteratur.

Berg, S.H. 2015. "Creative Cluster Evolution: The Case of the Film and TV Industries in Seoul, South Korea." *European Planning Studies* 23 (10): 1993–2008. https://doi.org/10.1080/09654313.2014.946645.

Bergman, E.M. 2007. "Cluster Life Cycles: An Emerging Synthesis." In *Handbook of Research on Cluster Theory*, ed. C. Karlsson, 114–32. Cheltenham, UK: Edward Elgar.

Bertolini, L. 2007. "Evolutionary Urban Transportation Planning? An Exploration." In *Applied Evolutionary Economics and Economic Geography*, ed. K. Frenken (ed.) Cheltenham: Edward Elgar, 279–310.

Beugelsdijk, S., and T. Van Schaik. 2005. "Differences in Social Capital between 54 Western European Regions." *Regional Studies* 39 (8): 1053–64. https://doi.org/10.1080/00343400500328040

BioPeople. 2012. "Denmark's Innovation Network for Health & Life Sciences." Online at http://www.biopeople.dk/index.php?id=52&no_cache=1.

BioPeople. 2017. "BioPeople Information." May. Online at https://biopeople.eu/fileadmin/user_upload/Editor/Biopeople_Information_may17.pdf.

BIO (Biotechnology Industry Organization). 2012. "State BioScience Industry Development 2012." Online at http://www.bio.org/sites/default/files/v3battelle-bio_2012_industry_development.pdf.

BIO (Biotechnology Industry Organization. 2013. "About BIO." Online at http://www.bio.org/articles/about-bio.

Birch, K. 2017. *Innovation, Regional Development and the Life Sciences, Beyond Clusters*. New York: Routledge.

Bizikova, L., D. Swanson, S. Tyler, D. Roy, and H.D. Venema. 2018. "Policy Adaptability in Practice." *Policy Design and Practice* 1 (1): 47–62. https://doi .org/10.1080/25741292.2018.1436376.

Blazek, J., and P. Zizalova. 2010. "The Biotechnology Industry in the Prague Metropolitan Region: A Cluster within a Fragmented Innovation System?" *Environment and Planning C: Government and Policy* 28 (5): 887–904. https:// doi.org/10.1068/c09113.

BMS Institute. 2010. "Bridging the Gap from Research to Commercialization." Online at http://www.idg.a-star.edu.sg.

Boekholt, P., and B. Thuriaux. 1999. "Public Policies to Facilitate Clusters. Background, Rationales and Policy Practices in International Perspective." In *Cluster Analysis and Cluster-based Policy Making in OECD Countries*, ed. T. Roelandt and P. den Hertog, 381–413. Paris: Organisation for Economic Co-operation and Development.

Bogomolny, L., C. Gagne, B. Guthrie, and D. Calleja. 2004. "Biotech Nation." *Canadian Business* 77 (19): 19–70.

Borgatti, S.P., and M.G. Everett. 1999. "Models of Core/Periphery Structures." *Social Networks* 21 (4): 375–95. https://doi.org/10.1016/S0378 -8733(99)00019-2

Borrás, S. 2011. "Policy Learning and Organizational Capacities in Innovation Policies." *Science and Public Policy* 38 (9): 725–34. https://doi.org/10.3152 /030234211X13070021633323

Borrás, S., and D. Tsagdis. 2008. *Cluster Policies in Europe: Firms, Institutions and Governance.* Cheltenham, UK: Edward Elgar.

Boschma, R. 2005. "Proximity and Innovation: A Critical Assessment." *Regional Studies* 39 (1): 61–74. https://doi.org/10.1080/0034340052000320887.

Boschma, R. 2014. "Towards an Evolutionary Perspective on Regional Resilience." *Regional Studies* 49 (5): 733–51. https://doi.org/10.1080 /00343404.2014.959481.

Boschma, R., and K. Frenken. 2006. "Why Is Economic Geography not an Evolutionary Science? Towards an Evolutionary Economic Geography." *Journal of Economic Geography* 6 (3): 273–302. https://doi.org/10.1093/jeg/lbi022.

Boschma, R., and K. Frenken. 2011. "The Emerging Empirics of Evolutionary Economic Geography." *Journal of Economic Geography* 11 (2): 295–307. https://doi.org/10.1093/jeg/lbq053.

Boschma, R., and R. Martin, 2010. *Handbook of Evolutionary Economic Geography* Cheltenham, UK: Edward Elgar.

Boschma, R., A. Minondo, and M. Navarro. 2012. "Related Variety and Regional Growth in Spain." *Papers in Regional Science* 91: 241–56. https:// doi.org/10.1111/j.1435-5957.2011.00387.x.

Bosman, J., and M. Davey. 2017. "Illinois lawmakers override budget veto, ending twoy-year stalemate." *New York Times*, 6 July. Online at https://

www.nytimes.com/2017/07/06/us/illinois-budget-shutdown
-states-rauner.html?action=click&contentCollection=U.S.&module
=RelatedCoverage&region=EndOfArticle&pgtype=article&_r=0.

Bosworth, S.J. 2013. "Social Capital and Equilibrium Selection in Stag Hunt Games." *Journal of Economic Psychology* 39 (December): 11–20. https://doi.org/10.1016/j.joep.2013.06.004.

Boynton, A.C., and R.W. Zmud. 1987. "Information Technology Planning in the 1990's: Directions for Practice and Research." *MIS Quarterly* 11 (1): 59–71. https://doi.org/10.2307/248826.

Braun, D. 2008. "Organising the Political Coordination of Knowledge and Innovation Policies." *Science and Public Policy* 35 (4): 227–39. https://doi.org/10.3152/030234208X287056.

Brenner, T. 2004. *Local Industrial Clusters: Existence, Emergence and Evolution.* London: Routledge.

Brenner, T., and C. Schlump. 2011. "Policy Measures and Their Effects in the Different Phases of the Cluster Life Cycle." *Regional Studies* 45 (10): 1363–86. https://doi.org/10.1080/00343404.2010.529116.

Brenner, T., U. Cantner, D. Fornahl, M. Fromhold-Eisebith, and C. Werker. 2011. "Regional Innovation Systems, Clusters and Knowledge Networking." *Papers in Regional Science* 90 (2): 245–9. https://doi.org/10.1111/j.1435-5957.2011.00368.x.

Breschi, S., and F. Lissoni. 2001. "Knowledge Spillovers and Local Innovation Systems: A Critical Survey." *Industrial and Corporate Change* 10 (4): 975–1005. https://doi.org/10.1093/icc/10.4.975.

Bresnahan, T., and A. Gambardella. 2004. "Old-Economy Inputs for New-Economy Outcomes, What Have We Learned?" In *Building High-Tech Clusters: Silicon Valley and Beyond*, ed. T. Bresnahan, and A. Gambardella, 331–58. Cambridge: Cambridge University Press.

British Columbia. 2017a. Ministry of International Trade. "British Columbia Canada, Life Sciences." Vancouver. Online at https://www.britishcolumbia.ca/TradeBCPortal/media/Marketing/bc-lifesciences-mit.pdf.

British Columbia. 2017b. Ministry of Health. "Leading health research with Genome BC." *BC Government News*, 23 March. Online at https://news.gov.bc.ca/releases/2017HLTH0063-000785.

British Columbia. 2020. "Life Sciences in British Columbia: Sector Profile." Online at https://www2.gov.bc.ca/assets/gov/british-columbians-our-governments/initiatives-plans-strategies/technology-industry/lifesciencesinbc_sectorprofile_finalweb.pdf.

Brydon, R., N. Chesterley, B. Dachis, and A. Jacobs. 2014. "Economic Growth and Innovation, Measuring Innovation in Canada: The Tale Told by Patent Applications." *E-brief*, 28 November. Toronto: C.D. Howe Institute. Online at https://www.cdhowe.org/sites/default/files/attachments/research_papers/mixed/e-brief_191.pdf.

Buenstorf, G., and J.P. Murmann. 2005. "Ernst Abbe's Scientific Management: Theoretical Insights from Nineteenth-Century Dynamic Capabilities Approach." Papers on Economics and Evolution 0312.

Burt, R.S. 1992. *Structural Holes: The Social Structure of Competition*. Cambridge, MA: Harvard University Press.

Burt, R.S. 2002. "Bridge Decay." *Social Networks* 24 (4): 333–63. https://doi.org/10.1016/S0378-8733(02)00017-5.

Cantwell, J. 2005. "Innovation and Competitiveness." In *The Oxford Handbook of Innovation*, ed. J. Fagerberg, D. Mowery, and R. Nelson, 543–68. Oxford: Oxford University Press.

Carpinetti, L., and R. Lima. 2013. "Institutions for Collaboration in Industrial Clusters: Proposal of a Performance and Change Management Model." *International Journal of Production Management and Engineering* 1 (1): 13–26. https://doi.org/10.4995/ijpme.2013.1502.

Casper, S. 2007. "How Do Technology Clusters Emerge and Become Sustainable? Social Network Formation and Inter-firm Mobility within the San Diego Biotechnology Cluster." *Research Policy* 36 (4): 438–55. https://doi.org/10.1016/j.respol.2007.02.018.

Cecil, B.P., and M.B. Green. 2000. "In the Flagships' Wake: Relations, Motivations and Observations of Strategic Alliance Activity among IT Sector Flagship Firms and Their Partners." In *Industrial Networks and Proximity*, ed. M.B. Green and R.B. McNaughton, 165-88. Aldershot, UK: Ashgate.

Chapple, K., and B. Lester. 2007. "Emerging Patterns of Regional Resilience." Working Paper 2007-13. Berkeley, CA: University of California, Institute of Urban and Regional Development.

Chesbrough, H. 2003. *Open Innovation: The New Imperative for Creating and Profiting from Technology*. Boston: Harvard Business School Press.

Chia, L. 2017. "Action taken against around 50 firms after failing to give locals a fair chance when recruiting." *Channel News Asia*, March.

Chuan, T.Y. 2016. "Stricter rules of Employment Pass approval." *Straits Times*, 9 April. Online at https://www.straitstimes.com/singapore/stricter-rules-for-employment-pass-approval.

Clegg, S., and C. Hardy. 1996. "Conclusion: Representations." In *Handbook of Organisation Studies*, ed. S. Clegg, C. Hardy, and W.R. Nord, 676–709, London: SAGE.

Coenen, L., J. Moodysson, and B.T. Asheim. 2004. "Nodes, Networks and Proximities: On the Knowledge Dynamics of the Medicon Valley Biotech Cluster." *European Planning Studies* 12 (7): 1003–18. https://doi.org/10.1080/0965431042000267876.

Cohen, W.M., and D.A. Levinthal. 1990. "Absorptive Capacity: A New Perspective on Learning and Innovation." *Administrative Science Quarterly* 35 (1): 128–52. https://doi.org/10.2307/2393553.

Coleman, J. 1990. *Foundations of Social Theory*. Cambridge, MA: Harvard University Press.

Cooke, P. 2002a. "Business Processes in Regional Innovation Systems in the European Union." In Regional Innovation, Knowledge and Global Change, ed. Z. Acs, 53–71. London: Pinter.

Cooke, P. 2002b. *Knowledge Economies*. London: Routledge.

Cooke, P., C., De Laurentis, F. Tödtling, and M. Trippl. 2007. *Regional Knowledge Economies, Markets, Clusters and Innovation*. Cheltenham, UK: Edward Elgar.

Cooke, P., and K. Morgan. 1999. *The Associational Economy: Firms, Regions and Innovation*. Oxford: Oxford University Press.

Cooke, P., M.G. Uranga, and G. Etxebarria. 1997. "Regional Innovation Systems: Institutional and Organisational Dimensions." *Research Policy* 26 (4-5): 475–91. https://doi.org/10.1016/S0048-7333(97)00025-5.

Costa, C., and R. Baptista. 2015. "The Impact of Clusters on Firm Performance in the Growth and Sustainment Stages of the Cluster Lifecycle." DRUID Society. Online at https://conference.druid.dk/acc_papers/2s8hfjboc7yqujcheaje5gj7dffd.pdf.

Council of Canadian Academies. 2013. "Paradox Lost: Explaining Canada's Research Strength and Innovation Weakness." Ottawa. Online at http://www.scienceadvice.ca/uploads/eng/assessments%20and%20publications%20and%20news%20releases/synthesis/paradoxlost_en.pdf.

Crespo, J., R. Suire, and J. Vicente. 2014. "Lock-in or Lock-out? How Structural Properties of Knowledge Networks Affect Regional Resilience." *Journal of Economic Geography* 14 (1): 199–219. https://doi.org/10.1093/jeg/lbt006.

Crespo, J., J. Vicente, and F. Amblard. 2016. "Micro-Behaviours and Structural Properties of Knowledge Networks: Toward a "One Size Fits One" Cluster Policy." *Economics of Innovation and New Technology* 25 (6): 533–52. https://doi.org/10.1080/10438599.2015.1076199.

Dansk Biotek 2012. "The Danish Biotech Industry." Online at http://www.danskbiotek.dk/uk/danish-biotech-industry.

Dasgupta, P. 2000. "Trust as a Commodity." In *Trust: Making and Breaking Cooperative Relations*, ed. D. Gambetta, 49–72. Oxford: Oxford University Press.

Davis, C.H., D. Arthurs, E. Cassidy, and D. Wolfe. 2006. "What Indicators for Cluster Policies in the 21st Century?" Paper prepared for Blue Sky II 2006, Ottawa, September 2006. Online at https://www.oecd.org/sti/inno/37443546.pdf.

Delgado, M., M. Porter, and S. Stern. 2014. "Clusters, Convergence and Economic Performance." *Research Policy* 43 (10): 1785–99. https://doi.org/10.1016/j.respol.2014.05.007.

Deloitte. 2016. "2016 Global Life Sciences Outlook: Moving Forward with Cautious Optimism." Online at https://www2.deloitte.com/content/dam

/Deloitte/global/Documents/Life-Sciences-Health-Care/gx-lshc-2016-life
-sciences-outlook.pdf.

Denmark. 2013. "Strategy for Denmark's Cluster Policy." Copenhagen:
Ministry of Science, Innovation and Higher Education.

Denti, L. 2013. "Measuring Innovation Part 1: Frequently Used Indicators."
*Innovation Management*, 15 February. Online at https://
innovationmanagement.se/2013/02/15/measuring-innovation-part-1
-frequently-used-indicators/.

Dhanaraj, C., and A. Parkhe. 2006." Orchestrating Innovation Networks."
*Academy of Management Review* 31 (3): 656–69. https://doi.org/10.5465
/amr.2006.21318923.

Dohse, D. 2007. "Cluster-based Technology Policy: The German Experience."
*Industry and Innovation* 14 (1): 69–94. https://doi.org/10.1080
/13662710601130848.

Doloreux, D., and S. Dionne. 2008. "Is Regional Innovation System
Development Possible in Peripheral Regions? Some Evidence from the Case
of La Pocatière, Canada." *Entrepreneurship & Regional Development* 20 (3):
259–83. https://doi.org/10.1080/08985620701795525.

Doss, H. 2013. "Trust, Innovation and Ronald Coase." *Forbes*, 3 September.
Online at http://www.forbes.com/sites/henrydoss/2013/09/03/trust
-innovation-andronald-coase/.

Doz, Y.L., and G. Hamel. 1998. *Alliance Advantage: The Art of Creating Value
through Partnering*. Boston: Harvard Business School Press.

Dudek, M. 2013. "Four West Side hospitals back Illinois Medical District
expansion plan." *Chicago Sun-Times*, 23 April.

Dunkel, T. 2004. *Der Einfluß institutioneller Rahmenbedingungen auf die
nationalen Innovationssysteme in Frankreich und Deutschland*. Kassel:
University of Kassel.

Duranton, G. 2011. "California Dreamin': The Feeble Case for Cluster
Policies." *Review of Economic Analysis* 3: 3–45.

Dutton, T. 2018. "An Overview of National AI Strategies." *Politics and AI*, 28
June. Online at https://medium.com/politics-ai/an-overview-of
-national-ai-strategies-2a70ec6edfd.

EDB (Economic Development Board). 2016." Looking Ahead for
Singapore's Biomedical Sciences Sector." Singapore. Online at https://
www.singaporebusiness.com/2016/looking-ahead-for-singapores
-biomedical-sciences-sector.html?utm_source=futurereadysingapore
.com&utm_medium=redirect&utm_campaign=Domain0Tracking.

EDB (Economic Development Board). 2017a. "Healthcare, Background."
Singapore. Online at https://www.edb.gov.sg/content/edb/en/industries
/industries/healthcare.html.

EDB (Economic Development Board. 2017b. "Monthly Manufacturing
Performance." *Media Release*, July. Singapore.

EDB (Economic Development Board. 2019. "Overview of the Singapore PharmBio Sector." Online at https://vcf.mycareersfuture.sg/resources/content/0b87b993ce809dddd521c3088c3c4bcf.pdf.

Edquist, C. 1997. "Systems of Innovation Approaches – Their Emergence and Characteristics." In *Systems of Innovation: Technologies, Institutions and Organizations*, ed. C. Edquist, 1–35. London: Pinter.

Edquist, C. 2005. "Systems of Innovation: Perspectives and Challenges." In *The Oxford Handbook of Innovation*, ed. J. Fagerberg, D. Mowery, and R. Nelson, 181–209. Oxford: Oxford University Press.

Edquist, C., L. Hommen, and L. Tsipouri. 2000. *Public Technology Procurement and Innovation*. Dordrecht: Kluwer Academic.

El-Taliawi, O.G., and Z. Van der Wal. 2019. "Developing Administrative Capacity: An Agenda for Research and Practice." *Policy Design and Practice* 2 (3): 243–57. https://doi.org/10.1080/25741292.2019.1595916.

Enright, M.J. 2003. "Regional Clusters: What We Know and What We Should Know." In *Innovation Clusters and Interregional Competition*, ed. J. Bröcker, D. Dohse, and R. Soltwedel, 99–129. Berlin: Springer.

Enright, M.J., and the Competitiveness Institute. 2000. "Survey on the Characterization of Regional Clusters, Initial Results." Working Paper 19. Hong Kong: University of Hong Kong, Institute of Economic Policy and Business Strategy. Online at https://www.researchgate.net/publication/228599616_Survey_on_the_characterization_of_regional_clusters_initial_results.

Environmental Working Group. 2012. "Corn subsidies in the United States totaled $81.7 billion from 1995–2011." Online at https://farm.ewg.org/progdetail.php?fips=00000&progcode=corn.

Ernst & Young. 2011. *Beyond Borders, Global Biotechnology Report*. Online at https://www.scribd.com/document/62971873/Beyond-Borders-Global-Biotechnology-Report-2011.

ESCA (European Secretariat for Cluster Analysis). 2017. "European Secretariat for Cluster Analysis and Regional Development." Online at https://www.cluster-analysis.org/.

Estrin, S., J. Korosteleva, and T. Mickiewicz. 2014. "Entrepreneurial Growth Aspirations, Innovation Propensity and National Knowledge Intensity: Unveiling the Complexity of the Relationship, using GEM Data." GRINCOH Working Paper 3.08.2. Online at http://www.grincoh.eu/media/serie_3_knowledge__innovation__technolog/grincoh_wp_3.08.2_estrin-korosteleva-mickiewicz.pdf.

Etzkowitz, H. 2003. "Innovation in Innovation: The Triple Helix of University-Industry-Government Relations." *Social Science Information* 42: 293–337. https://doi.org/10.1177/05390184030423002.

Etzkowitz, H., and L. Leydesdorff. 2000. "The Dynamics of Innovation: From National Systems and "Mode 2" to a Triple Helix of University-Industry -Government Relations." *Research Policy* 29 (2): 109–23. https://doi.org /10.1016/S0048-7333(99)00055-4.

European Cluster Observatory. 2016. "European Cluster Panorama 2016." Online at http://ec.europa.eu/DocsRoom/documents/20381.

European Commission. 2002. "Regional Clusters in Europe." *Observatory of European SMEs* 2002 (3). Online at http://ec.europa.eu/regional_policy /archive/innovation/pdf/library/regional_clusters.pdf.

European Commission. 2016. "Smart Guide to Cluster Policy." Online at https://www.cluster-analysis.org/downloads/smart-guide-to -cluster-policy.

European Commission. 2017a. "European Innovation Scoreboard 2017." Online at https://www.rvo.nl/sites/default/files/2017/06/European _Innovation_Scoreboard_2017.pdf.

European Commission. 2017b. "Regional Innovation Scoreboard 2017." Online at http://ec.europa.eu/docsroom/documents/23881.

European Commission. 2018. "S3 Cluster Organizations, Smart Specialization Platform." Online at https://s3platform.jrc.ec.europa.eu/cluster-organisations.

Fai, L.K., and X. Kek. 2016. "Government commits S$19b to new 5-year plan for R&D initiatives RIE2020." *Channel News Asia*, 8 January. Online at https://declara.com/collection/ff1f5393-d76d-40bc-8b32-11d5fda23307 /post/adced0d7-bdf8-4a16-8e2e-7c95a7ab4e61.

Feldman, M.P., and R. Florida. 1994. "The Geographic Sources of Innovation: Technological Infrastructure and Product Innovation in the United States." *Annals of the Association of American Geographers* 84 (2): 210–29. https://doi .org/10.1111/j.1467-8306.1994.tb01735.x.

Feldman, M.P., and J.L. Francis. 2004. "Homegrown Solutions: Fostering Cluster Formation." *Economic Development Quarterly* 18 (2): 127–37. https:// doi.org/10.1177/0891242403262556.

Feldman, M.P., and S. Tavassoli. 2014. "Something New: Where Do New Industries Come from?" CITR Electronic Working Paper Series 2014/2. Center for Innovation and Technology Research. Online at https://www .bth.se/wp-content/uploads/2018/02/14_WP-2014_2_FeldmanTavassoli_1 .pdf.

Ffowcs-Williams, I. 2005. "Cluster Development: The How, Five Phases, Twelve Steps." Presentation to TCI Annual Conference, Hong Kong.

Filieri, R., R. McNally, M. O'Dwyer, and L. O'Mallet. 2014. "Structural Social Capital Evolution and Knowledge Transfer: Evidence from an Irish Pharmaceutical Network." *Industrial Marketing Management* 43 (3): 429–40. https://doi.org/10.1016/j.indmarman.2013.12.011.

Finegold, D., P.-K. Wong, and T.-C. Cheah. 2004. "Adapting a Foreign Direct Investment Strategy to the Knowledge Economy: The Case of Singapore's Emerging Biotechnology Cluster." *European Planning Studies* 12 (7): 921–41. https://doi.org/10.1080/0965431042000267830.

Fischer, M.M., T. Scherngell, and E. Jansenberger. 2006. "The Geography of Knowledge Spillovers between High Technology Firms in Europe: Evidence from a Spatial Interaction Modeling Perspective." *Geographical Analysis* 38 (3): 288–309. https://doi.org/10.1111/j.1538-4632.2006.00687.x.

Flanagan, K., E. Uyarra, and M. Laranja. 2011. "Reconceptualising the 'Policy Mix' for Innovation." *Research Policy* 40 (5): 702–13. https://doi.org/10.1016/j.respol.2011.02.005.

Florida, R. 1995. "Toward the Learning Region." *Futures* 27 (5): 527–36. https://doi.org/10.1016/0016-3287(95)00021-N.

Florida, R. 2005. *Cities and the Creative Class*. Oxford: Routledge.

Florida, R. 2017. "Venture capital remains highly concentrated in just a few cities." *Bloomberg CityLab*, 3 October. Online at https://www.bloomberg.com/news/articles/2017-10-03/the-geographic-concentration-of-venture-capital.

Foley, M.W., and B. Edwards. 1999. "Is It Time to Disinvest in Social Capital?" *Journal of Public Policy* 19 (2): 141–73. https://doi.org/10.1017/S0143814X99000215.

Fornahl, D., R. Hassink, and M.-P. Menzel. 2015. "Broadening Our Knowledge on Cluster Evolution." *European Planning Studies* 23 (10): 1921-31. https://doi.org/10.1080/09654313.2015.1016654.

Fornahl, D., S. Henn, and M.P. Menzel, eds. 2009. *The Emergence of Clusters. Theoretical, Empirical and Political Perspectives on the Initial Stage of Cluster Evolution*. Cheltenham, UK: Edward Elgar.

Frenken, K., E. Cefis, and E. Stam. 2013. "Industrial Dynamics and Economic Geography: A Survey." Discussion paper. Tjalling C. Koopmans Research Institute, Utrecht School of Economics.

Frenken, K., F.G. van Oort, and T. Verburg. 2007. "Related Variety, Unrelated Variety and Regional Economic Growth." *Regional Studies* 41 (5): 685–97. https://doi.org/10.1080/00343400601120296.

Genome British Columbia. 2015. *Strategic Plan 2015-2020: Powering BC's Bioeconomy*. Vancouver. April. Online at https://www.genomebc.ca/wp-content/uploads/2017/10/GBC_StrategicPlan_2015-2020.pdf.

Genome British Columbia. 2017a. "Industry Innovation Program (I²)." Online at https://www.genomebc.ca/funding-opportunity/industry-innovation-program/.

Genome British Columbia. 2017b. "Who We Are." Online at https://www.genomebc.ca/about/who-we-are/.

Gerolamo, M.C., L.C.R., Carpinetti, G. Seliger, and E.V.C. Galdamez. 2008. "Performance Management of Regional Clusters and SME Cooperation

Networks." *International Journal of Business Excellence* 1 (4): 457–83. https://doi.org/10.1504/IJBEX.2008.018844.

Gertler, M.S., and U. Quach. 2005. "Biomedical Innovation Systems: A Comparative Analysis of Six Canadian Regions." PowerPoint Presentation. Toronto: University of Toronto, Munk Centre for International Studies. Online at https://www.powershow.com/view1/1fcad9-ZDc1Z/Biomedical _Innovation_Systems_A_Comparative_Analysis_of_Six_Canadian_Regions _powerpoint_ppt_presentation?varnishcache=1.

Giest, S. 2015. "Network Capacity-Building in High-Tech Sectors: Opening the Black Box of Cluster Facilitation Policy." *Public Administration* 93 (2): 471–89. https://doi.org/10.1111/padm.12131.

Giest, S. 2016. "The Challenges of Enhancing Collaboration in Life Science Clusters: Lessons from Chicago, Copenhagen and Singapore." *Science and Public Policy* 44 (2): 163–73. https://doi.org/10.1093/scipol/scw046.

Giest, S. 2017. "Overcoming the Failure of 'Silicon Somewheres': Collective Learning in Innovation Networks." *Policy and Politics* 45 (1): 39–54. https://doi.org/10.1332/030557316X14779412013740.

Giest, S. 2019. "Trust Dynamics in Innovation Networks: The Chicago Life Science Cluster." *Administration & Society* 51 (2): 325–43. https://doi.org/10.1177/0095399717701522.

Giuliani, E. 2005. "Absorptive Capacity: Why Do Some Clusters Forge Ahead and Others Lag Behind?" *European Urban and Regional Studies* 12 (3): 269–88. https://doi.org/10.1177/0969776405056593.

Giuliani, E., and M. Bell. 2005. "The Micro-determinants of Meso-level Learning and Innovation: Evidence from a Chilean Wine Cluster." *Research Policy* 34 (1): 47–68. https://doi.org/10.1016/j.respol.2004.10.008.

Glaeser, E.L., S.S. Rosenthal, and W.C. Strange. 2010. "Urban Economics and Entrepreneurship." *Journal of Urban Economics* 67 (1): 1–14. https://doi.org/10.1016/j.jue.2009.10.005.

Glouberman, S., P., Campsie, M. Gemar, and G. Miller. 2003. "A Toolbox for Improving Health in Cities." Ottawa: Caledon Institute for Social Policy.

Glückler, J., and P. Doreian. 2016. "Editorial: Social Network Analysis and Economic Geography – Positional, Evolutionary and Multi-level Approaches." *Journal of Economic Geography* 16 (6): 1123–34. https://doi.org/10.1093/jeg/lbw041.

Godin, B. 2006. "The Knowledge-based Economy: Conceptual Framework or Buzzword?" *Journal of Technology Transfer* 31: 17–30. https://doi.org/10.1007/s10961-005-5010-x.

Goduscheit, R. 2014. "Innovation Promoters – A Multiple Case Study." *Industrial Marketing Management* 43 (3): 525–34. https://doi.org/10.1016/j.indmarman.2013.12.020.

Gordon, I.R., and P. McCann. 2000. "Industrial Clusters: Complexes, Agglomeration and/or Social Networks?" *Urban Studies* 37 (3): 513–32. https://doi.org/10.1080/0042098002096.

Graham, M. 2016. "Illinois to invest $220M in venture funds focused on tech startups." *Chicago Tribune*, 26 January. Online at https://www.chicagotribune.com/business/blue-sky/ct-frerichs-tech-venture-funds-bsi-20160126-story.html.

Granovetter, M. 1985. "Economic Action and Social Structure: The Problem of Embeddedness." *American Journal of Sociology* 91 (3): 481–510. https://doi.org/10.1086/228311.

Grillitsch, M., and B. Asheim. 2015. "Cluster Policy: Renewal through the Integration of Institutional Variety." Papers in Innovation Studies 2015/21. Lund, Sweden: Lund University, Center for Innovation, Research and Competences in the Learning Economy.

Gulati, R. 1995. "Does Familiarity Breed Trust? The Implications of Repeated Ties for Contractual Choices in Alliances." *Academy of Management Journal* 38 (1): 85–112. https://doi.org/10.5465/256729.

Guy, S. 2013. "An audacious expansion is coming to the Illinois Medical District." *Chicago Grid*, 25 May. Online at http://www.suffredin.org/news/newsitem.asp?language=english&newsitemid=5815.

Halkier, H. 2011. "Regional Policy in Transition – A Multi-level Governance Perspective on the Case of Denmark." *European Planning Studies* 9 (3): 323–38. https://doi.org/10.1080/09654310120037603.

Hansen, P.A., and G. Serin. 2008. "The Interaction between Public Science and Industry and the Role of the Øresund Science Region's Platform Organisation." In *Innovation and the Creative Process: Towards Innovation with Care*, ed. L. Fuglsang, 169–92. Cheltenham, UK: Edward Elgar.

Hardin, R. 2002. *Trust and Trustworthiness*. New York: Russell Sage.

Harvey, C.J., K.K. Bartz, J.R. Davies, T.B. Francis, T.P. Good, A.D. Guerry, M.B. Hanson, et al. 2010. "A Mass-Balance Model for Evaluating Food Web Structure and Community-Scale Indicators in the Central Basin of Puget Sound." NOAA Technical Memorandum NMFS-NWFSC-106. United States, Department of Commerce, National Oceanic and Atmospheric Administration. Online at https://www.webapps.nwfsc.noaa.gov/assets/25/1335_08042010_120050_MassBalanceModelTM106WebFinal.pdf.

Hassink, R. 2009. "Locked in Decline? On the Role of Regional Lock-ins in Old Industrial Areas." In *The Handbook of Evolutionary Economic Geography*, ed. R. Boschma and R. Martin, 450–70. Cheltenham, UK: Edward Elgar.

Hassink, R. 2010. "Regional Resilience: A Promising Concept to Explain Differences in Regional Economic Adaptability?" *Cambridge Journal of Regions, Economy and Society* 3 (1): 45–58. https://doi.org/10.1093/cjres/rsp033.

Hassink, R., and C. Klaerding. 2010. "Evolutionary Approaches to Local and Regional Development Policy." In *Handbook of Local and Regional Development*, ed. A. Pike, A. Rodrıguez-Pose, and J. Tomaney, 139–48. London: Routledge.

Heinemann, J.A., M. Massaro, D.S. Coray, S.Z. Agapito-Tenfen, and J.D. Wen. 2014. "Sustainability and Innovation in Staple Crop Production in the US Midwest." *International Journal of Agricultural Sustainability* 12 (1): 71–88. https://doi.org/10.1080/14735903.2013.806408.

Hira, A., M. Howlett, A. Bwenge, and S. Giest. 2013. "Explaining the Success of Clusters: A Framework for the Study of Global Wine Industry Dynamics." In *What Makes Clusters Competitive? Cases from the Global Wine Industry*, ed. A. Hira, 3–56. Montreal; Kingston, ON: McGill-Queen's University Press.

Holbrook, J.A., M., Salazar, N., Crowden, S., Reibling, K. Warfield, and N. Weiner. 2003. "The Biotechnology Cluster in Vancouver." Vancouver: Simon Fraser University, Centre for Policy Research on Science and Technology. Online at http://blogs.sfu.ca/departments/cprost/wp-content/uploads/2012/06/0306.pdf.

Holling, C.S. 1978. *Adaptive Environmental Assessment and Management*. New York: John Wiley.

Hon, D. 2008. "QT Inc: A Place Called Hope." *BC Business*, September 2008. Online at https://www.bcbusiness.ca/qlt-inc-a-place-called-hope.

Hospers, G.-J., P. Desrochers, and F. Sautet. 2009. "The Next Silicon Valley? On the Relationship between Geographical Clustering and Public Policy." *International Entrepreneurship and Management Journal* 5: 285–99. https://doi.org/10.1007/s11365-008-0080-5.

Howlett, M. 2009. "Policy Analytical Capacity and Evidence-based Policymaking: Lessons from Canada." *Canadian Public Administration* 52 (2): 153–75. https://doi.org/10.1111/j.1754-7121.2009.00070_1.x.

Howlett, M. 2011. *Designing Public Policies: Principles and Instruments*. London: Routledge.

Huggins R., A. Johnston, and P. Thompson. 2012. "Network Capital, Social Capital and Knowledge Flow: How the Nature of Inter-organizational Networks Impacts on Innovation." *Industry and Innovation* 19 (3): 203–32. https://doi.org/10.1080/13662716.2012.669615.

Hughes, M., R.E. Morgan, R.D. Ireland, and P. Hughes. 2014. "Social Capital and Learning Advantages: A Problem of Absorptive Capacity." *Strategic Entrepreneurship Journal* 8 (3): 214–33. https://doi.org/10.1002/sej.1162.

Ibata-Arens, K. 2003. "Review Article: The Comparative Political Economy of Innovation." *Review of International Political Economy* 10 (1): 147–65. https://doi.org/10.1080/0969229032000048862.

iBIO (Illinois Biotechnology Industry Organization). 2013. "What We Do." Online at http://www.ibio.org/ABOUT/what-we-do.html.

Illinois. 2013. Department of Commerce and Economic Development. "Invest Illinois Venture Fund." Online at http://www.illinoisbiz.biz/dceo/Bureaus/Advantage+Illinois/Invest+Illinois+Venture+Fund.

Illinois Innovation Network. 2013. "Governor Quinn announces Illinois a national leader in biotechnology employment and economic impact." Press release, 22 April. Online at http://www.illinoisinnovation.com/2013/04/4242013-governor-quinn-announces-uic-health-technology-research-hub/.

Illinois Innovation Network. 2017. "About the Network." Online at https://www.illinoisinnovation.com/about-the-network.

IMDC (Illinois Medical District Commission). 2013. "Welcome." Online at http://www.imdc.org/about/welcome.

Innes, J.E., and D.E. Booher. 2007. "Consensus Building and Complex Adaptive Systems: A Framework for Evaluating Collaborative Planning." *Journal of the American Planning Association* 65 (4): 412–23. https://doi.org/10.1080/01944369908976071.

IRIS Group. 2009. "Towards a Strong Biotech Cluster in the Copenhagen Region: An Analysis of the Key Success Factors for Internationally Leading Biotech Regions." Online at http://www.danskbiotek.dk/sites/default/files/nyhedsbreve/Towards_a_strong_biotech_cluster.pdf.

Isaksen, A., and M. Trippl. 2016. "Path Development in Different Regional Innovation Systems: A Conceptual Analysis." In *Innovation Drivers and Regional Innovation Strategies*, ed. M. Parilli, D. Fitjar, and A. Rodriguez-Pose, 66–84. London: Routledge.

ISTP (Illinois Science and Technology Park). 2013. "The Science Park." Online at http://www.scienceparkillinois.com/science-park.

James, C. 2010. "Global Status of Commercialized Biotech/GM Crops: 2010." ISAAA Brief 42-2010. International Service for the Acquisition of Agri-biotech Applications.

Jenkins, T., B. Dahlby, A. Gupta, M. Leroux, D. Naylor, and N. Robinson. 2011. "Innovation Canada: A Call to Action." Online at http://rd-review.ca/eic/site/033.nsf/vwapj/R-D_InnovationCanada_Final-eng.pdf/$FILE/R-D_InnovationCanada_Final-eng.pdf.

Jensen, O.B., and T. Richardson. 2004. "Constructing a Transnational Mobility Region: On the Øresund Region and Its Role in the New European Union Spatial Policy." In *The Nordic Regions and the European Union*, ed. S. Dosenrode and H. Halkier, 139–58. Aldershot, UK: Ashgate.

JETRO (Japan External Trade Organization). 2003. "Report: The US Midwest Biotechnology Industry." Tokyo. March. Online at https://www.jetro.go.jp/ext_images/jfile/report/05000628/05000628_003_BUP_0.pdf.

Jones Lang LaSalle. 2014. "Life Sciences Cluster Report." Online at http://lifescience.pl/wp-content/uploads/2015/04/2014-global-life-sciences-report-JLL.pdf.

Jothen, K.A. 2017. *Human Capital Policy and Practice in British Columbia: Growing the Province's Economy and Potential through Talent*. [Vancouver]: Business Council of British Columbia. Online at https://bcbc.com /dist/assets/publications/human-capital-policy-and-practice-in-british -columbia-growing-the-provinces-economy-potential-through-talent /Human-Capital-Policy-and-Practice-in-BC.pdf.

Jung, D., A. Wu, and C.W. Chow. 2008. "Towards Understanding the Direct and Indirect Effects of CEOs' Transformational Leadership on Firm Innovation." *Leadership Quarterly* 19 (5): 582–94. https://doi.org/10.1016 /j.leaqua.2008.07.007.

Karlsen, J., A. Isaksen, and O. Spilling. 2011. "The Challenge of Constructing Regional Advantages in Peripheral Areas: The Case of Marine Biotechnology in Tromsø, Norway." *Entrepreneurship and Regional Development* 23 (3-4): 235–57. https://doi.org/10.1080/08985620903233945.

Kenney, M., and D. Patton. 2006. "The Coevolution of Technologies and Institutions: Silicon Valley as the Iconic High-Technology Cluster." In *Cluster Genesis*, ed. P. Braunerhjelm and M.P. Feldman, 38–60. Oxford: Oxford University Press.

Kenney, M., and U. von Burg. 1999. "Technology and Path Dependence: The Divergence between Silicon Valley and Route 128." *Industrial and Corporate Change* 8 (1): 67–103. https://doi.org/10.1093/icc/8.1.67.

Ketels, C. 2003. "The Development of the Cluster Concept – Present Experiences and Further Developments." Presentation to NRW conference on clusters, Duisburg, Germany, 5 December. Online at https://www .researchgate.net/publication/268059813_The_Development_of_the _cluster_concept-Present_experiences_and_further_developments.

Ketels, C. 2013. "Recent Research on Competitiveness and Clusters: What Are the Implications for Regional Policy?" *Cambridge Journal of Regions, Economy and Society* 6 (2): 269–84. https://doi.org/10.1093/cjres/rst008.

Klepper, S. 1997. "Industry Life Cycles." *Industrial and Corporate Change* 6 (1): 145–81. https://doi.org/10.1093/icc/6.1.145.

Klepper, S. 2007. "Disagreements, Spinoffs and the Evolution of Detroit as the Capital of the US Automobile Industry." *Management Science* 53 (4): 616–31. https://doi.org/10.1287/mnsc.1060.0683.

Klijn, E.-H., V. Sierra, T. Tsa, E. Berman, J. Edelenbos, and D.Y. Chen. 2016. "The Influence of Trust on Network Performance in Taiwan, Spain and the Netherlands: A Cross-Country Comparison." *International Public Management Journal* 19 (1): 111–39. https://doi.org/10.1080/10967494.2015 .1115790.

Kotsemir, M.N., and D. Meissner. 2016. "Conceptualizing the Innovation Process towards the 'Active Innovation Paradigm' – Trends and Outlook." *Journal of Innovation and Entrepreneurship* 5 (14): 1–18. https://doi.org /10.1186/s13731-016-0042-z.

KPMG. 2016. *British Columbia Technology Report Card: Scaling Up BC's Tech Ecosystem.* Available at: https://assets.kpmg.com/content/dam/kpmg/ca/pdf/2016/10/BC-tech-report-card-FY16.pdf.

Kuemmerle, W. 1996. "Home Base and Foreign Direct Investment in Research and Development: An Investigation into the International Allocation of Research Activity by Multinational Enterprises. Thesis (D.B.A.), Harvard University, Graduate School of Business Administration.

Kumar, S., and S. Siddique. 2010. *The Singapore Success Story: Public-Private Alliance for Investment Attraction, Innovation and Export Development.* Santiago, Chile: United Nations, ECLAC, Division of International Trade and Integration.

Lai, A.Y. 2011. "Organizational Collaborative Capacities in Disaster Management: Evidence from the Taiwan Red Cross Organization." *Asian Journal of Social Science* 39 (4): 446–68. https://doi.org/10.1163/156853111X597279.

Lane, P.J., B.R. Koka, and S. Pathak. 2006. "The Reification of Absorptive Capacity: A Critical Review and Rejuvenation of the Construct." *Academy of Management Review* 31 (4): 833–63. https://doi.org/10.5465/amr.2006.22527456.

Lee, B. 2012. "Driving innovation in Singapore." *Straits Times*, 3 March.

Lee, K. 1993. *Compass and Gyroscope: Integrating Science and Politics for the Environment.* Washington, DC: Island Press.

Leifer, R., and A. Delbecq. 1976. "Organizational/Environmental Interchange: A Model of Boundary Spanning Activity." *Academy of Management Review* 3 (1): 40–50.

Lerner, J. 2009. *Boulevard of Broken Dreams: Why Public Efforts to Boost Entrepreneurship and Venture Capital Have Failed – and What to Do about It.* Kauffman Foundation Series on Innovation and Entrepreneurship, Princeton, NJ: Princeton University Press.

Leydesdorff, L., and H. Etzkowitz. 1998. "The Triple Helix as a Model for Innovation Studies." *Science and Public Policy* 25 (3): 195–203. https://doi.org/10.1093/spp/25.3.195.

Leydesdorff, L., and M. Meyer. 2006. "Triple Helix Indicators of Knowledge-Based Innovation Systems." *Research Policy* 35 (10): 1441–9. https://doi.org/10.1016/j.respol.2006.09.016.

Liao, S., W. Fei, and C. Chen. 2007. "Knowledge Sharing, Absorptive Capacity, and Innovation Capability: An Empirical Study of Taiwan's Knowledge-Intensive Industries." *Journal of Information Science* 33 (3): 340–59. https://doi.org/10.1177/0165551506070739.

LifeSciences BC. 2007. "Submission to the British Columbia Conversation on Health, Open Letter from the Chair of Life Sciences British Columbia."

Online at http://www.lifesciencesbc.ca/files/PDF/LSBC_COH
_Submission_Sept_27_2007_Final.pdf.

LifeSciences BC. 2015. "The Life Sciences Sector in BC: Economic Impact Now
and in the Future." Vancouver. Online at http://www.lifesciencesbc.ca
/wp-content/uploads/2015/06/LifeSciences-BC-Sector-Report-2015.pdf.

LifeSciences BC. 2017a. "LifeSciences BC Members by Sector." Online at
http://lifesciencesbc.ca/membership/lifesciences-bc-members-by-sector.

LifeSciences BC. 2017b. "LifeSciences BC Policies." Online at http://
lifesciencesbc.ca/advocacy/lifesciences-bc-policies/.

Lin, S. 2008. "Illinois looks to attract more biotechnology and pharmaceutical
businesses." *Medill Reports*, 5 June. Online at http://news.medill
.northwestern.edu/chicago/news.aspx?id=92909.

Lindqvist, G., C. Ketels, and Ö. Sölvell. 2013. *The Cluster Initiative Greenbook
2.0*. Stockholm: Ivory Tower.

List, F. 1841. *The National System of Political Economy*. London: Longmans,
Green.

Lundvall, B.-Å. 1992. *National Systems of Innovation: Towards a Theory of
Innovation and Interactive Learning*. London: Pinter.

Lundvall, B.-Å. 2001. *Innovation, Growth and Social Cohesion: The Danish Model*.
Cheltenham, UK: Edward Elgar.

Lundvall, B.-Å., and J.L. Christensen. 2003. "Broadening the Analysis of
Innovation Systems: Competition, Organisational Change and Employment
Dynamics in the Danish System." In *Innovation, Competence Building and
Social Cohesion in Europe: Towards a Learning Society*, ed. P. Conceição, M.V.
Heitor, and B.-Å. Lundvall, 144–79. Cheltenham: Edward Elgar.

Lundvall, B.-Å., B. Johnson, E. Andersen, and B. Dalum. 2003. "National
Systems of Production, Innovation and Competence-Building." *Research
Policy* 31 (2): 213–31. https://doi.org/10.1016/S0048-7333(01)00137-8.

Lybecker, K. 2012. "Canada needs to improve intellectual property rights."
*Waterloo Region Record*, 9 March. Online at http://www.therecord.com
/opinion-story/2597876-canada-needs-to-improve-intellectual-property
-rights.

MacKinnon, D., A. Cumbers, A. Pike, K. Birch, and R. McMaster. 2009.
"Evolution in Economic Geography: Institutions, Political Economy, and
Adaptation." *Economy Geography* 85 (2): 129–50. https://doi.org/10.1111
/j.1944-8287.2009.01017.x.

Maier, G., B. Kurka, and M. Trippl. 2007. "Knowledge Spillover Agents and
Regional Development: Spatial Distribution and Mobility of Star Scientists."
Dynamic Regions in a Knowledge-Driven Global Economy Lessons and
Policy Implications for the EU (DYNREG), Working Papers. Dublin:
Economic and Social Research Institute.

Majocchi, A., and M. Presutti. 2009. "Industrial Clusters, Entrepreneurial Culture and the Social Environment: The Effects on FDI Distribution." *International Business Review* 18 (1): 76–88. https://doi.org/10.1016/j.ibusrev.2008.12.001.

Malecki, E.J. 1994. "Entrepreneurship in Regional and Local Development." *International Regional Science Review* 16 (1-2): 119–53. https://doi.org/10.1177/016001769401600107.

Malmberg, A., and P. Maskell. 2002. "The Elusive Concept of Localization Economies: Towards a Knowledge-Based Theory of Spatial Clustering." *Environment and Planning A: Economy and Space* 34 (3): 429–49. https://doi.org/10.1068/a3457.

Marshall, A. 1890. *Principles of Economics*. London: Macmillan.

Martin, B. 2012. "The Evolution of Science Policy and Innovation Studies." *Research Policy* 41 (7): 1219–39. https://doi.org/10.1016/j.respol.2012.03.012.

Martin, H., and L. Coenen. 2015. "Institutional Context and Cluster Emergence: The Biogas Industry in Southern Sweden." *European Planning Studies* 23 (10): 2009–27. https://doi.org/10.1080/09654313.2014.960181.

Martin, R., and P. Sunley. 2003. "Deconstructing Clusters: Chaotic Concept or Policy Panacea?" *Journal of Economic Geography* 3 (1): 5–35. https://doi.org/10.1093/jeg/3.1.5.

Martin, R., and P. Sunley. 2006. "Path Dependence and Regional Economic Evolution." *Journal of Economic Geography* 64 (4): 395–437. https://doi.org/10.1093/jeg/lbl012.

Martin, R., and P. Sunley. 2011. "Conceptualizing Cluster Evolution: Beyond the Life Cycle Model?" *Regional Studies* 45 (10): 1299–318. https://doi.org/10.1080/00343404.2011.622263.

Martin, R., and M. Trippl. 2014. "System Failures, Knowledge Bases and Regional Innovation Policies." *disP - The Planning Review* 50 (1): 24–32. https://doi.org/10.1080/02513625.2014.926722.

Maskell, P. 2004. "Learning in the Village Economy of Denmark: The Role of Institutions and Policy in Sustaining Competitiveness." In *Regional Innovation Systems: The Role of Governance in a Globalized World*, ed. P. Cooke, M. Heidenreich, and H.-J. Braczyk, 154–86. London: Routledge,.

Maskell, P., and A. Malmberg. 1998. "Explaining the Location of Economic Activity: Ubiquitification." Presented at the Association of American Geographers Annual Meeting, Boston, March.

Maskell, P., and A. Malmberg. 1999. "Localised Learning and Industrial Competitiveness." *Cambridge Journal of Economics* 23 (2): 167–85. https://doi.org/10.1093/cje/23.2.167.

Maskell, P., and A. Malmberg. 2007. "Myopia, Knowledge Development and Cluster Evolution." *Journal of Economic Geography* 7 (5): 603–18. https://doi.org/10.1093/jeg/lbm020.

Mayntz, R. 1983. *Implementation Politischer Programme II: Ansätze zur Theoriebildung*. Opladen, Germany: Westdeutscher Verlag.

McEvily, B., V. Perrone, and A. Zaheer. 2003. "Trust as an Organizing Principle." *Organization Science* 14 (1): 91–103. https://doi.org/10.1287/orsc.14.1.91.12814.

McEvily, B., and A. Zaheer. 2004. "Architects of Trust: The Role of Network Facilitators in Geographical Clusters." In *Trust and Distrust in Organizations: Dilemmas and Approaches*, ed. R. Kramer and K. Cook, 189–213. New York: Russell Sage Foundation,.

Medrisch, P. 2008. "Singapore Pharma Report." Focus Reports.

Menzel, M.-P., and D. Fornahl. 2010. "Cluster Life Cycles: Dimensions and Rationales of Cluster Evolution." *Industrial and Corporate Change* 19 (1): 205–38. https://doi.org/10.1093/icc/dtp036.

Mesquita, L.F. 2007. "Starting Over When the Bickering Never Ends: Rebuilding Aggregate Trust among Clustered Firms through Trust Facilitators." *Academy of Management Review* 32 (1): 72–91. https://doi.org/10.5465/amr.2007.23463711.

Mirowski, P. 2012. "The Modern Commercialization of Science Is a Passel of Ponzi Schemes." *Social Epistemology* 26 (3-4): 285–310. https://doi.org/10.1080/02691728.2012.697210.

Moodysson, J., L. Coenen, and B.T. Asheim. 2010. "Two Sides of the Same Coin? Local and Global Knowledge Flows in Medicon Valley." In *Business Networks in Clusters and Industrial Districts: The Governance of the Global Value Chain*, ed. F. Belussi and A. Sammarra, 356–77. London: Routledge.

Moore, G., and K. Davis. 2004. "Learning the Silicon Valley Way." In *Building High-Tech Clusters, Silicon Valley and Beyond*, ed. T. Bresnahan and A. Gambardella, 7–40. Cambridge: Cambridge University Press.

Morgan, K. 1997. "The Learning Region: Institutions, Innovation and Regional Renewal." *Regional Studies* 31 (5): 491–503. https://doi.org/10.1080/00343409750132289.

Mroczkowski, T. 2012. *The New Players in Life Science Innovation: Best Practices in R&D from Around the World*. Upper Saddle River, NJ: FT Press.

Murphy, L., R. Huggins, and P. Thompson. 2016. "Social Capital and Innovation: A Comparative Analysis of Regional Policies." *Environment and Planning: Government and Policy C* 34 (6): 1025–57. https://doi.org/10.1177/0263774X15597448.

MVA (Medicon Valley Alliance). 2011. "Beacon Initiative." Online at http://www.mva.org/system/files/public/2%20-%20PROJECTS%20%2526%20INITIATIVES/Beacons/Beacon%20Initiative_jan2013.pdf.

MVA (Medicon Valley Alliance). 2012. "The Life Science Ambassador Program." Online at https://ec.europa.eu/research/iscp/pdf/brussels-2012/dk_ambassadors_programme.pdf.

MVA (Medicon Valley Alliance). 2016. "State of Medicon Valley 2016: An Analysis of Life Science in Greater Copenhagen." Online at http://mva .org/wp-content/uploads/2015/02/State_of_Medicon_Valley_2016_the _full_report_20161107.pdf.

MVA (Medicon Valley Alliance). 2017. "Frequently Asked Questions." Online at http://mva.org/about-mva/frequently-asked-questions/.

Nahapiet, J., and S. Ghoshal. 1998. "Social Capital, Intellectual Capital, and the Organizational Advantage." *Academy of Management Review* 23 (2): 242–66. https://doi.org/10.2307/259373.

Nallari, R., and B. Griffith. 2013. *Clusters of Competitiveness*. Washington, DC: World Bank.

Narula, R. 2004. "Understanding Absorptive Capacities in an 'Innovation Systems' Context: Consequences for Economic and Employment Growth." Danish Research Unit for Industrial Dynamics (DRUID) Working Paper 04-02. Copenhagen Business School and University of Oslo.

Nauwelaers, C. 2001. "Path-Dependency and the Role of Institutions in Cluster Policy Generation." In *Cluster Policies – Cluster Development?* ed. Å. Mariussen, 93–107. Stockholm: Nordregio.

Nauwelaers, C., and R. Wintjes. 2008. "Conclusions and Perspectives: Adapting Old Policy Institutions to New Challenges." In *Innovation Policy in Europe: Measurement and Strategy*, ed. C. Nauwelaers, and R. Wintjes. Cheltenham, UK: Edward Elgar.

Nauwelaers, C., K. Maguire, and G.A. Marsan. 2013. "The Case of Øresund (Denmark-Sweden) – Regions and Innovation: Collaborating across Borders." OECD Regional Development Working Papers 2013/21. Paris: OECD Publishing. Online at https://www.oecd.org/cfe/regionaldevelopment /publicationsdocuments/Oresund.pdf.

Nelson, R.R. 1996. *The Sources of Economic Growth*. Cambridge, MA: Harvard University Press.

Nijkamp, P., and P. van Hemert. 2009. "Knowledge Infrastructure and Regional Growth." *Regional Symbiosis* 17, 1–10.

Nilsson, A. 2001. "Biotechnology Firms in Sweden." *Small Business Economics* 17: 93–103. https://doi.org/10.1023/A:1011101818877.

Normaler, Ö., and B. Verspagen. 2016. "River Deep, Mountain High: Of Long Run Knowledge Trajectories within and between Innovation Clusters." *Journal of Economic Geography* 16 (6): 1259–78. https://doi.org/10.1093/jeg /lbw035.

Novo Nordisk Foundation. 2013." The Foundation, Vision and Mission." Online at http://novonordiskfonden.dk/en/content/vision-and-mission.

Nusca, A. 2013. "Here are your top 20 U.S. cities for venture capital investment." *Between the Lines*, 17 June. Online at http://www.zdnet.com /here-are-your-top-20-u-s-cities-for-venture-capital-investment-7000016910.

O'Connor, K., and A. Scott. 1992. "Airline Services and Metropolitan Areas in the Asia Pacific Region, 1970–1990." *Review of Urban and Regional Development Studies* 4 (2): 240–53. https://doi.org/10.1111/j.1467-940X.1992.tb00045.x.

OECD (Organisation for Economic Co-operation and Development). 2001. "STI Scoreboard: Towards a Knowledge-Based Economy." Paris: OECD.

OECD (Organisation for Economic Co-operation and Development). 2005." A Framework for Biotechnology Statistics." Paris: OECD.

OECD (Organisation for Economic Co-operation and Development). 2009. "Biotechnology Statistics 2009." Paris: OECD. Online at http://www.oecd.org/sti/sci-tech/42833898.pdf.

Orton, J.D., and K.E. Weick. 1990. "Loosely Coupled Systems: A Reconceptualization." *Academy of Management Review* 15 (2): 203–23. https://doi.org/10.5465/amr.1990.4308154.

Pack, H., and K. Saggi. 2006. "The Case for Industrial Policy: A Critical Survey." Policy Research Working Paper 3839. Washington, DC: World Bank. Online at http://www.ycsg.yale.edu/focus/gta/case_for_industrial.pdf.

Painter, M., and J. Pierre. 2005. "Unpacking Policy Capacity: Issues and Themes." In *Challenges to State Policy Capacity*, ed. M. Painter and J. Pierre, 1–18. Basingstoke, UK: Palgrave Macmillan,.

Peck, F., and C. Lloyd. 2008. "Cluster Policies and Cluster Strategies." In *Handbook of Research on Innovation and Clusters: Cases and Policies*, ed. C. Karlsson, 393–410. Cheltenham, UK: Edward Elgar.

Pendall, R., K.A. Foster, and M. Cowell. 2007. "Resilience and Regions: Building Understanding of the Metaphor." Macarthur Foundation Research Network on Building Resilient Regions. Berkeley, CA: Institute of Urban and Regional Development.

Pennings, J.M. 1981. "Strategically Interdependent Organizations." In *Handbook of Organization Design*, ed. P.C. Nystrom and W.H. Starbuck, 433–55. New York: Oxford University Press.

Perren, L., and J. Sapsed. 2013. "Innovation as Politics: The Rise and Reshaping of Innovation in UK Parliamentary Discourse 1960-2005." *Research Policy* 42 (10): 1815–28. https://doi.org/10.1016/j.respol.2013.08.012.

Pessoa, A. 2013. "Competitiveness, Clusters and Policy at the Regional Level: Rhetoric vs. Practice in Designing Policy for Depressed Regions." *Regional Science Inquiry, Hellenic Association of Regional Scientists* 5 (1): 101–16.

Pisano, G. 2006. *Science Business*. Cambridge, MA: Harvard University Press.

Porter, M. 1990. *The Competitive Advantage of Nations*. New York: Free Press.

Porter, M. 1998. "Clusters and the New Economics of Competition." *Harvard Business Review* 76: 77–91.

Porter, M. 2001. "Regions and the New Economics of Competition." In *Global City- Regions: Trends, Theory, Policy*, ed. A.J. Scott, 139–52. Oxford: Blackwell.

Porter, M.E. 2003. "The Economic Performance of Regions." *Regional Studies* 37 (6-7): 549–78. https://doi.org/10.1080/0034340032000108688.

Potter, A.J., and H.D. Watts. 2008. "Evolutionary Agglomeration Theory: Increasing Returns, Diminishing Returns and the Industry Life Cycle." University of Sheffield, Department of Geography. Mimeo.

Powell, W.W., and S. Grodal. 2005. "Networks of Innovators." In *The Oxford Handbook of Innovation*, ed. J. Fagerberg, D.C. Mowery, and R.R. Nelson, 56–86. New York: Oxford University Press.

Powell, W.W., K.W. Koput, and L. Smith-Doerr. 1996. "Interorganizational Collaboration and the Locus of Innovation: Networks of Learning in Biotechnology." *Administrative Science Quarterly* 4 (1): 116–45. https://doi.org/10.2307/2393988.

PricewaterhouseCoopers. 2011. "Uncovering Excellence in Cluster Management." Online at https://www.pwc.com/gx/en/psrc/pdf/cluster_management.pdf.

PROPEL. 2013. "About Us." Online at http://www.ibiopropel.org/about/index.html.

Provan, K.G., A. Fish, and J. Sydow. 2007. "Interorganisational Networks at the Network Level: A Review of the Empirical Literature on Whole Networks." *Journal of Management* 33 (3): 479–516. https://doi.org/10.1177/0149206307302554.

Provan, K.G., K.R. Isett, and H.B. Milward. 2004. "Cooperation and Compromise: A Network Response to Conflicting Institutional Pressures in Community Mental Health." *Nonprofit and Voluntary Sector Quarterly* 33 (3): 489–514. https://doi.org/10.1177/0899764004265718.

Provan, K.G. and P. Kenis. 2007. "Modes of Network Governance: Structure, Management and Effectiveness." *Journal of Public Administration Research and Theory* 18 (2): 229–52. https://doi.org/10.1093/jopart/mum015.

Putnam, R. 1993. *Making Democracy Work: Civic Traditions in Modern Italy*. Princeton, NJ: Princeton University Press.

Putnam, R. 2000. *Bowling Alone: The Collapse and Revival of American Community*. New York: Simon & Schuster.

Raines, P. 2003. "Cluster Behaviour and Economic Development: New Challenges in Policy Evaluation." *International Journal of Technology Management* 26 (2–4): 191–204. https://doi.org/10.1504/IJTM.2003.003369.

Ratanawaraha, A., and K.R. Polenske. 2007. "Measuring the Geography of Innovation: A Literature Review." In *The Economic Geography of Innovation*, ed. K.R. Polenske, 30–59. New York: Cambridge University Press.

Reagans, R., and B. McEvily. 2003. "Network Structure and Knowledge Transfer: The Effects of Cohesion and Range." *Administrative Science Quarterly* 48 (2): 240–67. https://doi.org/10.2307/3556658.

Reynolds, P.D., S.M. Camps, W.D. Bygrave, E. Autio, and M. Hay. 2001. "Global Entrepreneurship Monitor – 2001, Executive Report." Kansas City, MO: Kauffman Center for Entrepreneurial Leadership.

RIE Secretariat. 2011. "Research> Innovation> Enterprise, Singapore's Future 2015." Online at http://www.mti.gov.sg/ResearchRoom/Documents/app.mti.gov.sg/data/pages/885/doc/RIE2015.pdf.

Roberts, N.C., and R.T. Bradley. 1991. "Stakeholder Collaboration and Innovation." *Journal of Applied Behavioral Science* 27 (2): 209–27. https://doi.org/10.1177/0021886391272004.

Rocha, H.O. 2004. "Entrepreneurship and Development: The Role of Clusters." *Small Business Economics* 23 (5): 363–400. https://doi.org/10.1007/s11187-004-3991-8.

Rodríguez-Pose, A., and M. Di Cataldo. 2014. "Quality of Government and Innovative Performance in the Regions of Europe." *Journal of Economic Geography* 15 (4): 673–706. https://doi.org/10.1093/jeg/lbu023.

Rosen, M. 2009. "IBIO: A Twelve-Year Retrospective on Biotechnology in Illinois." *Yer Biotech Blues*, 24 March. Online at http://wtnnews.com/articles/5778/.

Rosenberg, N. 1982. *Inside the Black Box: Technology and Economics*. Cambridge: Cambridge University Press.

Rothwell, R. 1994. "Towards the Fifth-Generation Innovation Process." *International Marketing Review* 11 (1): 7–31. https://doi.org/10.1108/02651339410057491.

Rutter, J., R. Malley, A. Noonan, and W. Knighton. 2012. *It Takes Two: How to Create Effective Relationships between Government and Arm's-Length Bodies*. London: Institute for Government.

Sainsbury, D. 1999. "Biotechnology Clusters." London: Department of Trade and Industry. Online at https://studylib.net/doc/7715896/uk-biotechnology-clusters-report.

Sammarra, A., and F. Belussi. 2006. "Evolution and Relocation in Fashion-Led Italian Districts: Evidence from Two Case-Studies." *Entrepreneurship & Regional Development* 18 (6): 543–62. https://doi.org/10.1080/08985620600884685.

Saxenian, A. 1994. *Regional Advantage: Culture and Competition in Silicon Valley and Route 128*. Cambridge, MA: Harvard University Press.

Schilling, M.A. 2015. "Technology Shocks, Technological Collaboration and Innovation Outcomes." *Organisation Studies* 26 (3): 668–86. https://doi.org/10.1287/orsc.2015.0970.

Schmitz, H. 1995. "Collective Efficiency: Growth Path for Small-Scale Industry." *Journal of Development Studies* 31 (4): 529–66. https://doi.org/10.1080/00220389508422377.

Schneider, A., and H. Ingram. 1990. "Behavioral Assumptions of Policy Tools." *Journal of Politics* 52 (2): 510–29. https://doi.org/10.2307/2131904.

Schretlen, J., K. Dervojeda, W. Jansen, and B. Schaffmeister. 2011. *Uncovering Excellence in Cluster Management*. Amsterdam: PriceWaterhouseCoopers.

Schrier, D. 2017. *Profile of the British Columbia Technology Sector: 2017 Edition*. Victoria: BC Stats. Online at https://squamish.ca/assets/ED-resources /2481bfb3f9/Profile-of-the-British-Columbia-Technology-Sector -2017-Edition.pdf#:~:text=PROFILE%20OF%20THE%20BRITISH %20COLUMBIA%20TECHNOLOGY%20SECTOR%3A%202017, clusters.%20Firms%20in%20the%20technology%20sector%20tend%20to.

Seawright, J., and J. Gerring. 2008. "Case Selection Techniques in Case Study Research." *Political Research Quarterly* 61 (2): 294–308. https://doi.org /10.1177/1065912907313077.

Seliger, G., L. Carpinetti, and M. Gerolamo. 2008. "Promoting Innovative Clusters and Cooperation Networks: The European Commission Observatories of SMEs and the Context of Berlin-Brandenburg." *International Journal of Networking and Virtual Organizations* 5 (2): 204–23. https://doi.org/10.1504/IJNVO.2008.017011.

Serapio, M.G., and D.H. Dalton. 1999. "Globalization of Industrial R&D: An Examination of Foreign Direct Investments in R&D in the United States." *Research Policy* 28 (2-3): 303–16. https://doi.org/10.1016/S0048 -7333(98)00109-7.

Simmie, J., and R. Martin. 2010. "The Economic Resilience of Regions: Towards an Evolutionary Approach." *Cambridge Journal of Regions, Economy and Society* 3 (1): 27–43. https://doi.org/10.1093/cjres/rsp029.

Singapore. 2012. Ministry of Trade and Industry. "About MTI." Online https://www.mti.gov.sg/About-Us/About-MTI#.

Singapore. 2013. "A Sustainable Population for a Dynamic Singapore." Population White Paper. Singapore: Strategy Group, National Population and Talent Division.

Singapore. 2017. "Research Innovation Enterprise 2020 Plan: Winning the Future through Science and Technology." Singapore: Prime Minister's Office, National Research Foundation. Online at https://www.nrf.gov.sg /rie2020.

Siren, E. 2017. "The quirks and quarks of keeping the Vancouver biotech ecosystem afloat." *Financial Post*, 10 February. Online at http://business .financialpost.com/entrepreneur/the-quirks-and-quarks-of-keeping-the -vancouver-biotech-ecosystem-afloat.

6, P., N. Goodwin, E. Peck, and T. Freeman. 2006. *Managing Networks of Twenty-First Century Organisations*. Basingstoke, UK: Palgrave Macmillan.

Skowronek, S. 1982. *Building a New American State: The Expansion of National Administrative Capacities, 1877–1920*. Cambridge: Cambridge University Press.

Skyrms, Brian. 2004. *The Stag Hunt and the Evolution of Social Structure*. New York: Cambridge University Press

Small Business Innovation Research. 2013. "The SBIR Program." Online at http://www.sbir.gov/about/about-sbir.

Snyder, W.M., and E. Wenger. 2010. "Our World as a Learning System: A Communities-of-Practice Approach." In *Social Learning Systems and Communities of Practice*, ed. C. Blackmore, 107–24. Milton Keynes, UK: Springer.

Sölvell, Ö. 2008. *Clusters: Balancing Evolutionary and Constructive Forces.* Stockholm: Ivory Tower.

Sölvell, Ö., G. Lindqvist, and C. Ketels. 2003. *The Cluster Initiative Greenbook.* Stockholm: Ivory Tower.

Spolaore, E., and R. Wacziarg. 2012. "How Deep Are the Roots of Economic Development?" NBER Working Paper 18130. Cambridge, MA: National Bureau of Economic Research.

Steiner, M., and M. Ploder. 2008. "Structure and Strategy within Heterogeneity: Multiple Dimensions of Regional Networking." *Regional Studies* 42 (6): 793–815. https://doi.org/10.1080/00343400701861310.

Sternberg, R. 2010. "Defining a great university." *Inside Higher Education*, 29 November. Online at https://www.usd259.org/site/handlers/filedownload.ashx?moduleinstanceid=11718&dataid=6445&FileName=Defining%20a%20Great%20University.pdf.

Stevens, G.A., and J. Burley. 1997. "3,000 raw ideas = 1 commercial success!" *Research-Technology Management*, May-June, 16–27.

Stimson, R.J., and R.R. Stough. 2009. *Leadership, Institutions and Regional Endogenous Development.* Cheltenham, UK: Edward Elgar.

Stough, R.R., R.J. Stimson, and P. Nijkamp. 2011. "An Endogenous Perspective on Regional Development and Growth. In *Drivers of Innovation, Entrepreneurship and Regional Dynamics*, ed. K. Kourtit, P. Nijkamp, and R.R. Stough, 3–20. Heidelberg: Springer.

Strambach, S. 2010. "Path Dependence and Path Plasticity: The Co-evolution of Institutions and Innovation – The German Customized Business Software Industry." In *The Handbook of Evolutionary Economic Geography*, ed. R. Boschma and R. Martin, 406–31. Cheltenham, UK: Edward Elgar.

Streijffert, B. 2008. "Øresund Science Region: Cross-border Triple Helix Collaboration." Øresund Star Briefing. Online at http://ec.europa.eu/regional_policy/en/projects/best-practices/sweden/1369/download.

Swanson, D.A., S. Barg, S. Tyler, H.D. Venema, S. Tomar, S. Bhadwal, S. Nair, et al. 2010. "Seven Tools for Creating Adaptive Policies." *Technological Forecasting & Social Change* 77 (6): 924–39. https://doi.org/10.1016/j.techfore.2010.04.005.

Swanstrom, T. 2008. "Regional Resilience: A Critical Examination of the Ecological Framework." IURD Working Paper 2008-07. Berkeley: University of California, Berkeley, Institute of Urban and Regional Development.

Tangkjær, C. 2000. "Øresund as an Open House Strategy by Invitation."
In *Invoking a Transnational Metropolis. The Making of the Øresund Region*,
ed. P.O. Berg, A. Linde-Laursen, and O. Löfgren, 165–90. Lund, Sweden:
Studentlitteratur.

Tavassoli, S., and D. Tsagdis. 2014. "Critical Success Factors and Cluster
Evolution: A Case Study of the Linkoping ICT Cluster Lifecycle."
*Environment and Planning A: Economy and Space* 46 (6): 1425–44. https://doi
.org/10.1068/a46258.

Telleman, P., and M. Dinnetz. 2005. "Nanoscale Science and Technology in the
Øresund Region."

Temouri, Y. 2012. "The Cluster Scoreboard: Measuring the Performance of
Local Business Clusters in the Knowledge Economy." OECD Local Economic
and Employment Development (LEED) Working Papers 2012/13. Paris:
OECD Publishing. Online at http://dx.doi.org/10.1787/5k94ghq8p5kd-en.

T-Net. 2017. "Genome BC invests in BC Biotechnology Company Augurex."
6 February. Online at http://www.bctechnology.com/news/2017/2/6
/Genome-BC-Invests-in-BC-Biotechnology-Company-Augurex.cfm.

Tödtling, F., and M. Trippl. 2004 "One Size Fits All? Towards a Differentiated
Policy Approach with Respect to Regional Innovation Systems." SRE
Discussion Papers 2004/01. Vienna: WU Vienna University of Economics
and Business.

Trippl, M., B. Asheim, and J. Miorner. 2015. "Identification of Regions with
Less Developed Research and Innovation and Innovation Systems." Papers
in Innovation Studies 2015/1. Lund, Sweden: Lund University, Centre for
Innovation, Research and Competence in the Learning Economy.

Trippl, M., and A. Otto. 2009. "How to Turn the Fate of Old Industrial Areas:
A Comparison of Cluster-based Renewal Processes in Styria and the
Saarland." *Environment and Planning A: Economy and Space* 41 (5): 1217–33.
https://doi.org/10.1068/a4129.

UNDP (United Nations Development Programme). 2011. *Capacity
Development: A UNDP Primer*. New York: UNDP. Online at https://www
.undp.org/content/dam/aplaws/publication/en/publications/capacity
-development/capacity-development-a-undp-primer/CDG_PrimerReport
_final_web.pdf.

University Technology Park. 2011. "Governor Quinn opens new Incubator
at IIT's University Technology Park." *Illinois Tech Mediaroom*, 2 November.
Online at https://web.iit.edu/mediaroom/press-releases/2011/nov/02
/governor-quinn-opens-new-incubator-iits-university-technology.

Uyarra, E. 2010. "What Is Evolutionary about Regional Systems of Innovation?
Implications for Regional Policy." *Journal of Evolutionary Economics* 20 (1):
115–37. https://doi.org/10.1007/s00191-009-0135-y.

Uyarra, E., and R. Ramlogan. 2016. "The Impact of Cluster Policy on Innovation." In *Handbook of Innovation Policy Impact*, ed. J. Edler, P. Cunningham, A. Gök, and P. Shapira, 196–225. Cheltenham, UK: Edward Elgar.

Uzzi, B. 1996. "The Sources and Consequences of Embeddedness for the Economic Performance of Organizations." *American Sociological Review* 61 (4): 674–98. https://doi.org/10.2307/2096399.

Vaekstmotor. 2013. "Attraction of International Labour and Companies." Online at http://www.vaekstmotor.dk/english/activities/attraction-of -international-labour-and-companies.

Vancouver Economic Commission. 2011. "The Vancouver Economic Action Strategy: An Economic Development Plan for the City." Online at https:// vancouver.ca/files/cov/vancouver-economic-action-strategy.pdf.

Vaz, E., T. de Noronha Vaz, P.V. Galindo, and P. Nijkamp. 2014. "Modelling Innovation Support Systems for Regional Development: Analysis of Cluster Structures in Innovation in Portugal." *Entrepreneurship & Regional Development* 26 (1-2): 23–46. http://dx.doi.org/10.1080/08985626.2013 .860193.

Visser, E.-J., and O. Atzema. 2008. "With or Without Clusters: Facilitating Innovation through a Differentiated and Combined Network Approach." *European Planning Studies* 16 (9): 1169–88. https://doi.org/10.1080 /09654310802401573.

Wallsten, S. 2004. "The Role of Government in Regional Technology Development." In *Building High-Tech Clusters: Silicon Valley and Beyond*, ed. T. Bresnahan and A. Gambardella, 229–79. Cambridge: Cambridge University Press.

Webb, A. 1991. "Co-ordination: A Problem in Public Sector Management." *Policy and Politics* 19 (4): 229–41. https://doi.org/10.1332 /030557391782454188.

Wee, J. 2017. "SPRING Singapore." *Singapore Infopedia*, National Library. Online at http://eresources.nlb.gov.sg/infopedia/articles/SIP_301_2005-02-02.html.

Williams, P. 2002. "The Competent Boundary Spanner." *Public Administration* 80 (1): 103–24. https://doi.org/10.1111/1467-9299.00296.

Williams, P. 2010. "Special Agents: The Nature and Role of Boundary Spanners." Paper presented to the ESRC Research Seminar Series, University of Birmingham, February. Online at http://www.download.bham.ac.uk /govsoc/pdfs/special-agents-paper.pdf.

Williamson, O.E. 1995. "Hierarchies, Market and Power in the Economy: An Economic Perspective." *Industrial and Corporate Change* 4 (1): 21–50. https:// doi.org/10.1093/icc/4.1.21.

Wixted, B., and J.A. Holbrook. 2011. "Innovation, Cities and Place: An Empirical Study of the Knowledge System in Vancouver and Its Place on the

Pacific Rim." CPROST Report 11-01. Vancouver: Simon Fraser University, Centre for Policy Research on Science and Technology. Online at http://blogs.sfu.ca/departments/cprost/wp-content/uploads/2012/08/1101.pdf.

Wolfe, D.A. 2008. "Cluster Policies and Cluster Strategies: Implications of the ISRN Cluster Study." Presentation to the Policy Day of the 10th Annual Meeting of the Innovation Systems Research Network, Montreal, 30 April.

Wolfe, D.A. 2010. "The Strategic Management of Core Cities: Path Dependence and Economic Adjustment in Resilient Regions." *Cambridge Journal of Regions Economy and Society* 3 (1): 139–52. https://doi.org/10.1093/cjres/rsp032.

Wolfe, D.A., and T. Creutzberg. 2003. "Community Participation and Multilevel Governance in Economic Development Policy." Paper prepared for the Panel on the Role of Government, Toronto, August. Online at http://www.utoronto.ca/progris/pdf_files/Community%20Participation%20and%20Economic%20Development%20Policy%20Pa%85.pdf.

Wolfe, D.A., and M.S. Gertler. 2004. "Clusters from the Inside and Out: Lessons from the Canadian Study of Cluster Development." *Urban Studies* 41 (5-6): 1071–93. https://doi.org/10.1080/00420980410001675832.

Wong, J. 2011. *Betting on Biotech: Innovation and the Limits of Asia's Developmental State*. Ithaca, NY: Cornell University Press.

Wong, P.-K. 2006a. "Commercializing Biomedical Science in a Rapidly Changing 'Triple Helix' Nexus: The Experience of the National University of Singapore." *Journal of Technology Transfer* 32 (4): 367–95. https://doi.org/10.1007/s10961-006-9020-0.

Wong, P.-K. 2006b. "Toward an Ecosystem for Innovation in a Newly Industrialized Economy." *Industry & Higher Education* 20 (4): 231–6.

Woodhouse, A. 2006. "Social Capital and Economic Development in Regional Australia: A Case Study." *Journal of Rural Studies* 22 (1): 83–94. https://doi.org/10.1016/j.jrurstud.2005.07.003

Wu, X., M. Ramesch, and M. Howlett. 2015. "Policy Capacity: A Conceptual Framework for Understanding Policy Competences and Capabilities." *Policy and Society* 34 (3-4), 165–71. https://doi.org/10.1016/j.polsoc.2015.09.001.

Yeung, H.W. 2010. "Situating Regional Development in the Competitive Dynamics of Global Production Networks: An East Asian Perspective." In *Globalizing Regional Development in East Asia Production Networks, Clusters and Entrepreneurship,* ed. H.W. Yeung, 5–32 London: Routledge.

Zeller, C. 2001. "Cluster Biotech: A Recipe for Success? Spatial Patterns of Growth of Biotechnology in Munich, Rhineland and Hamburg." *Small Business Economics* 17 (1-2): 123–41. https://doi.org/10.1023/A:1011182624329.

Zucker, L.G., and M.R. Darby. 1996. "Star Scientists and Institutional Transformation: Patterns of Invention and Innovation in the Formation of the Biotechnology Industry." Proceedings of the National Academy of Sciences of the United States of America 93, 12709–16. Online at https://www.pnas.org/content/93/23/12709.

Zucker, L.G., and M.R. Darby. 2006. "Movement of Star Scientists and Engineers and High-Tech Firm Entry." NBER Working Paper 12172. Cambridge, MA: National Bureau of Economic Research

Zucker, L.G., M.R. Darby, M.B. Brewer, and Y. Peng. 1995. "Collaboration Structure and Information Dilemmas in Biotechnology: Organizational Boundaries as Trust Production." NBER Working Paper 5199. Cambridge, MA: National Bureau of Economic Research.

zu Köcker, G.M., and T. Lämmer-Gamp. 2017. "Core Design Features of an Integrated Cluster Policy." In The Life Cycle of Clusters: A Policy Perspective, ed. D. Fornahl, and R. Hassink, 135–50. Cheltenham, UK: Edward Elgar.

zu Köcker, G.M., and J. Rosted. 2010. "Promoting Cluster Excellence: Measuring and Benchmarking the Quality of Cluster Organizations and Performance of Clusters." Berlin: VDI/VDE Innovation + Technik GmbH, FORA Danish Enterprise and Construction Authority. Online at https://irp-cdn.multiscreensite.com/bcb8bbe3/files/uploaded/doc_2900.pdf.

# Index

**Studies in Comparative Political Economy and Public Policy**